MW00357038

CC

STONE COLD

STONE COLD

The True Story of Michael Stone and The Milltown Massacre

Martin Dillon

HUTCHINSON
London

© Martin Dillon 1992

The right of Martin Dillon to be identified as Author of this
work has been asserted by Martin Dillon in accordance with the
Copyright, Designs and Patents Act, 1988

This edition first published in 1992 by
Hutchinson, an imprint of Random House UK Limited,
20 Vauxhall Bridge Road, London SW1V 2SA

Reprinted 1992

Random House Australia (Pty) Ltd
20 Alfred Street, Milsons Point, Sydney, NSW 2061, Australia

Random House New Zealand Ltd,
18 Poland Road, Glenfield, Auckland, New Zealand

Random House South Africa (Pty) Ltd
PO Box 337, Bergvlei, 2012, South Africa

A CIP catalogue record for this book is
available from the British Library

ISBN 0 09 177410 1

Photoset by Raven Typesetters, Ellesmere Port
Printed in England by Clays Ltd, St Ives plc

Contents

I dedicate this book to my friends Gladys Shelley, America's greatest-living songwriter and Chad Paine, a fine musician and constant source of support.

Foreword

Martin Dillon is the greatest living authority on Irish terrorism. He is our Virgil to that Inferno, in all the varieties of its torments. 'All the varieties' include the activities of the various sets of Catholic (Republican) and Protestant (Loyalist) terrorists, and also the illegal aspects of the activities of members of the different branches of the security forces.

In *Political Murder in Northern Ireland* and in *The Dirty War*, Martin Dillon examined the general pattern of terrorism in the Province. Other works in the Dillon cycle – as we can now designate it – are more specialised. Thus, *Rogue Warrior of the SAS*, was concerned with an example of what might be called 'official terrorism' (alias counter-terrorism). In *The Shankill Butchers* he examined a particularly horrific set of Loyalist-sectarian murders. In *Killer In Clowntown* he followed the career of a leading member of the IRA. In *Stone Cold*, he returns to the Protestant/Loyalist side of the divide.

Martin Dillon's greatest gift as an enquirer into terrorism is his extraordinary capacity for getting all sorts of people to talk to him. This is particularly striking in *Stone Cold*, which contains something resembling an autobiography of a terrorist, in the form of the profuse confidences which Michael Stone poured out to the author. Stone is best known for the Milltown Massacre, a lethal attack on mourners at a Republican funeral. The record of the feelings of *attraction* which the killer experienced as he attended an earlier Republican funeral (see p. 150) is of great psychological interest, as is the whole of Stone's self-portrait, together with Dillon's subtle and critical comments on it.

In relation to other (necessarily unnamed) participants in the struggle, *Stone Cold* contains many other notable examples of Dillon's capacity to get people to talk. See, for example, the confession of a former intelligence officer (pp 136–7); the analysis by 'a source now retired from the intelligence community' (pp 161–2) and the account by 'a Special Branch contact' of his 'concerns about Military Intelligence operations' (pp 208–9).

The particular neck of this sinister wood which Martin Dillon is exploring in *Stone Cold* is the world of the Loyalist paramilitaries and of their undercover allies in various branches of the security forces. Readers of *Stone Cold* who have not read *The Dirty War* may get the impression that most of the troubles of Northern Ireland are due to the Loyalist paramilitaries in collusion with the security forces. This would be a misleading impression. In what remains of this foreword I shall try to put these matters into perspective.

Most of the troubles of Northern Ireland are due to the offensive of the Provisional IRA which began twenty-one years ago and still continues. The object of that offensive is to drive Northern Ireland out of the United Kingdom, contrary to the known wishes of the great majority of its inhabitants. The tactics used in that offensive include the murder of Northern Ireland Protestants (including ordinary civilians as well as RUC and UDR) with the objective of weakening and ultimately breaking the will of the Protestant community to remain in the United Kingdom. The tactics also include the murder of British soldiers in Northern Ireland and occasional attacks on other British targets with the objective of weakening and ultimately breaking the will of the British to keep Northern Ireland as part of the United Kingdom.

A subsidiary but important objective of the Provisional offensive is to provoke a massive Protestant backlash, which would probably precipitate British withdrawal. They have had some success along those lines – as the career of Michael Stone exemplifies – but on a lesser scale so far than what would be required to precipitate British withdrawal. They are still working on this.

What the Provisionals *have* succeeded in eliciting, however, is a tacit alliance between Loyalist paramilitaries and significant elements in the security forces. This is hardly surprising. Both the RUC and the UDR are part of the community whose will the IRA is trying to break, by a sustained campaign of murder. In the circumstances it is not surprising that some members of these forces should regard the Loyalist paramilitaries as their allies against a common enemy. It is to the credit of most members of the

RUC that they appear to have resisted that temptation; some, clearly, have not.

Among the regular British soldiers in Northern Ireland some are prepared to make use of the Loyalist paramilitaries as irregular and deniable allies. The only paramilitaries who are killing British soldiers are the Republican ones. Protestant areas are places of rest and recreation for the troops (as Martin Dillon mentions). Catholic areas are places of deadly danger. In these conditions the emergence of a tendency to see Protestants as 'friendly' and Catholics as 'hostile' is predictable. And in some cases – chronicled by Martin Dillon – this can result in the turning of blind eyes to the crimes of Loyalist paramilitaries or even in some cases, partnership in such crimes.

In principle, of course, the authorities have a duty to clear all that up. In practice, this is exceedingly hard to do. Those tendencies among the security forces on the ground in Northern Ireland are inherent in the nature of the situation, and likely to continue as long as the IRA offensive does. The only thing the British can do that will effect a radical change is to disengage from Nothern Ireland. But in that event the result would be an Irish civil war in which the first week's casualties would be likely to exceed the combined casualties of twenty-one years of *incipient* civil war.

Conor Cruise O'Brien

1

Meeting an Assassin

To an outsider Belfast seems an attractive place surrounded by mountains and hills, with little evidence of the violence, hatred or destruction lurking within its streets and alleyways: it is a city enveloped by a countryside more easily accessible than any British counterpart.

On a sunny morning in August 1990 I drove from Belfast along the M1 motorway towards the town of Lisburn. In my rear-view mirror, the Cave Hill, redolent with historical imagery, dwarfed North Belfast, and to my left industrial estates sprawled across reclaimed land once known as the Bog Meadows. For any southbound traveller, Belfast retains one powerful reminder of its testimony to violence, an interruption to an otherwise tranquil scene. Milltown Cemetery and its thousands of headstones reaches from the Falls Road to the high fences separating it from the motorway. This is hallowed IRA ground where the Provisionals bury their dead to the accompaniment of historical phrases and the quivering echoes of rehearsed gunfire volleys. I knew the cemetery from boyhood, those Sunday excursions to family graves – my aunts; a school friend; my grandparents.

Milltown always intrigued me with its untidiness and quietude, different from London graveyards with their well-cut verges, fresh flowers and pervading sense of order. In spring Milltown was a place for wild flowers irrepressible among the rusted grave surrounds and weather-beaten headstones. Now, as I drove by, it was overgrown with weeds and high grass awaiting the autumn, winter and rebirth.

The cemetery's prominent feature is a large plot and monument dedicated to IRA dead. The IRA needed such commemoration to remind others of their 'sacrifice', to elevate death, to recruit: their stone monument dwarfs the graves of other mortals. The emergence of a renewed conflict in 1969 began to transform Milltown into a shrine where IRA orations were frequently delivered at the burials of those scores of IRA volunteers killed 'on active service'. Throughout this past twenty years, the constant tramping of marching men in balaclavas, and the attention of the world's media, brusquely erased my quiet family Sunday memories.

My journey on the motorway past Milltown was also a search for the past – but not mine. Twenty minutes later, I was driving along narrow roads, skirting the town of Lisburn, context of two contemporary reminders of violence: headquarters of the British Army in Northern Ireland – and, my destination, the Maze Prison which housed many of the world's most dangerous terrorists from within the Catholic and Protestant communities.

Catholics rarely use the term 'Maze Prison', preferring to call it 'Long Kesh'. In 1971 the prison site housed an internment camp reminiscent of Second World War prisoner-of-war camps, on the location of a disused airfield called Long Kesh. Then, it was surrounded by barbed wire, and within its boundaries were scores of Nissen huts. The introduction of internment in 1971 trans-formed Long Kesh into a frightening illustration of how politicians and military strategists react to such chaos. Extra barbed wire, with machine-gun turrets and searchlights became a permanent feature of the landscape. When internment was phased out in 1975 the British government opened a modern prison on the site with cell blocks shaped in the form of the letter H, and created one of the most modern prison systems in Europe – but it still failed to erase Catholic memories of Long Kesh, and the use of that old name persisted. The H-blocks of the Maze became notorious worldwide when IRA inmates staged their 'dirty protest', smearing walls with excreta; ten hunger-striking republicans starved to death.

My memory of the Maze was limited to standing at the front gate in 1971 interviewing a prison spokesman. Now, I was about to be afforded the opportunity of seeing beyond the barbed wire, the high corrugated fences and the guard posts. High above me, cameras were strategically placed to record the movement of all traffic on the periphery of the prison. Entry to the compound was unhindered and I drove through a large doorway into a spacious car-park. The only clue that I was within the confines of a prison were the watchtowers and cameras. In the car glove compartment, sat a visitor's permit:

Inmates ref no: A385. Name. M.A. Stone
Location H-8.
The above inmate has requested a visit from the following:
  Martin Dillon.
Attention.
Do not give anything to or receive anything from a prisoner during a visit.
If in doubt please ask the officer supervising the visit.
This permit is only valid for the date and day shown.
For sentenced inmates a maximum of three adults and two children may be admitted. For unconvicted inmates a maximum of two adults and two children may be admitted.
If visitors are different from those listed above, you should notify the Visitor's Reception Officer on arrival.

Through a turnstile, I was directed into a portakabin and led to a narrow corridor which opened to a room partitioned by glass. Two prison officers examined my visitor's pass and personal identity documents and directed me through a security door into a room which resembled a community hall: a wooden floor, and rows of cheap tubular chairs of the type which fit one into another. Ahead of me, a heavy door operated electronically, the upper half a glass panel 6" by 6". Uncomfortably, I was being scrutinised from behind the door – which opened with a sharp resonant clicking, and a smiling prison officer beckoned. I was led into a narrow passage-way and the heavy door was shut. To my left were tiny cubicles each with a chair and wooden table: in one of these, a seated officer asked the purpose of my visit – a routine procedure, but also a security exercise to test the demeanour of a visitor for nervousness, betraying criminal intent or false identity. The seated officer watched my replies while his colleague stood alongside me, his eyes fixed on my profile. I was asked to remove all articles from my pockets: they examined the hoard of old train tickets, restaurant bills and assorted paper/scraps and placed them in a large envelope. To my consternation I was told I was not permitted to take my pen and notebook into the prison, but was allowed cigarettes, matches and coins for a coffee machine. The envelope containing the bulk of my possessions was sealed and I was asked to sign a declaration verifying the nature of the contents. They carried out a thorough body search, led me back to the corridor to another security door, and subsequently into a small room with more rows of tubular chairs, a more inviting area, with a television tuned to BBC1. The walls were painted with images of Mickey Mouse, Donald Duck and a host of other Disney characters – a fun atmosphere for the children of prisoners. I suddenly realised that from the moment I had entered the prison I had been deprived of a view of the prison proper: this room, like the others, contained no windows.

The others in the room included mothers with children, teenage girls and several elderly men: many of them knew each other but they all positioned themselves in separate groupings, mirroring the Catholic–Protestant divide. No evidence of animosity surfaced – and yet these were the relatives of people, sons or fathers who were bitter enemies, segregated outside in society and now in prison. I recalled a lunch with UDA leader John McMichael who had said he was always impressed by the way in which prison visitors behaved towards each other, and how Catholic and Protestant children arrived at the Maze as though dressed for Sunday School. His description of Catholic and Protestant visitors to the Maze, and the emotional way in which he described the children of inmates, contained poignant truth. No one spoke to me: I suspected they saw me as an outsider. Later I learned they were convinced by my clothing that I was a solicitor.

A security door opened and a heavily built prison officer entered the room, bearing a sheaf of visiting passes: he began reading the names of inmates. People in the room responded, and walked familiarly past the officer, through the security doorway and out of sight.

'No. 385 – Stone': I left the room and found myself in the open air: yards from the doorway an armoured van stood parked, its rear doors open. I was told to 'hurry along', and climbed into the vehicle which was equipped with a row of seating along its two sides. The other visitors looked bemused by my unfamiliarity with my surroundings. The windows in the van were blacked-out and when the rear doors were closed it resembled a tinfoil room on wheels. The interior was a silver hue and the only evidence of a driver was the van moving. Occasionally it negotiated road ramps and three metal gates. At each gate the rear doors were opened and a prison officer checked the number of visitors. Finally it came to a halt and we were asked to dismount: it was like leaving a cinema in the afternoon.

We were all in a holding area similar to the one we had left – but still without a view of the H-blocks. It grew increasingly apparent that we were permitted to see inmates but not their surroundings. The depressing room into which we were ushered had no Disney images: I suspected it to be part of the old Long Kesh complex – it resembled a Nissen hut rather than a portakabin.

They repeated the procedure of announcing inmates' names, and each visitor left on foot for the final journey to the real visiting area, having been handed our original visiting permits to enable us to negotiate security doors. Several prison officers examined my permit, told me Prisoner 385 was ready to meet me and directed me into a large hall with numbered rows upon rows of cubicles each separated by wooden uprights. I was told to proceed to Cubicle 15 at the rear of the room: in the cubicles to my right and left visitors spoke in whispers to inmates. Prison officers, strategically placed to observe, remained discreetly removed from individual cubicles.

I had come to meet Michael Anthony Stone, a loyalist hero, a notorious hitman who killed people with unparalleled ferocity. He was the assassin who unleashed a killing spree in front of the world's television crews in Milltown Cemetery on 16 March 1988. The British and Irish tabloid press labelled him 'Rambo', 'madman' and 'closet homosexual'. Local ballad-makers commemorated his exploits; graffiti extolled his killing methods, his hatred of Catholics. Stone was an enigma to the police, Army and intelligence services. One of the many theories suggested was that his hatred of Catholics derived from having been christened Roman Catholic.

I expected to see a dishevelled figure with long unruly dark hair, a beard and the looks of a man in his mid-forties. Such was the general image captured by newspapers and television cameras on that fateful day in Milltown Cemetery when Michael Stone, armed with guns and grenades, attacked an IRA funeral. The smiling, affable, heavily built man who greeted me did not resemble the Milltown assassin in age or appearance. He appeared younger than his 35 years and resembled a hippy from the 1960s. His hair was shoulder-length and only on close inspection betrayed a greying of age. He wore a wrangler jacket, denim jeans and an open-necked shirt. 'Pleased to meet you,' he said, his handshake that of a self-assured, powerful person. His eyes were light brown, enquiring – but capable of a coldness which questioned the honesty of his smile. Sitting down in the cubicle, he beckoned me to sit opposite.

During my years as a writer and reporter I had met many gunmen from republican and loyalist terror groups, meetings in bars, public places, or secret destinations with men who wore masks. Now I was sitting across a narrow table in what could easily have been intimate surroundings, and if my proximity to Stone in any way added to my discomfort, it also allowed me a closer inspection of his demeanour, and of his reactions to my enquiries.

His physical build bore evidence of someone who passed prison hours in intense physical exercises and weight training. Five feet nine, the muscles gave him squat proportions – this man had instilled a terrible fear in his victims. Loyalist assassins dragged young and old men off thoroughfares in Belfast, removed them to clubs or derelict houses, beat and tortured them before shooting or knifing them to death. It was difficult to detach the mind from such terrible events as Stone disarmingly reacted to my questions.

He talked quietly to avoid being overheard by republican inmates in nearby cubicles; I felt the eyes of other visitors on me, intrigued by my concern with the infamous Michael Stone. He seemed unaffected by the rigours, deprivation and solitariness of the life; his demeanour had the ordinariness of anyone 'outside', and he revealed that he had often frequented two Belfast bars which were the haunts of myself and several of my friends. I found the admission spine-chilling, and a reminder that Belfast was a dangerous city where it was not always easy to identify killers. Stone was determined to make me feel at ease by discussing places and people we knew. He talked of how he had enjoyed a hectic social life during his years as an assassin. His description of himself in the outside world betrayed a narcissism, given added, even poignant point, by his descriptions of the expensive, £250 suits he wore, and the multitude of women who found him irresistible.

Stone proved self-conscious about the way the tabloid press had portrayed his exploits in Milltown Cemetery: they described him as 'mad'. That description hurt him, pierced his ego and questioned his motivation for violence. He resented being labelled a psychopath, sectarian killer. He said, yes, he was sectarian in the early years of the conflict, but had erased that part of his past long before he entered the cemetery to kill IRA leaders. In talking of his childhood and his inherited politics, he denied the claim that he was once a Catholic. He assured me he was in prison for life but was content because he knew why he was there.

That first meeting I had with him ended at 12.30, and he was led away by prison officers while I made the return journey in the armoured van to the visitors' entrance. There, I signed a document, and retrieved the assortment of belongings considered a threat to prison security. As I drove away from the Maze I felt confused by my experience, unsure of the things I was told by Stone, but determined to examine the origins and actions of a very complex man. Even though I, and the world, knew why he was in prison, I had no sense or knowledge of the things that had shaped him, in particular, the nature of his early years and his life as a Protestant hitman before the fateful day in Milltown.

2

English and Catholic

In September 1990 I began the painstaking task of tracing Michael Stone's family history through the Office of the Registrar of Births in Belfast. The plethora of allegations that he had been christened Roman Catholic had first surfaced in 1988 in the *Sunday World*, one of Ireland's leading newspapers, and it reappeared in other publications. In the spring of 1991 the *Sunday World* resurrected its earlier story, and continued to assert that Stone had been born to Catholic parents, but lived in Protestant East Belfast. The newspaper believed that his religious persuasion had been hidden by the Stone family – a 'terrible secret' which conditioned his instinct to kill Catholics.

This kind of theory had applied to loyalist killers before. A similar story had emerged concerning Lenny Murphy, the most prolific mass murderer in British criminal history. Murphy led a killing squad, The Shankill Butchers, which became infamous for abducting innocent Catholics, torturing them and slitting their throats with butchery knives: he died in a hail of IRA gunfire. When I examined his life, I talked to Murphy's paramilitary associates, who convinced me that Murphy was Catholic, although his family lived in a Protestant area. One leading member of the Ulster Volunteer Force explained Murphy's hatred of Catholics by describing him as a 'super Prod', a definition intended to describe a man secretly a Catholic but publicly more antagonistic towards Catholics than his fellow Protestant paramilitaries. To survive within the loyalist community Murphy had to prove he could kill more Catholics than his associates. The theory grew more interesting when I discovered that he had lived close to a Catholic neighbourhood which housed a Murphy family. This other family contained three elderly men named John, Alexander and William; names which accorded with those of Lenny Murphy's brothers, leading me to suspect a relationship between the families – which appeared to confirm a Catholic dimension to the killer's history. The obvious conclusion seemed to be that the brothers had been named after uncles in the Catholic district. Then I traced the other family, and discovered they lived in the Falls area of West Belfast, several hundred yards from Lenny Murphy's home. There the similarity ended: no connection, no inter-community marriages, not even a tenuous link with Lenny Murphy's history. Yet, none the less, an overriding impression persisted in the Protestant community that the Shankill Butcher was, secretly, Catholic. At school he had been goaded about his name, and taunted: 'Murphy the mick'. Feeling doubtless un-fortunate to have a Catholic-sounding surname, he exorcised the suspicions of his co-religionists by becoming virulently anti-Catholic.

My experience in tracing Stone's history was similar: I knew he lived in a Protestant district, and some of his paramilitary colleagues had even defined him 'as not one of theirs'. In October 1991 I was approached by a contact from a loyalist enclave in North Belfast who told me he knew Stone's parents. He said they lived near him in Highfield Crescent and were Catholic. My contact said Stone's parents were Frank Stone from the Catholic Ardoyne district and Ivy Susan from Birmingham. They had lived in Highfield before the Troubles, but were forced to flee their home in 1969 during intimidating, city-wide 'pogroms' against many Catholics. Those who lived in or near Protestant areas proved particularly vulnerable, and found themselves petrol-bombed or threatened with firearms. Frank Stone, said my informant, his wife and three children, fled when their next-door neighbour, also Catholic, was shot dead. This convincing detail contradicted Stone, who told me, at that first prison meeting, his father's name – Cyril Alexander, his mother's, Mary. While debating whether to accept my contact's information I received a written note from Stone:

As you know my name is Michael Anthony Stone, date of birth 2/4/55. My natural parents were Cyril and Mary Stone. They met and married in Birmingham where my natural father was stationed. Cyril was in the Royal Corps of Signals. Like so many of these 'soldier–girl relationships', it lasted two years then sadly it was over. The marriage ended, my natural father brought me back to his family in Belfast and to his one sister, Margaret who lived in the Braniel in East Belfast.

Stone's account of his early life left me with the dilemma of whom to believe. Was Stone lying about the names of his parents to conceal his true religious identity? Or, for whatever family reasons, had he lived with his aunt, never aware that his parents also lived in Belfast.

Belfast's history is unsurprisingly riddled with mixed marriages and the possibility existed that Frank Stone's sister Margaret had married a Protestant. Was Michael born out of wedlock in Birmingham and quickly removed to Belfast? Steadily becoming exasperated, confused – and suspicious of Stone – I needed to confirm the existence of Frank and Ivy Stone, and whether they had a child named Michael born to them on 2/4/1955. Within weeks of receiving Stone's note I discovered that there was no record of the marriage of Francis Stone and Ivy Susan between 1944–54. However, a child, Joseph Alexander, had been born to Francis Stone and Ivy Susan Cotterill, a Birmingham girl, at Highfield Crescent in 1954, although no trace existed of a birth in 1955.

Many Protestants preferred to believe Stone was Catholic – content, perhaps, to think Protestants could not commit grisly murders, nor behave like 'mad Rambos'. In the Protestant psyche, therefore, Murphy and Stone committed awful crimes only 'because they were secretly Catholic'. Disturbingly, many Protestants were easily persuaded that people from within their community could not be inspired to commit barbaric acts unless there was 'something of the Catholic in them'. In the minds of many in the Protestant loyalist community the real violence was the violence of the IRA. My research had begun to confirm a tendency in one community – though not exclusive to that community – to remain oblivious to the violence in its midst. Catholics did not react against republican violence in the same manner – overtly or covertly they approved of it; it was an inextricable part of their history. The tendency among Protestants was to condemn all violence, particularly IRA atrocities, and then to seek to attribute grisly loyalist-inspired murder to the other community. The knowledge that Lennie Murphy existed in the Protestant community was dissipated by the myth that it was 'the Catholic in him' which motivated his appalling violence: likewise,

Michael Stone. A former loyalist terrorist, who knew Murphy and Stone, explained this tendency of Protestants to distance themselves from particular acts of violence.

Y'see there have been people, Catholics, men and women who married into the Protestant community and they were much more bitter. They lived like Protestants, lived in Protestant areas and assumed a Protestant identity. They were harder on the issues. They were the 'super Prods'. Many of us grew up on a diet of bigotry – so did Catholics. But we were made to believe Catholics were scum, animals, second-class citizens, less than human. Every Catholic was a member of the IRA, therefore every Catholic was a subversive. Now when y'believe that – killing Catholics, any Catholic, is politically and morally acceptable. Within the Protestant middle and upper class there is duplicity. They ran the State and taught us those values. They were the people who controlled our community and who kept control by convincing the rest of us Prods that Catholics threatened our country, religion and way of life. It's when y'come to the type of violence that nobody finds acceptable that the middle class, lower middle class and so-called do-gooders have difficulty. Murphy was not unique but he was prominent, and he was publicly identified as a Butcher from the Shankill which is the Protestant, loyalist heartland. The middle class etc. had to be seen to keep themselves well removed from his actions and the only way they could do it was to subscribe to the myth that he was really a Catholic. I mean – how could one of our people torture and butcher innocent people? Now Stone is another matter. Secretly they admire his 'Rambo' behaviour but publicly he is dubbed 'a mad bastard' so they can't be seen to support him. If he's mad and bad, he has Catholic blood in him.

That view, however revealing, did not resolve my dilemma in tracing Stone's parents, and verifying his claim about them, including his religious persuasion at birth. In January 1991, I wrote to the Superintendent Registrar of Birmingham City Council for his assistance: he sent me Michael Anthony Stone's birth certificate, No. 381.

It confirmed he was born on 2 April 1955 at Lordswood Hospital, 44 Lordswood Road, Harborne, to Cyril Alfred Stone and Mary Bridget Stone, née Sullivan. The parents' address was 200 Fentham Road, Birmingham, and Cyril Stone's occupation was lorry driver for a chemical manufacturer. It confirmed many of the points made by Michael Stone in his note though it left several matters unresolved, namely his religion and his claim that his father was a soldier. Mary Bridget Sullivan was indeed a Birmingham girl, but her name suggested an Irish Catholic connection. Cyril Alfred Stone was a Protestant but did not appear to be a member of the Royal Corps of Signals involved in 'one of these "soldier–girl relationships" '. From the Registry of Marriages in Birmingham I requested a marriage certificate for Cyril and Mary Stone. Bearing in mind Michael Stone's claim that the relationship 'lasted two years' I asked for the search to cover a five-year period either side of 1954. No such certificate existed, they said; write to a Merseyside registry which held records for the whole of England and Wales. Meanwhile the Belfast Registrar said no evidence existed in his files of a marriage between Cyril and Mary. At least I was in possession of a hitherto unknown fact – that Michael Stone was English, a fact which would lead me, at a later stage of my enquiry, to understand the motivation for some of his actions. If his father had been a soldier when first married, that might have provided an added impetus for Stone's commitment to eliminating the IRA.

While awaiting a reply from Merseyside I used other sources to trace the wider Stone family. Cyril Stone, it transpired, was also English, with an Ulster connection, which led to his sister, Margaret, returning to Belfast and marrying John Gregg.

Merseyside registry authorities finally found a marriage certificate for Cyril Stone and Mary Bridget Sullivan. They married in a London registry office in 1953 when Mary Bridget was 19. Cyril's occupation was not a soldier, as his son claimed, but – as Stone's own birth certificate stated – a lorry driver with a chemical manufacturer.

Stone did have a further correct detail: that their marriage had only lasted two years. In September 1955 Cyril and Mary Bridget parted and later remarried others and had children. Mary Bridget, for reasons unknown – perhaps the bitterness and shame of a broken marriage – walked out of the family home in Birmingham. She literally left Cyril holding the baby and never again saw her son: she was 21 years old. When Michael reached manhood he was told she had remarried and was middle class. In 1955, Cyril was unable to care for his baby boy, and took him to his sister Margaret in Belfast. She lived with John Gregg in the tiny coastal hamlet of Ballyhalbert on the shores of Belfast Lough. Michael was unaware of parental rejection in his formative years and regarded Margaret and John as his natural parents. They allowed the child to keep 'Stone' as his surname and protected him from his past. In 1959 the family moved to a new housing estate, the Braniel, on the edge of

East Belfast. In a letter to me from his prison cell, Stone reflected on his relationship with the Greggs:

John and Margaret have been my parents. They loved and cared for me. I grew up in a happy family-type environment. Our family are very supportive of each other to this day. My natural parents remarried and have their own life and families to look after. I sincerely hope they found happiness.

The Greggs were a typically working-class Protestant family living in a tidy new housing estate, which was an improvement on the overcrowded Catholic sidestreets of East and West Belfast where unemployment was rife and housing conditions appalling. John Gregg was a steel-worker in Harland and Wolff Shipyard, which employed a predominantly Protestant workforce. The shipyard was the symbol of the Protestant work ethic epitomising prosperity as well as domination. Its history mirrored sectarianism, and was frequently a focus for violent hatred of Catholics who dared enter the workforce. The shipyard cranes dwarfed East Belfast, and evoked the yard's vast building achievements, such as the *Titanic* and *Canberra* liners.

While East Belfast was the symbol of Protestant solidarity and prosperity, the Shankill district of West Belfast was the heartland of loyalism. The concept of God, Ulster and Britishness adorned street paintings in the east of the city. In John Gregg and Margaret Stone's home, photographs depicted the Stone family's commitment to Ulster and Britain.

There were photographs which gave an insight into my family and my hereditary sense of loyalism which I cherish. My grandfather, Cyril Stone, Royal Corps of Signals; greatgrandfather, Thomas Stone, ex English Regiment.

The photograph of Thomas Stone was taken while he was in Africa working on a British government engineering project, and depicted him holding his pet baboon 'Jacko'. Another wall-hanging contained a framed parchment commemorating the Solemn League and Covenant established in 1912 to resist British Home Rule for Ireland. The parchment bore a signature in blood of James Moore, Stone's great-grandfather and was dated 28 September 1912. Moore was in the Royal Irish Fusiliers but served in the staunchly Protestant paramilitary police auxiliary, the Ulster

Special Constabulary, from 1921–31. A photographic reminder of
Stone's natural father hung on a wall depicting him standing
beside a lorry. The significance of all the memorabilia was not lost
on Michael Stone who knew different images were to be found in
Catholic homes in Belfast.

Whilst they had framed pictures of the Sacred Heart and President
Kennedy, my home had the Queen, and portraits of my great grand-
fathers proud in their military uniforms, proud to have served 'King and
Queen' in two world wars and my grandfather's parchment signed in his
own blood.

When he reached primary-school age Margaret Gregg told him of
the existence of his natural father, and pointed to the photograph
of him. There was no mention of his mother, and Stone admits she
was an 'unmentioned subject'. His awareness of the existence of
his real father did not detract from his desire to regard the Greggs
as 'mum and dad', and his aunt Margaret ensured that he grew up
without knowing about the break-up of his parents' marriage.
Cyril occasionally sent postcards or telegrams to his son at
Christmas and on his birthdays, but Margaret placed that correspondence in a cupboard with the intention of giving it to the boy
when he reached maturity and would be better prepared to deal
mentally with his past.

Stone says his family were 'respectable working-class loyalists'
and he uses 'loyalists' to define Protestants who considered loyalty
to Queen and country an integral part of their religious conviction.
The use of language to link politics and religion was central to that
'God and Ulster' ethos crucial to the maintenance of Protestant
domination of Northern Ireland, accompanied by violence to
sustain Protestant ideals. Loyalty, Britishness, was represented
through attachment to monarchy, rather than via the constitutional link. It provided a convenient means of mixing religion
and politics, rendering violence a 'justifiable' way of ensuring
domination of Catholics who were 'Godless and anti-British'. The
use of the term 'loyalists' to define paramilitaries, and those
promoting violence against Catholics, obscured their prepared-
ness to sanction hatred and bigotry. Loyalism cloaked the true
nature of sectarianism and elevated those propagating it to
defenders of the British link – when in reality they sought to
guarantee religious as well as political supremacy within the State.
The defence of monarchy, as opposed to the constitutional

definition of Britishness, remained a curious feature of Ulster
Protestant thinking, a residue of the William of Orange era three
centuries earlier.

In the present conflict, the word 'loyalist' came into vogue with
the outbreak of Protestant-inspired violence in the late 1960s. It
remained the means by which to describe those harder on the
issues of opposing liberal measures towards Catholics. 'Loyalist'
defined those Protestants whose loyalty to Britain was conditional
upon British governments capitulating to Protestant demands. It
led to the creation of Ulster nationalism, and eventually a policy
that Ulster should break the link with Britain and seek independence. 'Loyalism' revealed a growing disillusionment with Protestant Unionist politics which had failed to prevent the abolition of
Northern Ireland's devolved parliament in 1972, and Unionists
had proven powerless to prevent the signing of the Anglo-Irish
Agreement in 1982.

In the late 1950s and early 1960s there was little evidence of the
presence of loyalists. Loyalism, domination and the supremacy of
the Protestant ethos were taken for granted, were not in jeopardy
and were not questioned. It surfaced in the late 1950s with the rise
of Protestant fundamentalism in Europe and the emergence of the
Revd Ian Paisley. He warned that liberal attitudes towards
Catholics were dangerous: they helped to increase the monolithic
structure of Roman Catholicism. Paisley remained a marginalised
figure until 1963, when a new Unionist prime minister, Terence
O'Neill, promised to reform Northern Ireland and put right many
of the wrongs against Catholics. O'Neill believed that the society
was in a desperate need of economic and social reform, and that
Protestants should behave like people in Britain. He miscalculated
the Protestant opposition to his ideas: his opponents demanded
the maintenance of Protestant domination, and discrimination in
every aspect of life. These were the loyalists: they contended that
concessions to Catholics weakened their legal, political and
religious heritage – hence the slogan 'For God and Ulster' and the
rise of loyalism to defend the Protestant heritage. While some were
prepared to overthrow O'Neill using political means, others
resorted to violence. Thus, the archetypal nature of Ulster
Protestant loyalism was resurrected in the early to mid-1960s in
order to oppose reforms, and to guarantee the shape of violent and
political conspiracy.

In 1963 Terence O'Neill none the less wooed Catholics with

promises of reform, and a new era dawned with the Catholic Nationalist Party accepting the role of official opposition in the previously structured one-party parliament at Stormont. The early 1960s were the quietest period in Northern Ireland's troubled history. In 1962 the IRA had terminated a six-year campaign, thereby recognising the failure of physical-force politics and acknowledging their rejection by the majority of Catholics.

Any search for the events which moved Northern Ireland towards its present conflict inevitably leads to an examination of the period 1962–70. The failure of IRA military traditionalism was a crucial element in providing republicans with the means and desire for emphasising political agitation in the 1960s.

That cessation of IRA gunmanship should have offered Protestants and their political leaders within the Unionist Party the opportunity properly to address themselves to the grievances of Catholics, in the knowledge that republicanism was no longer a threat to the existence of the State. For its part, the IRA leadership had decided that its politically barren militarism isolated it from the masses and that its volunteers should devote their energies to social issues which reflected the needs of the people. Republicans were not alone in seeking to alter the social status of Catholics. Young men such as John Hume and Austin Currie represented a growing intellectual clique who believed the State should be reformed. Catholics had always been excluded, with rare exceptions, from all but the most menial types of government employment. Protestant mistrust of Catholic subversion was embodied in an exceptional piece of legislation, the Special Powers Act, which was presided over by an openly partisan judicial system. (In 1963 the South African Minister for Justice, Vorster, referred to the Northern Ireland Special Powers Act while introducing a Coercion Bill in the South African Parliament, and commented he would be prepared to exchange his entire legislation for one clause of the Special Powers Act.) Today, there are several reputable historians who are prepared to amplify and explain the flagrant use of discrimination against Catholics, and an illustration of how discrimination was promoted in practice was contained within a report in the Belfast morning newspaper, the *Newsletter* on 6 March 1961. It quoted Robert Babington QC, later MP, advocating the following procedure:

Registers of unemployed loyalists should be kept by the Unionist Party and employers invited to pick employees from them. The Unionist Party should make it quite clear that the loyalists have the first choice of jobs.

Within the ruling Unionist establishment, awareness had grown of the need for reform, and Captain Terence O'Neill seemed a man with a vision. Arguing that Northern Ireland needed reforming if it were to address itself to a changing world, he told his followers that the image of the Province would be improved in the outside world if he were seen to carry through a programme of economic modernisation. According to the writer, Sarah Nelson, O'Neill's supporters held that being British meant behaving like modern British people, but the sentiment was an unfamiliar, if not revolutionary, notion among the rank-and-file Unionists. O'Neill recognised the failure of the 1956–62 IRA campaign as a unique opportunity for the Unionists to become magnanimous to the Catholic minority. Modernisation of the economy was, among other things, a prerequisite to convincing them that their future lay in a newly constructed Northern Ireland, and not within a united Ireland. Cynics have said that O'Neill thought he could buy allegiance to his dream, although some historians now contend that he was 'well-meaning but naive'. In some respects O'Neill was politically astute – and courageous. He recognised changing attitudes within the Irish Republic, notably a move away from the traditional Republican ethos that the national question of re-unification was a primary issue for Irish politics. O'Neill responded by establishing a rapport with Dublin, and took the historic and unprecedented step of inviting the Irish premier, Sean Lemass to visit Belfast. Many observers saw the subsequent meeting between the two leaders as the beginning of a new era in Anglo-Irish and British–Dublin relations.

However, O'Neill's own party contained men who believed that reform necessitated capitulation to Catholic demands – which would lead to a weakening of Protestant Unionist supremacy. Their discontent with O'Neill was duly exemplified in public denunciations by the messianic firebrand preacher, Ian Kyle Paisley. Paisley and those who supported him began to illustrate how O'Neill's dreams could be so easily compromised.

The degree to which Paisley influenced events was evident in 1964 when he threatened to organise a march to remove a tricolour from republican premises in a predominantly Catholic area. The police responded to political pressure and removed the flag with the result that serious rioting occurred and illustrated the fragile nature of the society.

In Britain Harold Wilson became prime minister in 1964 and was encouraged by the way O'Neill was running Ulster:

I was anxious that the Ulster Unionist government under Capt. O'Neill should be encouraged to press on with their programme of ending discrimination in housing allocation and jobs, and generally improving the lot of the minority in Northern Ireland. Since coming into office he had by Northern Ireland standards, carried through a remarkable programme of easement.

Wilson's apparent knowledge of what was happening hardly accorded with Jim Callaghan's observation – that when he became Home Secretary he discovered Northern Ireland was mystifyingly filed under 'London taxicabs'. Nor was Wilson's view of the situation shared by Catholic radicals, or by Labour backbenchers such as Stan Orme who were concerned about the pace of reform. Irrespective of Wilson's apparent intimacy with the issue, the evidence tends to prove that successive British governments including the 1964 Administration paid little attention to the way the Unionists ran the Province. As late as 1968, Richard Crossman was astounded to discover (according to his diaries) that it was virtually impossible to discover the extent of the financial subsidy to Northern Ireland. Callaghan should have been knowledgeable about the place because he had visited in 1954 and complained about 'blatant discrimination in housing and jobs'. However, between 1964–69 he concerned himself little with the issue. He later made the interesting observation in his book *Time and Change* that the ending of the IRA campaign provided the basis for change, but that Unionists had failed to grasp it, and had reverted to a policy of discrimination rather than reform. Callaghan identified 1966 as the year when prospects for change, for positive reform, were lost.

In East Belfast and other parts of the city new housing estates reflected some sort of changing society, with the arrival of small numbers of Catholic families who believed a new prosperity signalled a new era of peace. The Braniel was one such housing estate, where a small number of Catholic families co-existed with their Protestant neighbours. Catholics living in predominantly Protestant neighbourhoods (from my own experience) were tolerated, rather than accepted as good neighbours. Protestant neighbours talked freely about religion and paraded their politics while Catholics were frightened to express a view inconsistent with the predominant ethos of the State. Our neighbours were never violent, nor verbally abusive (ironically, a decade later, some of them found the area changed by the conflict, and newly populated by a majority of Catholic families).

Michael Stone's early years in a similarly structured community, were influenced by his local church, St John's Church of Ireland, and St Bridget's Church Hall in the Braniel. He regularly attended Sunday services and the Junior Boys' Brigade affiliated to the church. As a pupil at Braniel Primary, he is remembered as a 'tough kid', not particularly interested in learning. He was confirmed in St John's and joined the choir, excelling in hymn singing.

It would not be an exaggeration to say that I spent a significant part of my childhood in or around the tiny hall attached to St Bridget's. On one occasion a visiting cleric from the much larger St John's gave a sermon at our local church. I became the darling of the adult chorus line. The said Minister liked my vocalizing and virtually pinched me from my local choir. I later joined St John's and if I say so myself I wasn't a bad little chanter but with hindsight you do know that old saying 'all choirboys are bastards or bad bastards'.

The Gregg family expanded to five – two girls, two boys and Michael. He says life was, at times, hard but they 'looked after one another'. His reflections of the period could be applied in general to working-class families, Catholic and Protestant.

Times were hard and being one in a family of eight we had to care and look after one another. My elder brother was a shy, scholarly individual whereas I was outgoing, very boisterous. I had sisters to defend and I mean that literally. When you're young you naturally get into fights and my sisters kept me busy. Unlike other little girls who quarrel amongst each other, they fought tooth and nail with any fella who got too smart with their hands or mouth. It usually ended up with them calling for 'our Michael' to sort it out. I didn't mind fighting with slabbers, bully-boy types. It's just that they were always head and shoulders bigger than I.

The Greggs did not have a car and Michael's yearly vacation was a church Sunday School day-trip to the seaside at Helen's Bay, six miles from the Braniel. John Gregg worked long hours in the shipyard to keep his family clothed and well fed. Michael took a

part-time job delivering milk and newspapers in his neighbourhood. He gave his earnings to his 'mother' and she rewarded him
with 'surprises', small bags of assorted 'sweeties'. When he first
asked about his father, Margaret told him that Cyril was in the
merchant navy, constantly travelling the world. It may have been
her means of easing the boy's lack of contact with his father: his
natural mother was never a subject for conversation, which may
have reflected family bitterness towards her for abandoning the
child.

Michael Stone insists that he regarded the Greggs as his parents,
irrespective of whether his real parents had rejected him. Regarding early feelings towards his mother, he answered reticently,
remarking that she was never in his thoughts. The manner in
which he reacted to my questions about his natural mother implied
that he at least resented her for depriving him of a childhood in a
more lavish environment than East Belfast. He was able to cope
with his father's absence because there was a photograph to
remind him of his existence and his loyalty to the family's political
heritage.

In 1966 he left primary school for Lisnasharragh Secondary at a
time when the origins of the present conflict were beginning to
take a violent shape. In the same year, Protestant gunmen from a
terrorist organisation, the Ulster Volunteer Force, shot Catholics
and tried unsuccessfully to use violence to overthrow O'Neill. This
was the time when Stone's aunt, Margaret Gregg, decided he was
old enough to know a little about his natural parents and their
marriage break-up. She removed a bundle of letters, cards and
telegrams from a cupboard and handed them to him. Some
confirmed that Cyril had spent several years travelling the globe
with the merchant navy. Their expression of love and affection had
little bearing on the teenager beyond providing evidence of a
natural father.

I didn't regard Cyril as my real father. The cards and telegrams were only
proof of my natural father's existence. John Gregg was my real father and
Margaret my real mother.

Margaret told him that his mother had left the family home when
he was five months old, providing him with an image of women
who had babies but rejected them, and emphasising an uncaring
dimension to the character of a woman natural law says he should
have loved.

One aspect of his history pleased him: his nationality. His English parents gave him a greater claim to be British than any of his contemporaries in Northern Ireland. However, there still remained the question of his religious persuasion at birth.

I knew I was truly British. I was, after all, English and my father had served in the Royal Corps of Signals. Maybe my mother was Catholic but my father was Protestant and I was reared in the Protestant faith.

I suspect that he had been informed by someone regarding his natural mother's Catholicism. Did this later reinforce a view of the 'other' community, and of motherhood? One fact is not in doubt: Margaret Gregg had Michael christened in the Anglican Church of Ireland in 1955. Notwithstanding, the Catholic tag may well have remained a subliminal consideration in his own community because he was easily perceived as a bastard child living with in-laws; or because of the presence of the Catholic Stone family who lived in Protestant West Belfast; or because a family relative knew of the existence of Mary Bridget Sullivan, a name echoing to the ring of Irish Catholicism. There were other factors: his association with Catholics in his teens; Protestant rejection of certain types of violence within its midst; these were major contributory factors to the manner in which Stone was perceived as a Catholic thirty years later.

3

Violence and Uniforms

The year 1966 remains significant in the history of Northern Ireland – it signalled the origins of the present conflict. The schoolboy Michael Stone was unaware of a growing uneasiness within the Protestant community – that its domination was being questioned by Catholic nationalists protesting, albeit tentatively, about discrimination in jobs, housing and electoral practices. The mood of the time was for change, but only a few within the ruling Unionist Party recognised the need to address Catholic grievances. On the fringe of politics as yet, Ian Kyle Paisley was railing against change, inciting Protestant suspicion and delivering his own form of oratory against Roman Catholicism. Paisley recognised the inherited fear and prejudice within his community and exploited it. His speeches triggered deep-seated suspicions that Catholics with the IRA in their midst were preparing to undermine Protestantism and Ulster. Paisley openly questioned those few liberal Unionists who were advocating dialogue and branded them 'traitors'. Further inside the political system, hardliners within the Unionist political framework plotted the overthrow of Prime Minister Terence O'Neill, and when this failed they resorted to traditional methods.

Three men, two of them directly involved in the Unionist Party, reformed the Ulster Volunteer Force, a terrorist grouping which was originally a by-product of the 1920s; men who fought at The Somme in the 36th Ulster Division. The UVF was reconstituted to create violence which could be conveniently attributed to the IRA. Three political figures who were central to this period provided guns and explosives, and the UVF was quickly reborn. The timing of their decision was crucial; 1966 was the 50th commemoration of the Dublin Rising which evoked memories of IRA successes against the British. It would be marked with parades throughout Ireland. Conveniently, it was also the anniversary of the Battle of the Somme. The IRA was a spent force in 1966, contenting itself with leftist rhetoric, and involvement in nationalist agitation. It was easy, therefore, for Unionists who feared the loss of supremacy to reactivate Protestant fears of Irish republicanism; the advent of an IRA commemorative event assisted Unionist plotters.

The UVF placed bombs in reservoirs and the explosions were wrongly attributed to the IRA. This served to reinforce warnings from the Unionist hardliners that Catholics were subversives, and that it was dangerous to concede to demands for civil rights; placate the Catholics and Ulster would be weakened. The bombings undermined any potential within Unionism to adopt to a democratic form of government, even to the extent of allowing Catholics the basic principle of 'one man – one vote'. One of the lessons unfortunately ignored was that the formation of terrorist organisations was a tactic not easily controlled. Later that year several members of the UVF in the Shankill area shot dead a Catholic barman and his friend. The two men were drinking late at night in a Protestant pub and were singled out. Loyalism suddenly became a political force expressed through a gun barrel. The Shankill unit of the UVF responsible for the murder was apprehended and its leader, Gusty Spence, sentenced to life imprisonment: the shooting took place in Malvern Street and the victim was Peter Ward from the Catholic Falls district.

This event epitomised the historic battle between the two communities and proved a precursor to a larger conflict. Spence became a hero in his own community and a symbol of developing loyalism. I met Spence on many occasions, and his account of how he arrived at violence has a bearing on the society in which Michael Stone was growing up. Spence became one of Stone's heroes, and in any study of Stone, it is crucial to examine Spence's view of how he was drawn towards the use of violence in the context of the overpowering history surrounding him.

I was a bigot to a large degree. I was an unconscious bigot. Bigotry is not only a state of mind in Northern Ireland, it is a closely cultured state of mind. It was the people who held power who particularly cultured that state of mind. My mother could hardly write her own name and my father got no education until he joined the British Army. Many people were

illiterate and because they couldn't read, they couldn't think for themselves so they always depended on people who were their betters. It was
the local politicians or the churches. They didn't have any access to Irish
history so they believed what they were told. I knew William crossed the
Boyne in 1689, the Dublin Rising was in 1916 and the Somme was in 1916
because it had been handed down to me. But in the absence of fact you
have myth and legend and that's a dangerous thing. People had the
bigotry of the Shankill rather than the behind-the-hand bigotry of the golf
club. At election time it was easy for our politicians to whip up events by
telling people there was going to be assassination of a Unionist cabinet
minister or some sort of plot. Those people who were the bastions of
virtue, the pillars of society, carry a lot of responsibility for the bigotry.

Spence knew many of those 'pillars of society', particularly the
political figures who reformed the UVF. He first met Catholics
when he worked in a linen mill at the age of sixteen, found little
common ground with them and retreated into a mental trench
conditioned by his history, the geography of his birthplace, and
the divisions inherent in every aspect of life in Northern Ireland.
   Although Michael Stone was growing up in a similar society at
the time Spence resorted to the gun, their experiences differed
significantly. Several Catholic families lived in the Braniel and
wrongly believed that life in the early 1960s was peaceful and was
likely to remain so. Stone was aware of the degree of integration in
his neighbourhood and says some of his friends were 'RCs'.

Life then was carefree and a joy. My chums who were RCs were like
ourselves, were totally uninterested in politics or religion, during play.
We spent time in each others' homes sharing meals and sharing life. My
parents taught me to respect all creeds and cultures whilst telling me of
our own cultural and historical heritage. Looking back I'd say they were
quite liberal with their own views. There was no bigotry or sectarianism –
just the facts with a pinch of romanticism thrown in to maintain my
interest.

Questions arise from Stone's retrospective – if not revisionist –
analysis of his early years. Northern Ireland had never been devoid
of bigotry on both sides, nor of evidence of the acute divisions
between the communities. Stone's qualified use of 'during play'
suggests he believed that within their homes his friends were
interested in religion and politics which differed markedly from his
tradition. He must have been aware of the offensive anti-Catholic

sloganising and songs which featured prominently on gable walls, or during yearly Orange parades.

As a contemporary of Michael Stone I was conscious of the bigotry. Folk heroes were gunmen in both communities; the geography of Belfast was a sectarian fact. Family legends abounded. My uncle, a carpenter, told how he was intimidated in the shipyards, and forced to flee the workplace: he had been constantly subjected to anti-Catholic abuse and, eventually, violence. All such images had power, and they served to reinforce an awareness of difference and resentment.

In 1961 I went to school in England, thereby escaping from a society where turmoil rumbled just beneath the surface of life. When I returned in the mid-to-late 1960s, the situation had begun to change rapidly.

By 1968, Catholic agitation for reform was steadily increasing, but no one seems to have seen the inevitability of violence as a consequence of the resurgence of age-old traditions. The Catholic-nationalist caucus brought together republicans, nationalists, middle-class Catholics, and this merged into a Civil Rights movement, which also attracted a small number of liberal middle-class Protestants. On 5 October 1968 a Civil Rights march in Derry received the outrage and violence of the Unionist State. Police and 'B' Specials batoned the marchers, and from that moment events slid inexorably towards a breakdown of civil order. By the middle of 1969 new battle-lines had been drawn between the two communities.

During that first civil unrest, Michael Stone remained un-concerned with politics: more interesting things were occurring in his neighbourhood. He had become leader of a gang which labelled itself the Hole in the Wall. A formidable street-fighter, he defended his district not for political motives, but on account of a macho concern with territory. He was already feared: his repu-tation for violence prevented incursions into the Braniel by other street gangs from neighbouring parts of East Belfast. Any semblance of the choirboy had faded, and at thirteen he was quickly becoming a local thug, physically tough and capable of intimidating older boys. One of his contemporaries provided me with this description of that period.

Stone was either called Flint after the television programme 'The Flintstones', or Stoner. Other kids feared him because he could be really vicious. He really fancied himself and took an interest in all the girls in the area. Most of us were shy about girls but not Flint. He would go and stand alone outside Grosvenor High just to watch the talent. I remember he had an Alsatian and he would take it with him as protection, or because it gave him an air of authority. He used violence to impress, and was likely to attack some innocent kid just to prove how important he was.

Stone's preoccupation with violence is remembered by a colleague of mine who lived in East Belfast. He knew Stone's reputation, and once witnessed him attacking another schoolboy without provocation.

Stone's capacity for street violence was given greater impetus when political events impinged directly on life in the Braniel Estate. In August 1969, the violence on the streets of Belfast led to the intimidation of Catholic families throughout the city. The Braniel did not escape the chaos and Catholic homes were petrol-bombed. In the Braniel the Catholics who did not flee included members of the Hole in the Wall gang. Stone minimises the violence of the time, saying homes were not petrol-bombed: Catholics fled because they were frightened. Yet, August 1969 saw the largest displacement of the Catholic population of Belfast since the Second World War. Catholic families in Protestant areas proved particularly vulnerable and East Belfast witnessed a poignant, frightened exodus of many people carrying what remained of their belongings. Catholic homes in West and North Belfast suffered the greatest damage and that resulted in the arrival of the British Army. Protestants also suffered intimidation on a much smaller scale, although in one instance in Farrington Gardens in Ardoyne, I watched loyalist paramilitaries set fire to an evacuated Protestant street in order to deprive Catholics of the property. In later events, revenge attacks by republicans cost Protestant lives and caused damage to property. During August 1969, loyalist violence spread across the city: the majority of people at risk were Catholics. Thus, Stone watched not only the steady disintegration of his gang but of a way of life in the Braniel, events which, he says, affected him deeply.

The Hole in the Wall gang consisted of a mixed religious membership. Rat Todd along with several others were practising Catholics. But in those days that didn't mean Jack Shit to anyone. He and his co-religionists were put out, broken windows, etc. but no petrol-bombing. It was a result of republican burnings-out in the West and North Belfast. I have to admit emotionally I was shattered and so were the rest of the gang.

It is difficult to assess the veracity of Stone's assertion that he was 'emotionally shattered', but easy to contest his claim that religion 'didn't mean Jack Shit to anyone'. Perhaps an indication of his real state of mind may be found in his actions following the violence in his neighbourhood. The gang was disbanded by him, and he joined an emerging organisation of teenagers known as the Tartan gangs.

The Tartans were formed in response to the upsurge in sectarianism, and they became a focus for Protestant working-class teenagers to vent their hatred of Catholics. Gang members dressed up in tartan outfits which mirrored a Scots pop-group of the time – and satisfied a symbolic loyalist link with Scotland. Many of the Tartan gangs organised on a district basis, fermenting hatred by attacking Catholic homes or business premises. A lecturer at Queen's University who lived in East Belfast at that time reminded me that his teenage years were beset with a fear of the Tartans.

Stone assumed leadership of the Braniel Tartan, and his swift change in attitude from associating with Catholics to attacking them questions his claim that he was 'emotionally shattered' by the departure of Catholic friends. There may be a sense in which he now revises history to imply that sectarianism was never an element in his life. The more likely explanation for his behaviour in 1969 is that he was a product of a divided society, was reacting historically in a reflex way to events, and his propensity for violence was naturally channelled towards an organisation shaped for it.

I was a reporter in 1969 and thus witnessed the slide towards anarchy and the large number of young men in both communities drawn to violence as a means either of asserting identity, or defending their respective communities. I once visited a girlfriend who lived in a Protestant area of North Belfast and found myself watching the activities of a Tartan gang: it was in January 1970, on a Friday night following a day of sectarian rioting. My girlfriend phoned me to ask me if she and her parents should flee their home: her father was Protestant, her mother, a non-practising Catholic, and she had attended a Catholic convent school. They believed that irrespective of overt lack of religious commitment, they were branded 'Catholic'. I arrived at their home in the Oldpark at 10.00

p.m. and remained until the following morning. During those hours I stood at an upstairs window and watched the destruction of Catholic homes and businesses. The majority of the culprits were Tartans who looted homes and raided a licensed premises. Teenagers set fire to houses, and lugged cases of beer along nearby streets. Many of these gang members became recruits for paramilitary groupings and were then 'blooded' at an early stage. On that night policemen stood idly by, seemingly amused by events. Their inactivity added to the lawlessness, encouraging young men like Michael Stone to believe their actions had the approval of those employed to uphold the law.

The conflict widened and, irrespective of the presence of British soldiers, the city developed into sealed-off enclaves. In loyalist and republican areas the paramilitaries became the arbiters of law, order and punishment. Barricades were set up on roadways and street corners; self-styled vigilantes patrolled the streets. Belfast became a city of fear and uncontrolled ferocity. Amongst loyalists, the UVF was to be overshadowed by a new and much larger grouping, the Ulster Defence Association. Its members openly paraded in combat gear and balaclavas, presenting a new and formidable threat to Catholics and the British Army. The absence of law permitted barbarousness: aggressive psychopaths entered the ranks of the UDA and UVF.

By 1972 the Unionist monolith had begun to crumble on account of its inability to reform – and because the British government finally recognised the Northern Ireland parliament as anathema to progress. In March 1972 Unionist fears were exacerbated by the prorogation of the Stormont parliament and the imposition of direct rule from Westminster. Matters worsened when the British Cabinet flew IRA leaders to London to negotiate a political settlement to end the IRA campaign of violence. Loyalists reacted by terrorising sections of the Catholic population in revenge for the erosion of Unionist supremacy. The UDA and UVF launched a campaign of indiscriminate killing. Any Catholic male who found himself in the wrong part of Belfast at the wrong time was murdered. Tartan gangs in East Belfast were involved in abducting Catholics who passed through that part of the city or were travelling home drunk late at night. On what became known as 'dumping grounds', specific streets or alleyways, victims were unceremoniously left in their own blood.

One moment remains for me the most horrific in my record of

that period: the killing of 23-year-old Patrick Benstead, whose body was found by a man walking his dog in Templemore Avenue in East Belfast; a report of the incident had reached the *Belfast Telegraph* newsroom. A lone policeman at the entrance to the alley at Crossley Street wrongly believed I was a member of the police forensic team and gave me access. Ten yards ahead of me was a body wrapped in a blanket. A single bullet-wound to the head was the cause of death, but was probably a release from the torture he had endured. His killers used a red-hot poker to brand a cross on his back and the figure 4 and IRA. The palms of his hands and soles of his feet had burn marks. He had been in the hands of his killers for twelve hours in a derelict house or a club where victims were tortured. Loyalist paramilitaries called the torture houses 'romper rooms'. The origin of 'romper rooms' and 'rompering' as a euphemism for torture was a children's television programme, 'Romper Room', broadcast locally. Benstead, a grown man, behaved childishly, his speech evidence of his below-average intelligence. His mother pleased him by permitting him to run errands for her, and on the day of his abduction he was returning from a shopping trip and strayed too close to loyalist-held areas. The figure 4 was the killers' way of signalling it was their fourth victim. The same killers treated another victim, Henry Russell, to a grisly death and left his body on a railway track at Sydenham in East Belfast. The IRA retaliated, though not with grotesque individual torture: they bombed shopping centres, and killed soldiers and policemen.

East Belfast and North Belfast became the main killing grounds for loyalist groupings. The UDA and UVF were not alone in selecting targets, and were assisted by Tartans and two shady organisations known as Tara and the Red Hand Commando, both small in number, both run by homosexuals who had notorious reputations. The Red Hand Commandos was the creation of a firebrand loyalist John McKeague, who possessed a criminal record for buggery. McKeague recruited young men from Tartan gangs into his ranks and exploited them sexually as a precursor to violence. The Benstead, Russell and other killings were carried out by McKeague and his followers. Tara was led by William McGrath, a house warden at the Kincora Boys Home on the Newtownards Road in East Belfast. Unlike the Red Hand, Tara was established in the mid-1960s as an anti-Catholic, anti-communist group. It declared that the Catholic Church should be made illegal, and all

Catholic schools closed. In 1971 it urged loyalists to organise into platoons of twenty men and acquire weapons, and threatened that five Catholics would be assassinated for every dead Protestant. McGrath was, like many UDA leaders, a frequent visitor to Ian Paisley's church. An evangelical zealot who supported and attended Paisley's rallies in the 1960s, McGrath held the bizarre view that Northern Ireland Protestants were descended from the Lost Tribe of Israel. Like McKeague, McGrath was attracted to the violent anti-Catholic doctrine of Paisley but preferred to use his own organisation to further his ideas.

Both McGrath and McKeague were accepted and significant figures in a Protestant community which detested homosexuality. The 1967 legislation legalising homosexuality in Britain was resisted in Ulster by Unionists, and in particular by Paisley who orchestrated a 'Save Ulster from Sodomy' campaign. Acceptance of McKeague and McGrath within loyalism suggested a victory for virulently anti-Catholic rhetoric over traditional homophobia. Further than that, McGrath was accepted into the Orange Order, and McKeague invited to appear on political platforms with leading Unionists. No one in the Protestant community questioned their widely known – if never publicised – abuse of boys and young men. McGrath led a promiscuous life and it was not until 1981 that he was imprisoned for the sexual abuse of boys in his care at the Kincora Hostel. He was a secretive figure, whereas McKeague openly flaunted his paramilitary trappings.

In 1972 the Tartans displayed their potential for violence in the north of the city, killing a young Catholic, Victor Andrews. They beat him, stabbed him fifteen times and dumped his body near his home. Their actions signalled their value to McKeague and other paramilitary leaders. The UDA recruited many Tartans including Michael Stone and members of his gang. Membership of the UDA was not incompatible with membership of another terrorist grouping, and Stone found himself under the influence of John McKeague. He was 16 years old and was initiated into Tara and the UDA at the beginning of that year. Stone thereby took an irrevocable step towards committing his life to violence. His letters from prison and his remarks during visits refer to his fears, and his instinct to defend his own community. When he left school, where he had shown little interest in academic life, he followed his stepfather into the shipyard and attended day classes at a technical college. In the shipyard, he found himself in the midst of the gut politics of loyalism, although his entry into the UDA and the Red Hand Commandos was made easier by his local and Tartan reputation as a tough, uncompromising bully. He now says his paramilitary membership was an inevitable consequence of his association with things 'military'.

From an early age I wore a uniform in the Boys' Brigade and learned military mannerisms. I sang with pride *God Save the Queen* at the end of every parade. I am proud of my Britishness and from Senior Boys' Brigade I became an Army cadet in the Irish Guards.

Stone was conditioned to regard 'Britishness' as symbolised by military attributes; the photographs which adorned the walls of his home supported his belief. He admits that 'a number of loyalist acts of violence were sectarian' – to say the least, a gross over-simplification. Hundreds of innocent Catholics were murdered by loyalist killer squads between 1972–3. Stone concedes that he was 'sectarian' at that time, but does not admit direct involvement in killing. Yet, his presence in the Red Hand Commando, a tightly knit group, would have acquainted him with the thoughts, workings and methods of McKeague's private army. Today Stone admits being sectarian in his early terrorist career, but distances himself from murders in 1972–3.

A typical sectarian murder committed in North Belfast in 1972 illustrates the terrible hatred which existed in the minds of young men such as Stone. In the early hours of 12 July four Protestant men broke into the McClenaghan home. The men were Trevor Hinton, 23; Ronald Waller, 18; James McGleave, 19 and Terence Joseph Slavin, 22. In the house – Mrs Sarah McClenaghan, a middle-aged widow, mother of three children, her son David and a Protestant lodger, David Titherington. The McClenaghans were that endangered Belfast species, a Roman Catholic family living in a Protestant street. On the night prior to the attack Mrs McClenaghan and her children had been watching loyalist bonfires lit to celebrate the annual oncoming Twelfth of July celebrations commemorating the date of the 1690 victory of William of Orange over James I and his Catholic supporters. At midnight she returned home with her eldest child David and Mr Titherington; the two other children were staying with friends. At three o'clock the household was awakened by the sound of breaking glass. Mrs McClenaghan rose to find bullet holes in the glass panel of the front door and the walls of the hallway. Half an hour later Hinton, McCleave, Slavin and Waller forced their way into the house by reaching through the broken glass and opening the front door. The leader of the gang, Hinton, was unmasked, Waller wore a balaclava and the other two drew chair cushions down over their faces. By now the three occupants of the house had assembled in a downstairs room.

Hinton asked if the house contained guns, and the terrified Mrs McClenaghan replied that there were no weapons, nor had there ever been. Hinton demanded to know her religion and David Titherington, the lodger, intervened to protect her by admitting he was a Protestant. He was seized by Waller, marched upstairs, beaten, and burned under the chin with a cigarette lighter. Titherington produced an Orange sash and claimed that not only was he Protestant but so was Mrs McClenaghan. He lied and said she was his wife, but this did not impress the gang. Titherington was taken to an attic room and made to kneel on his sash. Waller was about to kill him but was distracted by shouting from downstairs. Waller rushed to investigate the noise and Titherington escaped through a skylight and made for the nearest Army post less than a quarter of a mile away.

Downstairs Hinton was having second thoughts about the religion of Mrs McClenaghan and her son. He turned to David who was mentally handicapped and uncomprehending of the exact nature of these transactions. Hinton asked him which church he attended and the boy replied 'Oldpark'. There was no church of that name but it was the district where they lived. There was however Oldpark Presbyterian Church and Mrs McClenaghan tried to convince Hinton that was what her son intended to say. Hinton doubted this and told the boy to fetch his prayerbook. The child dutifully obliged his captors and sealed his own fate. He left the room and returned with his mother's Roman Catholic Sunday missal and also rosary beads.

Completely satisfied he had come upon a 'nest of Fenians' Hinton ordered Mrs McClenaghan to take off her clothes. She refused and Hinton fired a warning shot above her head. A struggle followed and the gang ripped off her clothing and Hinton put her on a sofa. He raped her in front of her son and the other attackers. According to Mrs McClenaghan, McCleave also raped her. Afterwards she and her son were taken upstairs and made to lie face-down on the bed in her bedroom. Hinton told her there was a bullet for her and her son. Mrs McClenaghan threw herself across the body of her son to protect him. She pleaded with them not to touch the boy and pointed out he was handicapped. Hinton told her not to scream but she did, and he began firing. He fired three shots at David hitting him in the neck and chest. As Sarah McClenaghan tried to cover her son, Hinton fired three more rounds which struck her in the thigh and hand. The four men ran from the house but were later apprehended. Hinton and Waller were sentenced to life imprisonment; Slavin and McCleave were found 'not guilty' of murder but convicted on lesser charges, and given seven and eight years respectively.

In opening their trial the Crown Prosecutor said 'restraints of civilisation on human passions were non-existent in the McClenaghan case'. Hinton and his fellow criminals were members of the Ulster Defence Association; Waller was one year older than Michael Stone.

4

Bible, Gun and Absent Friends

Stone's transition from local Tartan gang member to fully fledged terrorist began when he formulated opinions about the conflict, and in a minor way, reacted to events in East Belfast. His awareness of the larger tribal conflicts in North Belfast coincided with the break up of the Hole in the Wall gang, and the moment at which sectarian strife touched his own family. His uncle Wesley lived in 105 Farringdon Gardens, on the edge of the Catholic Ardoyne district, and his house was one of the 307 Protestant households destroyed by rioting in 1969–70. This tragedy profoundly affected the teenage Stone, and he wrote to me about it from his cell in the Maze Prison.

My uncle Wesley was alerted by his loyalist neighbours that the IRA were on their way to burn them out. He being an only child and bachelor lived with and looked after his elderly parents. His loyalist neighbours fled taking what little possessions they could and he was left in the street with his parents as a large republican mob fronted by several armed IRA men arrived. He was severely beaten and a revolver was put to his head while most of the mob shouted 'Kill the Orange bastard'. One woman begged that he be spared saying 'he's only a big softie who looks after his ma and da'. They let him go for some unknown reason, and he walked up the street pushing his mother in a wheelchair, his father holding his hand. He wept as he left the burning street. The Protestants burned their own homes rather than let republicans take them.

Stone's account of a ghastly family experience was not the only factor which engendered resentment and hatred within him. He began to take an avid interest in radio and television news bulletins, and became informed of a steadily deteriorating situation. Tragedy struck again with fatal consequences and reinforced his commitment to become a 'loyalist volunteer'. Two friends, Harry Beggs and his sister Doreen, were frequent visitors to the Gregg home. Harry Beggs died in an IRA explosion in the electricity showrooms where he worked, and several months later Doreen and her two young children entered the Abercorn Restaurant in the centre of Belfast. It was a Saturday afternoon and most of the customers were women and their children. At 4.30 p.m. a bomb exploded without warning, killing two women and injuring 130 customers, among them Doreen Beggs and her children. The Provisional IRA denied responsibility and tried to attribute the bombing to loyalists. Members of the IRA's First Battalion from West Belfast left the bomb under one of the restaurant tables. The Abercorn tragedy occurred after Stone joined the ranks of terrorism but it undoubtedly hardened his resolve to retaliate. He describes his early role in terrorism both as 'combative and non-combative', which I interpret as a vague way of saying he was involved in terror, but not all of the time.

The person who offered him membership of the Ulster Defence Association was its East Belfast leader, Tommy Herron. A swearing-in ceremony was held in a youth club in the east of the city.

I was sixteen. I stood in a darkened back room before my superiors, a Browning pistol in my left hand, the Holy Bible in my right. I swore allegiance to 'God and Ulster'. Strange that all those years later I should stand in a cemetery with a Browning pistol in my left hand and a grenade in my right, still believing in God and Ulster.

His commitment to violence was recognised by Herron when Stone was a mere teenager. Herron, a powerful, ruthless man, controlled all UDA activities in East Belfast: he ran his operations from a headquarters building fronting the Newtownards Road. While the IRA remained a banned organisation, Herron was in control of legalised terror: to this day the British Government has refused to proscribe the UDA, even though it has a long record of murder convictions from its ranks.

Herron formed a close attachment to his new recruit, the formidable terrorist leader espousing a lowly volunteer. One reason was that Herron lived in the Braniel and had closely observed Stone's rise to prominence as a tough kid. The other, perhaps more significant, might derive from Herron's family history. His mother was a Catholic married to a Protestant and he may have felt protective towards Stone, suspecting, as others did, that they shared a common secret. Herron once displayed his penchant for violence when I was sent to interview him at UDA HQ. During the course of the interview, a UDA officer entered the room and informed Herron 'Billy's outside'. Herron withdrew a pistol from a holster, stood watching me momentarily, and then walked into a corridor. The door of the room remained open and I turned to see Herron standing in front of a terrified young man, the pistol pointed to his head. Herron shouted insults and proceeded to pistol-whip this person, leaving nasty gashes on his forehead and a trail of blood gushing to the floor. As quickly as the attack happened it ended. Herron strode back into the room and slammed the door closed behind him. He wiped the butt of the pistol against his trouser leg, replaced the gun in its holster and sat down. He smiled at me, remarked 'that will teach the bastard not to fuck with me' and asked me to proceed with the interview. His victim was a new recruit who questioned an order to extort money from a local bookmaker.

Herron exploited his position of privilege within the UDA and always appeared flush with money. He was vice-chairman and a member of the UDA Inner Council, the governing body which regularly met in an East Belfast hotel. Crime was rampant in Belfast because of lawlessness, and the UDA, particularly in East Belfast, was at the forefront of all racketeering. Households as well as business premises paid a weekly levy, collected by teenagers such as Stone. Householders paid upwards of 25p weekly for so-called protection, while businesses faced demands for £50–£100. UDA leaders used the profits from the rackets to purchase shops, pubs and caravans in seaside resorts on the County Down coast. The police ignored UDA activities, drank in the same pubs and clubs as terrorist leaders and, in some instances, provided them with weapons. Many UDA men, unemployed before the violence began, suddenly displayed wealth which did not derive from unemployment benefit. In local sweetshops, Herron's children presented large-denomination notes.

The UDA, like the IRA racketeers, laundered money derived from the large profits in illegal drinking clubs. In Protestant areas the clubs were also used for the ritualistic killings of Catholics. A Catholic apprehended was taken to a drinking club, interrogated and tortured in front of revellers. Detectives who visited one

Shankill Road club twenty-four hours after a killing found walls and floors spattered with blood. Speculation on loyalist involvement with ritual violence has suggested that the 'God and Ulster' ethos confirmed a politico-religious war against a godless enemy: dehumanising one's enemy, regarding him as godless, makes possible the most heinous crimes. Many victims of loyalists were 'interrogated in depth' before being killed, on the assumption that every Catholic was a secret republican who knew other republicans. To a lesser degree the IRA also engaged in the interrogation of victims but security records contain fewer examples of IRA torture, and rarely of the ritualistic kind. In the Red Hand Commando, McKeague's use of young and vulnerable personalities fuelled hatred which was then easily channelled into ritual slayings and bizarre practices.

A short time after leaving the UDA, Stone began a life of crime with some of his new acquaintances, and was caught. He appeared before a resident magistrate at Newtownards Petty Sessions three weeks after his seventeenth birthday and was found guilty of handling stolen goods from two robberies: he was given a twelve-month conditional discharge and ordered to pay compensation. No sooner was he out of trouble than his UDA superiors ordered him to steal weapons and ammunition from a sports shop in the town of Comber, eight miles from his home.

With an accomplice, he stole a car and gained entry to the shop under cover of darkness, where they removed shotguns and ammunition. A police informer helped detectives to trace Stone, and he was charged with possession of firearms and ammunition; auxiliary charges were preferred in respect of the burglary and car theft. He appeared at Saintfield Petty Sessions on 19 June 1972, pleaded guilty and was sentenced to six months' imprisonment. The magistrate, unaware of his terrorist links, ordered the prison term because Stone was on licence from the court for previous crimes. His first experience of life in prison was not in the city's Crumlin Road jail but a cell in the women's prison at Armagh. The upsurge in terrorism left the authorities with overcrowding, hence the use of a women's prison. Stone was startled to find he shared a cell with two young republicans, and, frightened that they might set about him, told them he was a common criminal who had committed a robbery for cash. His stay in Armagh was temporary and he was moved to Long Kesh internment camp.

I remember entering one of the large Nissen huts which held up to forty prisoners, republicans and loyalists. We all awaited to be claimed by our respective organisations. I looked around at the various groups of youths huddled together in corners of the hut. It was a case of safety in numbers. It was several weeks before we were checked out by men on the inside who sent messages to the various organisations. The UDA or the IRA in the camps needed to be sure someone was not a Special Branch plant. In the weeks we waited the atmosphere was electric with republicans and loyalists in the same hut. It was bizarre that prior to our arrests we had been trying to blow each other away. It was bizarre in the extreme.

One day as Stone sat on his bunk bed, a new batch of prisoners arrived and his attention was drawn to one of them. Closer inspection revealed it was James 'the Rat' Todd, an absent friend and one-time member of the Hole in the Wall gang. Stone approached him and asked 'how life was treating' him.

I thought he was an ODC, ordinary decent criminal, you know, rapists, thieves that type of thing. I said: 'What are you in for, mate?' He dropped his head and whispered: 'I can't say, Flint.' He walked away to a corner where some PIRA terrorists greeted him with open arms. I later scanned the press to discover he was a Provisional guilty of attempted murder. It later transpired that his cousin was the republican martyr hunger-striker, Bobby Sands. We never spoke after that encounter. I kept track of some of the old gang members. Some kept clear of the IRA while others were inevitably drawn into their ranks. They were once friends but became my and Ulster's enemies. Had I been ordered to take action against them as IRA activists it goes without saying they would have been history. All's fair in love and war. I love all those corny old clichés.

Stone says he built mental dossiers on anyone he considered a potential target.

   Within four weeks of entering Long Kesh he was accepted by the loyalist leadership and removed to loyalist compounds. He revelled in his new-found notoriety of being able to associate with the most notorious of killers. Among them was one of his heroes, Gusty Spence, overall commander of all the loyalist internees and convicted terrorists. Spence, a strict disciplinarian, ran his part of Long Kesh along military lines. Stone received weapons training and was taught the tactics of indiscriminate terror. He spent four months in the camp and it stiffened his resolve. When he returned to the streets of West Belfast he was applauded and welcomed by Tommy Herron and John McKeague.

Another person now appeared in his life, who was to have a significant influence on him. While Stone was in prison, 22-year-old Albert Walker Baker, a British Army deserter, arrived in East Belfast and offered his services to Herron. Baker, a native of the area, was indistinguishable from other UDA men, aside from an acquired English accent. Baker's military training with the Royal Irish Rangers made him an ideal recruit and bodyguard for Herron. It brought Baker into close contact with Stone, who was duly impressed with the deserter's knowledge of weaponry, his arrogance and assuredness. Baker swaggered through bars packing a .45 revolver and boasted about his military exploits and how he escaped the clutches of the British Army. Within one month of his arrival he walked into the Vulcan Bar on the Newtownards Road, the main thoroughfare in the east, produced his pistol and stole £821. The proceeds of the robbery were his pocket money which he shared with two accomplices, members of the UDA.

Whenever the UDA Inner Council met in the local hotel, Baker patrolled the building openly armed. Herron became concerned that one of the hotel waiters, Philip Anthony Fay, a Catholic, might be a security threat. He told Baker to eliminate him: 'Shoot him through the back of the head so that if he lives his brain will be damaged and he will not be able to testify.' Baker obliged and carried out the instruction to its fine detail. Fay was killed instantly on the doorstep of his home. Baker made him turn round and shot him in the back of the head. One other dimension to the murder sheds light on a clinical killing method used by Baker, and not contained in Herron's order. When Fay fell to the ground Baker crouched over him and fired three bullets into his head behind his ear, a technique used by SAS and other covert military groupings throughout the world. It served to illustrate that Baker did not require advice on assassination practices: it also begs the question of where he learned them.

Baker, convicted of this and several other killings, led a hit-squad known as the No. 1 Assassination Team, in East Belfast. In October 1972 this 'Team' kidnapped a 21-year-old Catholic, Paul McCartan, from a disco in the Park Avenue Hotel in East Belfast. They took him to the nearby Jones Club at Claremont Lane where they removed his coat and boots. Nine members of the Team were present, and each of them punched and kicked their victim while questioning him about the Provisional IRA. Baker ordered two men to lift McCartan upright from a kneeling position and extend his hands. He was repeatedly beaten with a wooden pickshaft until it broke in two. Baker produced a dagger and twice stabbed McCartan through the palm of his left hand and once through the palm of his right hand. They loosened the belt of his trousers, dropped them to his ankles and threatened 'to cut his balls off'. Baker ran the knife up his left buttock, opening up a large shallow incision. They tied a rope around one hand and another round his ankles, swung him round and dropped him downwards on a concrete floor.

Baker later said 'McCartan was in a bad way' and they decided to shoot him. They drove him to Connswater Bridge off the Newtownards Road, frog-marched him to a stretch of waste ground and placed a green cloth hood over his head. Baker shot him once through the back of the head with the pistol which killed Fay. When he fell, Baker crouched over him and fired three bullets through his right ear.

Stone, by now in the midst of such violent, bloody people, calls them 'a profound influence' on his life. Herron sanctioned such killings, but left the practicalities to men such as Baker and his associates.

In January 1973, Stone again appeared before Belfast Petty Sessions, charged with 'taking and driving away a motor vehicle'. He was sentenced to six months' imprisonment, but only served part of his sentence due to good behaviour in prison. When he returned to the streets, Baker and Herron were still in place, but suspicion was being directed towards the Team leader. The UDA leadership was puzzled at Baker's refusal to operate against British soldiers during a violent confrontation between the Army and loyalists in East Belfast in the spring of 1973. They also queried why RUC CID and Special Branch arrested other UDA men, but made no attempt to apprehend Baker, a man they knew as an Army deserter.

One or two senior UDA figures with secret contacts in republican organisations were told by the IRA that the Army was employing double agents in all terrorist organisations. The agents were being used in the role of *agents provocateurs*. The Provisionals believed that the sectarian killings by loyalists were being encouraged by the military to draw the IRA into a 'tit for tat' sectarian war, which would detach the IRA from their conflict with the

British. Historical evidence exists which, to a degree, validates the Provisional IRA thesis.

The Army recruited IRA men in 1971–2, trained them in counter-insurgency techniques and encouraged them to operate within the ranks of the Provisionals. These agents were part of a secret military unit known as the MRF, the Military Reconnaissance/Military Reaction Force. When the Provisionals uncovered the existence of the MRF, they successfully penetrated it and executed several of the double agents. News of this was leaked to the UDA leadership and Herron consequently began to scrutinise his volunteers. Baker received a tip-off that he was under suspicion and fled to England. He had every reason to believe that the UDA would have interrogated him, and extracted a 'confession' from him, irrespective of the truth. Baker knew too well the methods, ruthlessness and paranoia which characterised Herron and others. On 31 May 1973 Baker walked into Warminster county police station and confessed to four murders and eleven robberies. He claimed he had 'found God'.

Baker later received life sentences and during his time in prison was secretly interviewed by members of MI6. He made claims that he worked under cover. In 1992 he was released from Franklands Prison in England.

Baker's flight to England made Michael Stone feel uneasy, a warning, as it were, to choose his associates with greater care. In addition, Baker's 'betrayal' was also a factor in signalling the demise of Herron who was steadily trying to increase his power base. He believed he could remove the leadership of the organisation in West Belfast and seize overall command. Stone took over the role of bodyguard to his mentor, a dangerous decision. A majority of members of the UDA Inner Council had decided their vice-chairman was too ambitious, that racketeering was bringing the organisation into disrepute and that Herron was plotting against the life of Harding Smith, the West Belfast commander.

In September 1973 a woman lured Herron into a car outside his headquarters and encouraged him to drive to Drumbo, a rural townland between Belfast and Lisburn. Herron, a womaniser, had never been able to resist the prospect of an illicit sexual encounter. When the car halted in a laneway a gunman, hiding in the boot, pushed down the rear seat and shot Herron through the head. The UDA leader was carrying his personal weapon which was found beside his body.

Herron's death sounded a second warning to Stone of the risks of being prominent in the UDA. He was fortunate that his record as a volunteer drew such admiration – otherwise his association with Herron and Baker could have cost his life. The degree to which he was respected can be measured by the fact that after Herron's death he refused a senior promotion in the UDA. He fashioned a lower profile and maintained his connection with McKeague.

5

Women and Crime

Northern Ireland moved towards a political settlement between the two communities on 1 January 1974. A governmental body, the Northern Ireland Executive, took over parliament buildings at Stormont, an historic moment: Unionists and nationalists sharing responsibility for government for the first time in their history. The arrangement was opposed by loyalists because the new political structures were designed to create an eventual role for the Dublin government in Northern Ireland affairs. Republicans were equally opposed to it, believing any settlement within a British context an obstacle to their plans for the overthrow of British rule and the procurement of a united Ireland. Within five months, loyalist opposition hardened under an umbrella organisation, the Ulster Workers' Council, which included the UDA, UVF and other paramilitaries. The UWC controlled the power stations, which employed a majority-Protestant workforce and this provided a means of bringing Northern Ireland to a standstill. On 15 May, huge power-cuts closed several factories; and shipyard workers went on strike. Two days later car bombs in Dublin killed twenty-two people and five others died in an explosion in the town of Monaghan just over the border in the Irish Republic. The bombs were planted by units drawn from the UDA and UVF and were a warning that loyalists would not tolerate Dublin interference in their affairs.

Throughout Northern Ireland, loss of electrical power, and intimidation by loyalist thugs, brought the Province to a standstill. All workplaces closed and journeys were made only if permitted by the Workers' Council, who issued passes to broadcasting organisations, newspaper journalists and others deemed 'members of necessary services'. I remember acquiring passes for BBC management in Belfast to permit them freedom of travel. On one occasion I went to UWC HQ to talk to a contact and was led to a waiting room. Alongside me sat members of a family seeking permission to attend a funeral of a loved one. The city was controlled by masked men on barricades, who prevented people travelling to work and only allowed passage to those in possession of UWC permits. With the RUC powerless to act, the British Army refused to intervene: Army generals told Harold Wilson and his cabinet they were not prepared to confront the 'strikers'. The Army Chief of Staff attended a cabinet meeting on 23 May and outlined the Army's position. He said if soldiers moved into the power stations the strikers would wreck the installations causing irreparable damage, and he did not have the technicians capable of working sophisticated machinery. He argued that British public opinion would disapprove of military force against people regarded as legitimate strikers, and that such a move could be exploited by the IRA, leaving his men caught between two enemies. His defence of the Army position, with its experience of Northern Ireland, Cyprus, Aden and other political trouble-spots – albeit in this case a confronting of British civilians – involved a question of image, and, perhaps significantly, a concern that his soldiers might refuse to storm barricades. All fine to fight the IRA, 'real terrorists', killing soldiers, but not a community which supported the Army. Add in the danger that the RUC and the Ulster Defence Regiment might openly support the strike and oppose the Army. In order to prevent such a scenario, both groupings would have to be disarmed and such a move would lead to full-scale, loyalist-versus-republican civil war into which British generals had no desire to be drawn.

Wilson reluctantly accepted the Army view, and the new Northern Ireland Executive was forced to resign on 28 May. The following day the UWC abandoned the strike, and Merlyn Rees, Labour Secretary of State, observed that it was the rise of Ulster nationalism which led to the collapse of power-sharing.

During the UWC strike Stone was 'active', but is non-committal about the exact nature of his role. On 7 June he was back in court charged for an offence which was becoming a familiar feature of his life: 'attempting to take and drive away' a motor vehicle. He received a two-year probation order and considered himself lucky not to see a prison cell. The attempted theft of the car was related to his personal life, and a developing relationship with a girl from a town outside Belfast. In order to visit her, he stole cars, knowing he risked being caught and charged with not simply the theft of a vehicle but with having no driving licence or insurance. The girl was a Catholic from a middle-class family who became pregnant by Stone. Unaware of his paramilitary connections when they first met, only that the brash 19-year-old came from Belfast, her pregnancy ended the relationship, but she gave birth to a baby boy who now knows his father's notoriety. Stone never told his paramilitary colleagues of the relationship, or that he had a Catholic son. He enjoyed secret liaisons with many women and relished his ability to lead a double life. When a girl became pregnant he moved on, not wishing the responsibility of marriage. He worried constantly that a girlfriend or her in-laws might learn something of his past history. When this, his first 'serious' relationship ended, the pattern began of moving on to others, always ensuring that his past was hidden. Dressed in expensive clothes, he frequented trendy bars, picking up girls simply for sex. The Catholic girl represented an unusual feature for a man devoted to sectarian conflict. Though reluctant even now to discuss the relationship, he uses it to illustrate that he was not sectarian. He gives the impression of having enjoyed the idea of fathering a child, particularly to a middle-class Catholic. In the pubs of central Belfast, he enjoyed talking to fellow revellers whom he knew to be Catholic.

I used to go into the Beaten Docket and other bars in expensive gear. I drank with Catholics but they only knew me as Michael or Stoner. It was great knowing they were unaware they were standing beside someone who could blow them away.

He is forthcoming about his pursuit of women, as this note from prison testifies:

My relationships with the fairer sex? I have to admit I was always a bit of a flirt, always promiscuous. I enjoyed being with women, be it night-clubbing or out for a meal. I appreciated their company in or out of the sack. My way of life, i.e. my illegal activities, dictated the way I lived. If a relationship began to develop I always ended it before it had a chance to become permanent. This was a selfish attitude, but for obvious reasons I had to adopt a 'no one keeps tabs on me' policy.

Irrespective of his desire to determine the character of his sexual relations, he found himself drawn into longer-term arrangements, and lived with three women, fathering a child by each: the births of the children ended each relationship.

The mid-to-late 1970s was a period when he became preoccupied with his social life at the expense of his terrorist connections. I asked him why he fathered children when the births could have been prevented. He replied:

You won't believe this but the women never told me at the outset they were pregnant. I could have told them all to have abortions but I didn't agree with abortion. You may find it hard to believe that someone like me who has frequently taken life could be against abortion. Really I was. I value human life but not the lives of the people I've killed. Well maybe one or two who got in the way of an operation. I couldn't sanction abortion.

During his period as a wandering Casanova, Stone maintained contact with the Red Hand Commando, and in particular with Samuel Ferguson, one of his closest associates in the group. Ferguson also came from the Braniel, and the two were boyhood friends who operated together. 'Fergie', as he was affectionately known to Stone, was responsible for bombing Catholic-owned bars in East Belfast: two of his targets were the Hillfoot in the Braniel, and Paddy Lamb's on the Upper Newtownards Road. He served a prison term, and shortly after his release died in a road accident.

On 29 July 1975, Stone was convicted once again for a familiar criminal trait – driving without holding a licence or insurance – and received a six-month sentence in Magilligan Prison. He had 'no complaints' about the nature of justice, and the lenient way it treated him as a habitual offender. On his release he was rearrested and a magistrate sent him to the Maze Prison to serve an earlier six-month suspended sentence: as a model prisoner, he served less than four months. His return to East Belfast was marked by a change in his relationship with his former comrades. He began to spend less time in their company and undertook part-time jobs while collecting unemployment benefit. He also received money from his terrorist leaders, who provided active service volunteers with pocket money, yet he undertook robberies to fund his expensive suits. Although his life-style was flamboyant and clearly not financed from social benefits or part-time jobs, he remains reluctant to agree that he was criminally inclined, or involved in robberies, admissions which would weaken his assertion that he was a 'volunteer soldier' who desisted from 'ordinary criminal activity'. He attributes his car thefts to his role in terrorism – but sources close to him deny that.

In late summer 1976 his life changed dramatically, if only temporarily, when he fell in love with Marlene, an attractive Protestant girl. She was not prepared to tolerate his waywardness or a temporary relationship. He married her and tried to concentrate on being a husband and eventually a father. He 'stood himself down' from active service in the UDA and the Red Hand Commando and addressed himself to earning money honestly. However, he was never far from trouble, despite his best endeavours, and the opportunity for violence presented itself in a part-time job as a bouncer at a dance hall in the Braniel. One night while on duty, a group of tough young men from another district arrived at the dance and a fight broke out between locals and the outsiders. The leader of the outsiders was a large, heavily built individual with a reputation for being a 'hard man'. Stone and several friends attacked the intruders and a running fight developed in which many people were injured. Stone pursued the outsiders into the street and chased their leader until he caught up with him in a part of the estate where rebuilding was in progress. Unconcerned about the superior height and weight of his adversary, Stone, with blows from fists and feet, laid him low. He then lifted a concrete slab and dropped it on his victim's head.

Police arrived on the scene, quickly established Stone as the culprit and arrested him. The man he attacked was seriously injured and Stone faced a charge of attempted murder. He was remanded in custody but to his delight the charge was downgraded to one of inflicting grievous bodily harm. Concerned that he would face a prison term for the crime, he devised a way of encouraging the magistrate to treat him leniently: he persuaded Marlene, heavily pregnant, to attend his hearing and to sit at the front of the courtroom.

I reckoned that if she wore a tight-fitting dress that showed her big bump that the judge would take pity on her rather than me. It was a ploy I knew could be used in my defence. It worked a treat and I got a suspended sentence. The guy I hammered was in court and the damage to him was obvious and that was months later. I nearly killed him but there are wheels within wheels and I was lucky that the charge was reduced.

His court appearance forced him to rethink his way of life, and the notoriety he was acquiring in his own neighbourhood.

I began to realize that life was becoming too risky for me. The job as a bouncer brought me into contact with too many people in loyalist circles. I was always careful about personal security and limited my associates to people I trusted. I was coming to the attention of the police and that was dangerous. I decided to retreat into a quiet life. I moved away from the UDA and UVF and former colleagues. Times were changing and there were people joining the organisations who were not known. It was difficult to know who to trust. Some of the groups were penetrated with informers and the supergrass system was being put in place. I was still committed to action but I decided to lie low, to become a nobody until I could devise a way of operating without risk. It was no longer the mid-1970s when there was greater freedom of movement and people with you who could watch your back. There were informers, double agents, Military Intelligence groupings, MI6 and Special Branch targeting all of us. I moved into the background, into self-enforced retirement so that I would be forgotten.

Within marriage he was unable to remain faithful and secretly frequented Belfast city-centre bars and nightspots. Marlene was powerless to restrain him; his former associates took little notice of him and honoured his decision to 'retire'.

In East Belfast the UDA was trying to develop a political strategy under the leadership of its commander, Andy Tyrie, and his close adviser, John McMichael, the latter a shrewd tactician, politically and militarily. The UDA no longer claimed or publicly associated itself with violence and used the pseudonym Ulster Freedom Fighters to claim responsibility for bombings and shootings. The UFF was born of a tactic developed by the UDA in 1973 to prevent it being made a proscribed body. It employed the letters UFF as a cover for its paramilitary activities. The British government knew it was a cover name but did not act against the UDA: instead, it made illegal the UFF which represented once again a failure to deal effectively with the Province's largest paramilitary body. Banning the UFF was a futile exercise which permitted a legal terrorist organisation to claim responsibility for death and destruction under a bogus title. The creation of the UFF was set out in a secret UDA document, outlining its objectives. The identity of the document's author has remained secret: he was a Belfast lawyer.

Women and Crime 49

Permitting the UDA to exist was tantamount to legalising the IRA. It reflected the uneven nature of British policy-making in Northern Ireland. On the republican side the IRA was illegal but its political wing, Sinn Fein, was a lawful political body. The creation of the UFF exactly mirrored the situation and permitted the UDA gradually to adopt the IRA strategy of 'the ballot box and the Armalite'.

The arrival of John McMichael within the UDA leadership in East Belfast evidenced a progressive development of an IRA-type strategy. He moved the UDA towards politics, while secretly masterminding terrorism under the aegis of the UFF. The most lucid exposition of loyalist thinking – of the type which resided in Stone's mind throughout his career – was a 1973 UFF statement which had still remained in place as a loyalist thesis while Stone was reviewing his life in the late 1970s.

We accept that the Press of the world is sick of the sound and sight of Ulster, sick of our orgy of destruction, sick of our rancour and sick of our brutality. Why, therefore should you be interested in the self-delusive ravings of a band of extreme Protestants? A band of men cast in the role of wicked 'heavies', the 'bad guys' of the story, the narrow-minded bigots of Ulster, the cause of all the present troubles?
  Mountains of words have been written about us in the past four years and our role in the affair is cast by the Press in a certain way and all comments about us are based on these assumptions:
That we are narrow-minded. That we are fanatical. That we are similar to the IRA. That we hate all Catholics. That we are repressive, 'right-wing' fascists. That we cannot be reasoned with. With all that has been written about the Scots-Irish of Northern Ireland, you would have thought that someone would have eventually grasped the essential truth of it all. The real cause of the bloodshed, the real cause of the hatred. We think you, the Press, have done nothing of the sort, and it is high time that you did; for, if nothing else, we do feel you owe our people a little latitude. Just this once.
  It seems a lifetime ago that our competent, if partisan government came under fire from a civil rights movement, which, it has to be admitted, did have a justification for many of its grievances. Cast inevitably in the role of St Bernadette [*Bernadette McAliskey née Bernadette Devlin MP and political activist*] came a pint-sized lady of fiery oratory and poverty-stricken background. How the Press loved this little lady, pictured her swinging prettily in a garden as her victories over the repressing, misruling Unionists were announced.

You, the Press, made a heroine of this girl, and you bear a heavy responsibility for what happened. The blundering, incompetent, and seemingly repressive antics of our leaders confirmed your attitude that she and her associates were right and that we were wrong. The B Specials, the reactions of our police force, and the so-called ambush at Burntollet, hardened your views which, in turn, hardened ours and the die was cast. [*Burntollet was a townland where student activists were attacked by loyalists and members of the 'B' specials on 4 January 1969. Marchers were led by Bernadette Devlin and members of Queen's University Peoples' Democracy Movement. The PD believed civil rights were not enough and the State was irreformable. Their march from Belfast to Derry was provocative because it passed through staunchly loyalist strongholds. Eighty marchers were attacked at Burntollet Bridge by two hundred loyalists which transformed the civil rights struggle and pushed the situation towards sectarian strife.*]

It is such a pity that you do not consult your history books, for the real truth lies there, repeated over and over again, like a gramophone record. We are a hybrid race descended from men who colonised Scotland from Ireland in the fifth century and who then colonised Northern Ireland from Scotland in the seventeenth century. Our existence was not placid in Scotland but that was heavenly compared to our life in Ireland. For four hundred years we have known nothing but uprising, murder, destruction and repression. We ourselves have repeatedly come to the support of the British Crown, only to be betrayed within another twenty years or so by a fresh government of that Crown. What is happening now mirrors similar events in the seventeenth, eighteenth and nineteenth centuries.

We are not good at propaganda and not good at extolling our virtues or admitting our faults. We just stick to our point of view, bow our heads and pray for it all to die down for another fifty years or so. Gradually, however, we have come to realize that this time other factors have come into the age-old conflict of the Scots-Irish versus the Irish-Irish, or if you prefer it that way, the Protestants versus the Catholics in Ireland.

Traditionally the English politicians let us down – 'betrayal', we call it. The Catholics try to overwhelm us so we are caught between two lines of fire. Second-class Englishmen, half-caste Irishmen, this we can live with, and even defeat, but how can we be expected to beat the world revolutionary movement which supplies arms and training, not to mention the most sophisticated advice on publicity, promotion and expertise, to the IRA?

We do not have large funds from over-indulgent, sentimentally sick, Irishmen in America, who send the funds of capitalism to sow the seeds of communism here. We do not have the tacit support of the Government of Southern Ireland and we do not have the support or interest of the British people.

We are betrayed, maligned, and our families live in constant fear and misery. We are a nuisance to our so-called allies, we have no friends anywhere. Once more in the history of our people we have our backs to the wall, facing extinction in one way or another. This is the moment to beware, for Ulstermen in this position fight mercilessly until they or their enemies are dead.

We would like to remind you of a few salient facts:

The Russians, who condemn our people, have millions in slave labour camps, and their government is the biggest mass murderer since Adolf Hitler. Edward Kennedy, the heroic night swimmer of Martha's Vineyard, is hardly in a moral position to criticise his pet rabbit, let alone us. The ruler of Libya is a raving fanatic. If the Unionist Government of Northern Ireland was corrupt, it was as pure as the government of John Mary Lynch [*Jack Lynch, prime minister of the Irish Republic*].

If the Press likes scandals then let them examine the private fortunes of Government Ministers in the Lynch Republic. Fortunes made out of a divine intuition about future planning permissions. If Protestants in the South are content, then why do their numbers dwindle, and why do they never complain?

If the Southern Irish Government wants us, then it will have to win our hearts, rather than have us as bitterly hostile losers in a bombing war of attrition tacitly backed by them. Their own history should tell them this will never work. Our troubles destroyed their tourist industry, and a few well-planted disease-ridden animals could very rapidly destroy their economic growth. They too are not immune from trouble, and should not support evil men of violence lest it rebound on them.

The British Army in Ulster has good soldiers who are being set up like dummy targets. The orders of the politicians are tying both hands behind their backs. The British public says: 'Send the soldiers back home'. We say: 'Send the politicians and the officers home and leave us the men and weapons – or, why not send the soldiers home and leave us the weapons, and we will send you the IRA wrapped up in little boxes and little tins like cans of baked beans?'

The politicians who rule our lives from England do not understand us. They stop the Army from defending us properly and stop us from defending ourselves. We do not like these flabby-faced men with pop eyes and fancy accents. We do not like Edward Heath and we do not like his 'sidekicks'. We had to stomach Reggie Maudling until Poulsen saw him off, and Lord Lambton and Jellicoe went in a more interesting way [*three scandals, the last two of a sexual nature, which ruined British political careers*]. We should really like to see Willie [*Whitelaw, the Northern Ireland Secretary*] waddle off to cut the throats of his colleagues in Westminster, and leave us to sensible policies and ideas which will work.

We ourselves are not perfect. We ourselves do not always see eye to eye, but the time is coming near when the Scots-Irish of Ulster will have to reconsider their future actions. The bloodbath could very soon be a reality, and you who condemned us for it could have precipitated it unjustly on decent people, because they gerrymandered a few constituencies to avoid giving power to people who were educated and dedicated to destroying a way of life, and you gave a terrorist organisation all the publicity it desired. It was not an Irish leader of the IRA who said we were all fit to be bombed but a sick little pop-eyed Englishman with a false name and no Irish connections whatsoever. [*Ref: Sean Stevenson took the name Sean MacStiofain and became Chief of Staff of the Provisionals. He failed to fulfil a promise to die on hunger strike and was removed from his position in disgrace.*]

We the Scots-Irish are fighting for survival. We think we have been greatly wronged and we think you should watch events with extreme care.

This cogent statement of loyalist thinking was critical to UDA policy in the late 1970s. Stone regarded it as a definitive analysis of his position and admired McMichael for resurrecting it to reshape loyalist action. From time to time, Stone was tempted to resume a terrorist role because of Provisional IRA atrocities, and one which shocked him, and fanned his hatred of republicans, happened on the night of 17 February 1978. A three-man IRA unit from the Ballymurphy district of West Belfast travelled across the city towards the Braniel, and several miles beyond it to the La Mon Restaurant, a busy nightspot which attracted a Protestant clientele because its catchment area was East Belfast and the town of Comber. It was located in private grounds off a quiet country road, an easy target for the IRA. There were no security guards because it was believed unlikely the Provos would plant a no-warning bomb in a restaurant in the heartland of Protestant North Down. Even though this was a period when the IRA bombed commercial targets, including hotels, few would have believed that the IRA would travel deep into a predominantly Protestant area when they had many easier targets. La Mon, also a hotel, had a reputation for inexpensive, good food and a lively atmosphere. The IRA regarded hotels as targets because they represented a continuing growth potential in the tourist industry: the IRA aimed to destroy tourism as part of a 'scorched-earth' policy: it became one of the most damaging aspects throughout the conflict, and it also deprived Northern Ireland society of the facilities for relaxed enjoyment, and kept a generation from nightlife.

On Friday, 17 February, La Mon was crowded. The IRA unit

reached the car-park close to the hotel and removed a bomb from their car boot, a simple, cheap, but deadly incendiary device made from aluminium filings, recrystallised ammonium nitrate and one-gallon tins of petrol. The ingredients were easily assembled to make a devastating explosive, and the unit was experienced in the manufacture, placing, priming and detonation of bombs. They approached the restaurant, attached the bomb to a window grille and activated the device. Then, they drove to a public call-box to phone a bomb warning to the police but discovered that the phone had been vandalised – a predictable enough factor which, in a haphazard, callous way, had not been provided for: the majority of call-boxes in Northern Ireland were out of operation owing to vandalism at the time. The bombers decided to search for a phone in Belfast but were stopped at a military roadcheck while the bomb ticked towards zero.

The IRA unit negotiated the roadcheck, reached Belfast and phoned a warning to police. The timer on the bomb read two minutes to detonation, insufficient time for the security forces to prevent a catastrophe. When the bomb exploded it sent a fireball through the restaurant and hotel. Twelve people died horrifically and scores were badly injured. The incendiary effect was similar to that caused by napalm bombs in Vietnam.

Michael Stone was at home in the Braniel when a newsflash confirmed the deaths. He and a friend drove the short distance from the Braniel to La Mon to offer assistance to the emergency services. He vividly remembers his horror when he saw charred bodies lying in a row.

When I arrived it was chaotic. The police, soldiers, firemen and ambulance crews were doing their best. People were wandering round shocked and dazed. The injured, many of them badly disfigured, were being ferried away in civilian and military ambulances. What I will never forget was looking at a charred body which was being removed. It was smouldering and looked like a piece of wood. I thought, what is this fucking world coming to? Who is gonna do something about it? The experience of that night never left me.

During 1978–9, while he was living what was for him a normal life, Stone's sworn enemy, the IRA, had spectacular successes against the security forces. In an operation at Warrenpoint in County Down they killed eighteen members of the Parachute Regiment and at Bessbrook in Armagh a 1000-pound bomb claimed the lives of four policemen. Then came the event which truly horrified people world-wide – the assassination of Lord Louis Mountbatten of Burma. He was holidaying with family on his cruiser off the west coast of Ireland when a bomb hidden on the boat was remotely detonated. His 14-year-old grandson, Nicholas, and a local boy of the same age, died with him. Twenty-four hours later, the Dowager Lady Brabourne died of her injuries. Stone says he watched these events with increasing anger, and a resentment that no one within the loyalist paramilitaries was retaliating against the IRA.

The Provisionals, meanwhile, were restructuring their active service units into small cells to prevent penetration by informers, and the strategy was succeeding. The effect was to permit them to operate with greater efficiency and success. They published a secret British Army document written by Major-General James Glover, which provided a pessimistic assessment of the war against the IRA. It offered the Provisionals a propaganda coup by portraying them as a formidable fighting force which was nowhere near being defeated, was becoming more and more professional, and was likely to develop a growing expertise in terrorism.

John McMichael's response to all these events was to try to reshape the UFF along IRA lines, to create small active-service cells with varying degrees of expertise. He recommended the creation of similar ASUs, some with specialist experience of bombing, and others skilled in the use of firearms. He believed the UDA's history of sectarianism, and the strategy it fomented of revenge violence, was detrimental to establishing an organisation with an acceptable ideology. McMichael was convinced of a need to devise 'pre-emptive', not reflex, terror. He told me his reasons for this new policy in a Hillsborough restaurant in the early 1980s.

We didn't have the professionalism of the Provisional IRA. We were always reacting to events and it was too easy to simply go out and select any Catholic. We were not getting the real people – the IRA and their supporters. I knew people in our own community would respect us more if we chose prestige republican targets. We knew the Brits wouldn't mind the IRA being killed by us and would probably turn a blind eye to us operating in that way. We were constantly receiving intelligence files from contacts in the RUC, UDR and British Military Intelligence but nobody was acting on it. In border areas we used those contacts more than we did in the city. Down there it was simply a nod and a wink and our people would have all the necessary intelligence to do a hit. They would have files on the target, his address, his movements, as well as the movements of the security forces at the time we wanted to take him out. But it was all too haphazard. I reckoned we also needed more contact between ourselves and the UVF. In border areas there were lots of joint operations because people lived constantly under threat and there was no question of one-upmanship. Belfast and other major centres were very different. There was too much energy spent on racketeering and other pursuits. Some guys were in place from the early 1970s and ran their own private armies. I had to be careful not to tread on too many toes. The Provos taught me a lot about the control needed over volunteers. They were good at the politics and the terror. I believed if we could develop a clear political strategy as well as a more sophisticated armed strategy that we would also be a more formidable force.

McMichael was one of my best contacts within loyalist terror circles. He owned a bar in Lisburn and invited me to join him there on a number of occasions. Flirting with the notion of an independent Ulster, he was unsuccessful in attracting widespread support for his idea. Those who believed he was simply a loyalist politico found him an affable, straight-talking man. He was careful to distance this genial persona from acts of violence, and was a frequent contributor to radio and television debates. He travelled to university seminars in the Irish Republic to explain the loyalist cause but, like Stone, he led a double life. Behind the frank, friendly façade was a ruthlessness and a determination to kill.

His plans for the UFF gradually took shape and he began searching for new recruits. He set up a training programme, with the assistance of a former UDR officer. This man was English, possessed considerable military training, and undertook the task because of a passion for gambling which he was unable to finance. McMichael presented him with a lucrative means of supporting his life-style in return for his knowledge. The Ulster Defence Regiment provided a ready source of logistical and human resources for loyalist paramilitaries: soldiers in the regiment were earmarked for membership of the new UFF active-service units. McMichael recommended the creation of a detailed dossier of intelligence on republicans. He said it should constantly be upgraded with the aid of contacts within the security forces.

The UDR, a British Army regiment with a majority-Protestant membership, possessed a history of collusion with loyalist paramilitaries, and was an ideal source for intelligence on republican activists and non-combatants in the Catholic community who sympathised with the IRA cause. McMichael also preferred to think of himself as a non-sectarian ideologue, but his actions did not justify his image. He allowed the wild men within UFF ranks to kill innocent Catholics as a means of retaining their allegiance. There was always a need within loyalism to give vent to hatred and revenge, and he recognised the necessity for occasionally releasing that valve. It did not interfere with his plans for new active-service units capable of assassinating leading republicans.

Stone likewise was becoming impatient with loyalist inaction, with his own failure to remain faithful to his wife and with the loss of the comradeship of other terrorists. He was no longer prominent in loyalist circles, but this suited a concept which was steadily taking place in his mind. He was beginning to formulate new ways of operating as a hitman – without the attendant risks derived from operating within the UDA or Red Hand Commando.

6

A New Career

Stone's enforced isolation proved beneficial in removing him from the scrutiny of British Army and RUC surveillance teams. It distanced him from John McKeague of the Red Hand and William McGrath of Tara. Both these men had been accepted figures in loyalism during the turbulent years of the early 1970s, but by the end of the decade their homosexual exploits led to them being discredited. They remained friends because of their perverse interest in young boys, and their joint role in the systematic abuse of young men in an East Belfast hostel run by McGrath. The RUC also suspected McKeague of involvement in the unsolved murder of a 10-year-old Protestant boy, Brian McDermott, whose charred and dismembered body was found on the banks of the River Lagan in Belfast. The child disappeared while playing in a public park and a British intelligence file later identified McKeague as his abductor and murderer.

Military Intelligence analysts reckoned one motive for the killing could be witchcraft whereas the RUC were convinced the crime was sex-related. Details of these suspicions were leaked to the media and found their way into the loyalist community and McKeague was shunned. The RUC launched a separate enquiry to investigate McGrath's activities in the Kincora Boys Hostel in East Belfast. Previous attempts to examine matters at the home had failed – McGrath was shielded: he had been working for British intelligence from the mid-1950s. He was recruited by MI6, and in the 1950s and 1960s reported on the growth of communism within the IRA. During the early years of the present conflict he used Tara to cloak his secret activities. He also monitored the actions of his fellow loyalists, but his other life included the provision of boys for homosexual colleagues within the British intelligence community in Northern Ireland, and for several leading members of the British Establishment who visited Belfast regularly. Evidence exists he sent boys to parties organised by fellow homosexuals in London. The UDA and UVF knew that McGrath was abusing boys in the hostel, but overlooked his sexual predilections because he supported their cause.

In the mid-1970s they began to suspect him of attempts to discredit loyalist leaders – without proof, they decided to take no action. Their suspicions were correct: at the instigation of counter-insurgency experts within MI6, he circulated a document accusing leading Protestant politicians of homosexuality, wife-beating, and psychiatric illness. In 1979 a Military Intelligence liaison officer sabotaged RUC attempts to trace the history of McGrath and his British intelligence connection. A fear existed within the Secret Intelligence Service that Kincora would lead to a scandal which would damage the reputation of well-known homosexuals within the Military Intelligence community, and would also compromise others well known in British political life. An RUC officer leaked details of the cover-up surrounding McGrath to the *Irish Independent* newspaper reporter, Peter McKenna, whose revelations provided the catalyst for increased press speculation, eventually leading to an official inquiry and McGrath's conviction. The inquiry failed to unravel the history of Kincora, and McGrath went to prison with his secrets to serve a mere two-year sentence. McKeague was shot dead by an Irish National Liberation Army hitman before the judicial authorities could summon him to give evidence to the inquiry. Several others, who could also have provided valuable evidence, died by their own hands or mysteriously.

The controversy surrounding McGrath and, in particular, McKeague, convinced Stone that his self-enforced isolation was the essence of his survival. In prison McGrath was interrogated in a cell by a UDA officer for two hours, was eventually intimidated, broke down and revealed all the secrets of his espionage career. When the UDA officer was released shortly afterwards, he quickly rose to prominence within the UFF. He was murdered a short time later and took McGrath's secrets to his grave. An internal UFF investigation into his death concluded that his possession of highly sensitive information about MI6 activities in Ireland was a contributory factor to his demise.

A loyalist source, whom I met in 1990, was reluctant to discuss the matter with me but confirmed this story.

McGrath and Kincora was a dirty business. Many of us knew the rumours, and a few such as Herron knew the facts. The guy who interrogated McGrath in jail rose through the ranks, and there was a suspicion he had compromising information on someone within the UDA leadership, provided by McGrath. There was reason to believe it was someone high up in the East Belfast Command. The information linked this person to British intelligence. I'm not gonna point the finger at anybody – it's more than my life's worth to even discuss this. There are people who are very sensitive about this. Nobody talks about the McGrath business. There's a feeling it holds dangers for anybody who gets too close to it.

The only person in the East Belfast leadership with the authority to elevate people in rank was the UDA/UFF leader, John McMichael, but to point the finger firmly at him would not be possible without further evidence. Other journalistic investigators of the Kincora story uncovered startling evidence about McGrath's espionage activities and his codename within MI6. They received threats, one from an MI6 operative, and were left under no illusions as to the risks of unravelling homosexual loyalist connections with British intelligence.

The death of McKeague led Stone towards two other important influences in his life, and mirrored his earlier attachments to terrorist leaders. He was drawn firstly to John McMichael, but was uncertain about re-establishing a direct operational link with the UDA. He also favoured a connection with the outlawed UVF and its West Belfast commander, John Bingham, who resembled Herron, and possessed cunning and ruthlessness. Bingham was a charmer, with a personality which supported his often repeated contention 'he couldn't hurt a bird' – he was a pigeon fancier – but murdering Catholics, or known republicans, seems to have presented him with no conflict of conscience.

In spring 1980, Stone used a contact to inform McMichael he wished to meet him, secretly. McMichael was cautious, meticulous about his personal security and asked one of his intelligence operatives to 'run a check' on Stone. Within days a report was on McMichael's desk confirming Stone was an efficient volunteer, once highly regarded within the UDA and Red Hand. The UFF leader was rebuilding his units, and the prospect of a new recruit with no official police record for terrorism appealed to him.

McMichael used a third person from within his ranks to liaise with Stone, and a meeting was arranged in a car-park in the town of Comber away from prying eyes. The two sat in a car and Stone outlined his terrorist history. He stressed his desire to remain apart from mainstream terrorism because organisations were too easily penetrated by the security forces, and presented McMichael with a new concept of terror in which a freelance hitman operated independently of the UDA but claimed responsibility for successful acts on their behalf using the cover name, UFF.

McMichael listened intently as Stone displayed a detailed knowledge of terrorism and how it could be most effectively realised. Stone said he knew several other experienced activists who, like himself, might be tempted to operate as an independent unit. All they would require was logistical support and one contact within the UDA/UFF, namely McMichael. Stone's plan was that he, as a freelancer, would choose his targets and weapons, but was also prepared to consider targets selected by the UFF. He would require up-to-date intelligence before every job, and ground support from UFF personnel, and would always use an alias so that UFF volunteers who assisted him would never know his true identity. He told McMichael he was adept at leading the double life essential to his survival as a freelancer. McMichael was impressed, but said he needed time to consider the proposal. They agreed to meet at the same venue two weeks later.

Their subsequent get-together was devoted to a detailed analysis of Stone's proposal and a refinement of it. McMichael said Stone could not operate within East Belfast without the risk of someone identifying him, or being recognised by a 'fellow traveller' from the early 1970s. He would be of more use in towns or rural areas away from Belfast. Could his wife be trusted?

Stone replied she knew nothing of his terrorist background; his life-style was such he could disappear for days without incurring scrutiny.

McMichael said he favoured a deal with him, but an interim period of assessment was required. In the period pending agreement between them, Stone could use his expertise training new recruits to active-service units outside Belfast. This would provide him with a knowledge of the geography of rural operational areas, with necessary contacts, and the formation of a proper alias. Stone proffered the pseudonym, Colin Holmes, and it was agreed that he use it during his training lectures. McMichael said he required time to establish contact with Active Service Units and devise a means by which Stone could be introduced to relevant people. The meeting ended with a promise from McMichael that he would set things in motion and make contact with Stone through a third party.

The political situation in Northern Ireland was deteriorating rapidly because of a widespread support for republican protests within the H-blocks of the Maze Prison. These protests were the culmination of prison agitation from 1978, when the British government decided to end 'special category status', which accorded political prisoners privileges such as extra visits, food parcels, the wearing of civilian clothes and no requirement to undertake prison work. The special-category designation was a legacy from the Long Kesh era and was accorded to paramilitaries by William Whitelaw in 1972. By December 1974, the numbers of prisoners enjoying the status reached 1100.

The principle of having a growing population of prisoners with a political status conflicted with British plans to criminalise the paramilitaries and depict them as thugs; the creation of the Maze was central both to that plan, and to ending special-category status, especially as the Provisional IRA throve on the propaganda derived from an internationally held view – that political prisoners represented an indictment of British policy in Ireland. On 1 March 1976 the government began phasing out the special status by announcing that anyone convicted of a political offence after that day would not be accorded the 'Special Cat.' privileges. Within two years the number of special-category prisoners was reduced to 800. New prisoners, who would have been placed in compounds under the command of their own leaders before 1976, were now housed in cells in the modern H-blocks.

The Provisional IRA warned that it would not assist the new policy and told its men to refuse to wear prison clothes. They covered themselves in blankets, refused to wash or use toilets, vandalised the H-block cells and initiated a protest which became known as 'the dirty protest', in which they smeared their excreta on cell walls, and sat in empty cells wearing only prison blankets. Their plight, though self-inflicted, attracted media attention from around the globe, and increased IRA support in Ireland and the United States. From within the nationalist community, an organisation, the National H-Blocks/Armagh Committee, emerged as the spearhead of a campaign to draw the attention of the world to the dirty protest, and what became known as the 'five demands of the prisoners': own clothing and no prison work; freedom of association within prison; more visits and letters; extra recreational facilities; restoration of remission lost during the dirty campaign.

The campaign committee was an amalgam of disparate republican groupings and led by a number of highly intelligent, forceful propagandists and political agitators. Among them were – Bernadette McAliskey, née Devlin, who featured prominently in the 1973 UFF thesis of loyalist history; Miriam Daly, a Queen's University lecturer married to a prominent member of Provisional Sinn Fein; Ronnie Bunting, aged 27 years, a Protestant who converted to republicanism and was Director of Intelligence of the feared Irish National Liberation Army and adjutant of the Belfast Brigade. He was a former university graduate, prominent in the student Peoples' Democracy movement which, in 1969, pushed the Civil Rights campaign towards a violent outcome. His father, Major Ronald Bunting, was a rabid loyalist and an advisor to Ian Paisley in the early days of the conflict. Finally there was John Turnley aged 42, another Protestant convert to republicanism. Turnley came from an old landed Protestant family, with Unionist party affiliations. A teacher by profession, as a young man he had worked in Far East tea plantations, before living in Japan and marrying a Japanese girl. He returned to Northern Ireland, joined the SDLP, but left to become the leader of the Irish Independence Party which had its roots in traditional republican values. His party possessed formidable propagandist skills, and masterminded an ambitious international campaign to highlight the prison protests. They were also adept at street protest, and organised large demonstrations throughout Britain and Ireland.

McMichael watched a growing awareness of how the republican cause could be expertly packaged to appeal to an international market. It overshadowed the plight of loyalism and resurrected images of 1969 when the focus of the media was unfairly shaped to support a nationalist/republican portrayal of Northern Ireland.

Meanwhile Stone was training members of the UFF active-service units in parts of County Tyrone and Armagh under the alias 'Colin Holmes'. He regularly disappeared from home for days, refusing to tell Marlene of his whereabouts. His 'disappearances' steadily became longer, and placed tremendous strains on his family. The marriage was disintegrating, but his mind was devoted to a double life outside Belfast.

McMichael, in the meantime, was busy drawing up a hit-list of republican activists, namely those four most prominent in the H-block campaign, McAliskey, Daly, Bunting and Turnley. He was determined to test the effectiveness of two Active Service Units, and the first 'hit' was to be John Turnley, who in loyalist eyes, symbolised betrayal of a Protestant birthright.

Turnley was shot dead in his car in front of his wife and children on 4 June 1980, in the coastal village of Carnlough in County Antrim about fifty miles from Belfast. The hit squad, when later brought to justice, claimed links with British intelligence: their leader was ordered to make the claim by a UDA chief in East Belfast, who was acting under McMichael's instructions.

McMichael used the ploy of British involvement in the murder for several reasons all of which were essential to his strategy. He was in control of a policy of assassination which was only beginning, and was determined to shift blame from the UFF. Secondly, he had no wish to encourage people to believe the UFF capable of acting alone without the professionalism and expertise developed with local security force collusion. He preferred his enemy, the IRA, to be conditioned to believe that his assassination campaign was the work of British intelligence, not him or the UDA – although he did, however, have support from loyalists within the Ulster Defence Regiment, and from a small number of dissident policemen. McMichael was concerned to protect these sources by permitting speculation that a British hand was controlling loyalist violence. He knew this would worry and frighten the IRA, and was equally concerned not to encourage IRA retaliation towards loyalist leaders such as himself. Further, he was in the fortunate position of being free to voice publicly his political opinions, and did not wish to jeopardise that facility. There was an unspoken rule between the warring paramilitaries that terrorist leaders were not targets. Should the IRA suspect direct UDA leadership involvement in an assassination campaign he would be top of a Provisional hit-list.

Before the police apprehended John Turnley's killers, another Active Service Unit murdered Miriam Daly in her home in predominantly republican territory in the west of the city. They tied her hands and legs before using a cushion to deaden the sound of the six 9mm bullets which they fired into her head. The cool, clinical manner of the assassination fuelled speculation that SAS-type operatives were responsible. In other words, McMichael was quickly realising all his objectives with efficiency, and with a military professionalism hitherto never associated with loyalist assassins. The ability of Miriam Daly's killers to enter a republican stronghold where the British Army was prominent on the streets was achieved by means of intelligence acquired from within the UDR. Information availed of by the killers contained a detailed description of Daly, the layout of her house, her general move-ments, and – the most crucial detail – the exact location of security-force patrols in the 'killing area' before, during and after the assassination.

A particular feature of the murder was the manner of the shooting, and the use of a 9mm Browning pistol. The police report concluded that the killing bore 'a style of execution' and the murder weapon 'was a type which had not previously come to the attention of the police'. It was a legally held gun, belonging to a member of the security forces – an ideal weapon because it could not be traced; I was informed that it was 'borrowed' and returned to its owner. The use of such a gun would have accorded with McMichael's use of dissidents within the UDR and RUC. The Peoples' Democracy issued a statement condemning the murder and alleging British complicity:

We believe that the conception of this plan of assassination and the detailed planning and intelligence necessary are beyond the capacity of any of the loyalist groups. Theirs may be the hand on the trigger, but the brain is that of British Military Intelligence.

None of the speculation focused on a similar style of killing demonstrated by loyalists, namely Albert Walker Baker, Stone's mentor. Such expertise did, after all, exist within loyalist ranks and McMichael recognised it and fashioned it with success. Thereby, he developed a new style of political murder, and chose targets who symbolised his strategy of 'pre-emptive' violence. He even considered murdering the current Sinn Fein leader, Gerry Adams, but abandoned the plan because of a lack of up-to-the-minute intelligence on Adam's movements. The intention was to set up a bogus UDR roadblock and ambush Adams, as he travelled to a republican commemoration across the Irish Border.

McMichael's finger now moved to another target on his hit-list,

Ronnie Bunting, whom he hated for forsaking both his Protestant roots, and his father who had championed loyalism. The squad who killed Daly were selected to repeat the exercise, again in a republican enclave in West Belfast. Bunting lived with his wife Susan and three children in Andersonstown, and was the leading INLA strategist who ordered the assassination of Airey Neave, MP for Abingdon, a close friend and adviser to Margaret Thatcher. Neave had been critical of the British media for lending support to the PIRA, and advocated tough and uncompromising military action against republican terror groups. He was killed by a sophisticated booby-trap car-bomb as he drove from the underground car-park of the House of Commons on 30 March 1979. Bunting was a high-priority surveillance target for the security forces, and this did not escape the attention of McMichael in seeking data on his target's house and movements. McMichael acquired classified security files which showed the layout of Bunting's home, including sleeping arrangements. Planning for the 'hit' was meticulous and a date was only selected when there was sufficient information to guarantee unhindered access to the house and a safe exit. It required updated records on all security forces' schedules, and details of the presence of 'friendly' forces on the edge of the neighbourhood. In this case, the 'friendly' forces were an Ulster Defence Regiment mobile patrol scheduled for duty on the outskirts of Andersonstown. It was, according to McMichael's information, willing to permit the escape of the killers and, in the event of British soldiers pursuing them, would cover their tracks.

McMichael placed his hitmen on 'standby' with orders to operate at short notice. Briefed on the plan with an exactitude which exemplified military discipline, they were made intimate with the Bunting home. They were told that the hit would probably take place in the middle of the night when people were least prepared to react. The theory was that people awakened from sleep were vulnerable because their reaction time was lessened by suddenly being wakened. It was also a time when traffic was less likely to impede an escape.

On the night of 14 October, McMichael received a communication: Bunting was at home and had an 'interesting' visitor – Noel Lyttle, an INLA colleague, Miriam Daly's successor in the H-blocks campaign. My informant was unable to confirm whether the information on Lyttle came from Army, that is to say, Ulster

Defence Regiment, and/or RUC sources, but it was the type of intelligence which could only have been communicated from a person or persons involved in close military or police surveillance. It would be easy to blame the UDR because of McMichael's recruitment of its soldiers into his loyalist hit-squads, but there were others who would have been happy to see Bunting killed. In the world of Northern Ireland espionage and political assassination, sources or agents can have a variety of masters: one *agent provocateur* was run separately by handlers from Military Intelligence, Special Branch and a covert Army grouping, 14th Intelligence (known by several names). McMichael, therefore, may not always have known the exact route by which information reached him, or the true allegiance of his sources.

Before midnight on 14 October the hit-team was told 'it would soon go into action'. Its members were informed of Lyttle's presence, and where he would be sleeping. Orders to proceed with the planned assassination were only given at 3.00 a.m. At that time the Buntings and Lyttle were asleep in bed. Susan Bunting's recollection of events demonstrates the clinical ferocity and expertise of the killers.

At 3.00 a.m. we heard banging downstairs. We both jumped out of bed, but by the time we got up, the men were already pushing in the bedroom door. We tried to force it closed but the shooting started and I fell back on the bed. The next moment two men were in the room and started shooting Ronnie.

She was shot three times in the side, back and one hand.

While I struggled with one of the men, the other left, casual-like, without a care. As he walked downstairs, he shouted something like 'Come on Geordie' or 'Georgie'. The other man then left and as he walked to the stairs he shot me in the mouth. I turned and saw Ronnie. I knew he was dead. Noel was still alive because I could hear him breathing.

Lyttle was also shot as he tried to get out of bed and died en route to hospital. The killers wore ski masks, and green-ribbed pullovers with suede patches on the shoulders. While leaving the house they displayed military training, covering each other with handguns until all of them exited the house. According to my informant, the choice of green-ribbed pullovers was to give the impression that they were UDR soldiers: if stopped at a police or military roadcheck, they would probably be allowed free passage. Their car, which was described by eyewitnesses in the neighbourhood, was never traced and no one has ever been charged with the Bunting killing or that of Miriam Daly.

The type of men chosen by McMichael for the Daly/Bunting murders, UFF members, may have operated with excellent intelligence provided from sources within the security forces, but they were men with a history similar to that of Michael Stone. They had possessed a career in murder in the early 1970s and then faded from view until reactivated by McMichael and Bingham, and were retrained for the role designated by McMichael. The RUC officers who investigated the Turnley, Daly and Bunting murders were puzzled by the professionalism shown by the killers, and by their acquisition of information precise enough to enable such successful operations.

In December 1980 an IRA hunger strike in the Maze Prison ended after three weeks when the Provisional leadership were led to believe that the British government was prepared to capitulate to the demands of the 'dirty protesters'. In January 1981 the H-block protests resumed and the issue remained central to public consciousness. Then, McMichael chose his next target, Bernadette McAliskey or 'St Bernadette', as the UFF described her in its 1973 document. She lived with her husband in County Tyrone near the town of Coalisland. On 16 January, an SAS team was in place in the grounds surrounding her house. She was unaware of their presence or the fact that they had cut the telephone wires to her home. A UDA active-service team arrived, entered the house and shot her several times; they were arrested as they left the scene. An Army officer rushed to Bernadette McAliskey's side and kept her alive until a medical team arrived. The presence of the SAS has never been explained. Some observers have concluded that their behaviour proved a connection between the UFF and Military Intelligence and ten years later, this belief hardened the suspicion that McMichael was an agent of British intelligence. Whether he was, it seems certain that he would not always have known the true allegiance of some of his sources and contacts.

The capture of the Tyrone unit at Bernadette McAliskey's house signalled a lull in McMichael's assassination plans, and his best operators, including Stone, were ordered to 'lie low'. For eighteen months Stone remained apart from McMichael, though not wholly inactive. His relations with the UVF, and in particular with close associates of John Bingham, provided him with other opportunities for violent actions. He refuses to reveal the exact nature of these, but admits that while operating for the UVF he was given 'sanctions', a euphemism for orders, or offers, to kill. On one of my prison visits I asked him if he ever had rejected 'sanctions' from Bingham or McMichael. He replied:

I refused sanctions which could easily be deemed blatantly sectarian. Sure we were all involved in the sectarian thing in the early seventies. We've all feet of clay in that respect. But in the eighties I wasn't interested in that sort of thing. I turned down several sanctions to hit female members of the IRA. I examined the intelligence on them. Some of them were good-lookers [laughs]. The thing was they did not have criminal records. I knew if I hit them they would be described as innocent victims – wee girls murdered just because they were Catholics. Anyway, I didn't want to kill women. I had three 'sisters' and I loved all women [laughs].

In January 1991, I travelled to a secret location for a meeting with a former UVF intelligence officer who knew Bingham and Stone. My purpose was to ask him if he could shed light on a fascinating story I was given by another UVF contact.

The story concerned a 'sanction' offered to Stone in 1983 by a UVF commander whom I shall name Mr B: the details of the incident were confirmed to me by the former UVF officer, although Stone has refused to discuss the matter with me. At some time in 1983, probably the autumn, Mr B was approached by a stranger who appeared English, wishing to arrange a meeting – in England – and which was subsequently attended only by B. The bait to lure this UVF commander to the meeting was a promise of a consignment of weapons; the stranger said he was representing a third party willing to provide a consignment of Israeli-made Uzi submachine-guns in return for several killings. B asked to meet the 'third party', but was told it was neither possible nor preferable.

'The third party', the stranger added, 'wished to remain anonymous but could be depended on to guarantee safe shipment of the guns to Northern Ireland.'

My source for this story provided the following account of what transpired:

B was really taken with the promise of modern weapons and said there should be no problem in reaching a deal. He thought the targets would be IRA men and suspected there was no third party and the guy he was talking to was MI5, MI6 or Military Intelligence. Those were his first thoughts but he was in for a shock when he asked for the names of the targets. He was told they were students from the Middle East living in Belfast. There were three students and this guy said his 'third party' wanted them wiped. B wasn't happy about it, and said that if the UVF did the job, and it was ever discovered, it could be publicly damaging for his organisation. The stranger said there was a way round that, because the 'third party' didn't want them shot. They should be blown-up so that it could look as though they were making a bomb. B asked why go to those lengths, and was told the 'third party wanted it that way'. Stories could be leaked to the media that the students were involved in terrorism with the IRA. All of that would be left to the 'third party' to sort out. He told B that all he had to do was put a primed bomb into their flat. He also told him the names of the targets and their address in the University area of Belfast. B agreed to the deal but asked for several Uzis to be made available quickly as a sign of the third party's good faith. A small consignment of Uzis arrived in Belfast a week later.

B knew the job was potentially risky but he couldn't turn down an offer of new weapons. He didn't discuss the issue with too many people and kept it to a small number. He didn't want UVF operatives involved in the killing and decided he needed a freelancer whom he could trust. He chose Stone whose true identity was only known to a few of us. Others knew him by a variety of names and disguises. Sometimes Stone wore long hair, maybe even a beard. He would slick back his hair, grow a moustache and look like a hippie. He had a great ability to disguise himself. B knew he was a real pro, could operate alone and would keep his mouth shut. Stone was also someone who could not be easily traced. He had no recent terrorist record and the only thing was a robbery in the early 1970s. He was clean and that was essential to B's plan.

B provided Stone with the names of the students and the address of the flat where they lived or hung out. Apparently B was told by his contact that the students were photographed meeting Provos, and were a link between the IRA and Middle East Groups such as the PLO and Gadaffi. Stone was only too happy to consider the job because he hated the Provos. B told him that the students were probably the means by which the IRA made contact with their arms suppliers and arranged training for volunteers in PLO camps. Stone went away and spent a lot of time watching the students' flat, following them and 'casing' the building in which they lived. He arranged a meeting with B and told him it was possible to do the job, but he wasn't prepared to do it. B was shocked and disappointed. Stone was adamant that he wouldn't do it. He said it didn't feel right. I don't know exactly what he meant but I suspected he was frightened that if he was ever caught, everybody including B would deny any responsibility. Stone would be portrayed as mad, and no one would ever believe the story of B's contact and the third party. Stone was smart. I think he was worried that being caught for that sort of job would damage his image of himself as a loyalist hitman and hero. Killing three young students wouldn't have gone down well, even in our own community, especially when there was no proof of them doing anything. B dropped the idea and kept the Uzis. He wasn't going to use one of our guys who might get caught and name him as the planner.

The story fits neatly into the world of Northern Ireland's dirty war. B believed the mysterious Englishman was possibly MI6, and the third party, if one existed, was the Israeli intelligence service, Mossad. The former UVF intelligence officer who spoke to me was willing to concede that there was contact with Mossad, again through a third party, in relation to UVF intelligence on IRA activists.

One or two of our people supplied files on the IRA to the Israelis in return for guns. The Israelis were concerned about the spread of international terrorism and the IRA's Middle East connections. The Brits were never on good terms with the Israelis, so the Israelis approached us. The Englishman B met may not have been MI6. That was merely B's suspicion. Certainly the killing of three students, if made to look as if they were priming a bomb, would have suited Mossad. It would have forced the Western European governments to restrict the flow of such students into universities. The Israelis probably saw all Arab students as potential subversives. The murders would have provided great propaganda for the Mossad. I'm glad in a way it never took place. Everything gets out eventually.

I checked with a Provisional IRA source who said his organisation did not require assistance from Arab students at Queen's University. There were no Arab students assisting violence at that time or even meeting with members of the IRA. Stone's refusal to fulfil the sanction was illustrative of his cunning and desire for self-preservation. The Israeli connection will feature again in this book; at this stage I will simply confirm that I am aware of a former soldier in the Ulster Defence Regiment, who served in the Israeli Defence Force, returned to duty in Northern Ireland, and then passed classified security files on the IRA to a contact at the Israeli embassy in London.

Stone also travelled to England in 1983; his visit, which lasted several months, included working in a hotel in Scarborough. I pressed him for an explanation of his trip but he would only answer with a smile that he was 'on official business'.

While in England he fulfilled a dream to meet his father. He used terrorists with contacts within government departments in Belfast to find his father's address, and also acquired his father's personal telephone number but decided not to use it for fear his father would refuse to see him.

I opted for a direct approach and just went to his house and knocked at the door. When he came out he looked at me and then said: 'Michael?' I was suddenly looking at this tall man, but I didn't see him as my father. I walked straight into the house and there on a sideboard were photographs. He looked embarrassed. If I had phoned he might have removed them before I arrived. This way I was able to surprise him. I walked over and lifted the photos. There was one of him, my mother and me as a baby. There were others also of me. I looked at the one of my mother. She was 18 years old, a good-looker with long hair. She was really attractive. I stayed there for a couple of hours. I was proud he'd kept photos of me, but I didn't regard him as my father. He was like a big uncle. I never saw him again. At least I knew why he picked my mother. She looked the part. It was strange talking to him. I loved him as a big uncle. Harry Gregg was the man I regarded as my father, and Margaret as my mother.

Stone says his father was reluctant to discuss his marriage to Mary Bridget Sullivan, or the reasons for the break-up. He would only comment that she 'left him for a better life'.

If Stone secretly felt rejected by his mother, he now had justification for feelings of resentment and bitterness towards her. He says his father's revelations were not upsetting. 'I suppose one can understand it,' he told me.

He says he then 'seriously considered' applying to the Salvation Army's International Investigation Branch to seek help in finding his mother.

I often thought I should trace her and just arrive on her doorstep. I decided against it because she has her own life and family. She is happy and middle-class and it's best left that way.

Michael Stone's visit to his father ended his preoccupation with his natural parents and coincided with the forthcoming disintegration of his own marriage, and a final period of sustained violence as an assassin.

7

The Freelancer Strikes

In 1984 Stone's seven-year marriage ended and he left Marlene and their three sons. The marriage was doomed from the outset but, according to him, ended amicably. He wrote to me in 1991 and said 'his frequent disappearances' featured in his reasons for the break-up.

She was a good wife and now she's a dear friend. My frequent disappearances did not help and were, as now, my own business and mine alone. End of story.

When he left his wife, he had an 18-year-old girlfriend, Leigh-Anne. He found the younger woman irresistible, but didn't set up home with her for over a year. She, a native of East Belfast, knew nothing of her lover's history. Within a few months she was pregnant, at which point he informed his ex-wife and suggested she initiate divorce proceedings. Marlene had known for some time of her husband's new acquisition, and had resisted the temptation of divorcing him on grounds of adultery. She was prepared to wait two years and petition on the basis that they were not living as man and wife for that period. He was living with a girl whose age represented the age of his mother when she gave birth to him. To friends he bragged about the number of children he had fathered, and insisted that women found him irresistible; Leigh-Anne represented his power over women and their willingness to submit to him. Violence provided him with the opportunity further to enhance his self-image, and stamp his authority on the world.

Stone was not alone in behaving in this fashion. Lenny Murphy, the Shankill Butcher was a womaniser and a psychotic, thriving on the opportunities for self-projection provided by violence. Para-militarism created and licensed their means of expression, and allowed them to immerse themselves in violence, thus acquiring the means by which they could be accepted, admired and respected. In normal times Michael Stone would not have had the outlet for such abnormal expression, and might have been no more than an habitual 'common criminal'.

His behaviour as a father-figure provided an interesting insight into his fear of rejection, and his desire not to repeat the behaviour of his parents. He maintained ad-hoc arrangements for visiting, or meeting with, his children, or their mothers, and reacted violently to any suggestion by his former lovers that they intended to deny him access to his children, unable to cope with the thought that the mothers or children would not wish to see him. His reasons for choosing Leigh-Anne, or the previous women in his life, were not always clear. Most of them exhibited similar character traits: meekness, subservience, naïvety. In November 1990 he wrote to me and offered an explanation for his choice of Leigh-Anne.

She had no history. She was unquestioning and that's what attracted me to her. She was a great girl.

He married her within eighteen months but not without regrets:

I married her when I was, for the want of a better word, 'busy'. I must admit it was unfair to marry her in those circumstances. We had a great time together and it's a joy.

It appears she, by his testimony, was perfect for the maintenance of his double life. She never questioned his disappearances or where he acquired money; she was frightened of him, as was Marlene, on account of his fearsome displays of temper.

At the end of October 1984, while living alone in a flat in the Braniel, Stone received a secret communication from UFF leader, John McMichael, suggesting they meet in the County Down town of Comber, fifteen miles from Belfast, only half that distance from the Braniel. The venue was the car-park of a bar and restaurant on the edge of the town. Comber was predominantly Protestant, with a growing middle-class commuter population, and free from violence. With a part-time police station and small town square, it was designated a town, but resembled a village. Comber was imbued with a staunch loyalist history, and to this day many of the streets are painted or bedecked with loyalist symbols. Stone was familiar with adjacent towns such as Saintfield, Killyleagh and Newtownards, important recruiting areas for the UVF/UFF. Comber was an untypical venue for conducting terrorist business, and for that very reason it appealed to Stone's preoccupation with his personal security.

When he arrived for his meeting with McMichael, he found the UFF leader seated in his car. Nearby, a UFF bodyguard was seated in another vehicle with instructions to watch all movement, a precaution to ensure neither man was being followed. The bodyguard was told to note the registration numbers of cars entering the car-park. It was mid-afternoon, the restaurant was closed and the bar attracted little custom. The few cars expected by McMichael would be checked through the RUC computer with the aid of a UFF source.

McMichael invited Stone to sit beside him in his car. No one in the building behind would have seen the two men or, in the event of spotting them, have been unduly suspicious. McMichael made it clear that he required Stone to undertake a 'sanction'; the target – an IRA intelligence officer from West Belfast. Stone asked for proof that his intended victim was IRA and McMichael replied that the UFF possessed security forces' files on the target. Stone said he was prepared to 'do the hit', provided he was given access to the files to reassure himself that the target was a Provo. McMichael promised to provide Stone with copies of the files within twenty-four hours. He said Stone should read them, destroy them and request whatever weapons and manpower he needed for the killing.

Stone received files containing detailed police and Army surveillance notes on 35-year-old Paddy Brady, a Catholic from St James's Crescent on the Upper Falls Road of West Belfast. Security photographs and documents claimed that Brady was regularly seen with IRA men, and he had been photographed in the company of known activists by undercover surveillance teams. The documents confirmed that he was a member of Sinn Fein and that his brother, Martin, had served eleven years of a lengthy prison term for bombing the Old Bailey in London. It revealed the name of Brady's wife as Patricia and his daughters, Frances and Patricia. The documentation was extensive and provided Stone with a clear profile of his target. Some of the papers within the file were similar to intelligence assessments provided to police, UDR and British Army personnel.

The most critical information for the would-be assassin was Brady's place of work, and his working pattern. He was a milkman who travelled by private car each morning to Kennedy Bros Dairy on the Boucher Road in South Belfast. He picked up a fully laden milk-float and drove to West Belfast: the journey from home to work took him five minutes by car.

From the available information, Stone knew the limited number of routes available to Brady on his daily trip to the dairy, and the approximate time he started work. He was aware of the advantage to be gained from killing Brady in the early morning, when there was little traffic to hamper an escape, and a reduced risk of eye-witnesses. Between 6.00 and 6.30 a.m. there were few people about – in cars or on foot – and, aside from Kennedy Bros, Boucher Road was a sprawling area of industrial sites, which did not open until 8.30 a.m. Aside from the written documentation on Brady, Stone received a video depicting him standing, arms folded, on the speakers' platform at a Provisional Sinn Fein annual conference (Ardfheis) in Dublin.

Stone was not only prepared to take the 'sanction', he was happy about the prospect of killing Brady. The documentation, while confirming Brady's membership of Sinn Fein, proved inconclusive about his IRA connections, but this deterred neither Stone nor McMichael from assuming and then asserting that Brady was an 'IRA intelligence officer'. The possession of security documents containing suspicions, allegations and, often, circumstantial evidence connecting people to the IRA, was always sufficient to convince loyalist hit-squads of the guilt of their victims. Phrases which recurred in many of the documents were: 'suspected of passing information to PIRA', 'Drinks with known PIRA', 'has brother within PIRA', 'Republican sympathiser'. The latter phrase, like so many others, denoted a legal political aspiration, but in the context of what loosely became known as 'wanted files' created a lethal juxtaposition.

For several days Stone travelled in the early mornings to Kennedy Bros Dairy and watched Brady alight from his 340 Volvo car and walk into the premises. Brady was easily recognised by his twenty-stone frame, bald head and the folds of flesh under his chin. The location of the dairy presented Brady with an ever-present threat which he had failed to perceive. If he had read accounts of Boucher Road, and its prominence as an escape route for loyalist killers in the early 1970s, he might have been more circumspect about working there. In 1972–3 UDA/UVF assassins made use of Boucher Road, the M1 motorway and the streets of the nearby Village area, to mount attacks into Catholic West Belfast, and as escape routes which linked numerous roads and sidestreets leading into and out of the city centre.

Stone selected 16 November to fulfil his 'sanction' and requested the assistance of two accomplices. They were UFF volunteers and their instructions were to meet him at approximately 5.30 a.m. at a shopping precinct at the entrance to the Taughmonagh housing estate in South Belfast; Stone would flash car headlights to warn them of his arrival. He named his killing weapon as an automatic shotgun and recommended cartridges size 4 which contained heavy lead shot.

At close quarters this is a fearsome weapon. If you are not close enough to do a head job with a pistol, a shotgun blast to the head is lethal. Its good if you're mobile and ready for a quick getaway. I favoured a shotgun when working close to a target.

He also asked for a revolver which he intended to use if the shotgun jammed. He told McMichael that he preferred to examine the weapons on the morning of the 'sanction', and that his accomplices should be in possession of them when he arrived at Taughmonagh.

Paddy Brady was oblivious of danger, and unaware that he was being stalked by an assassin. He was a committed republican, prominent in Sinn Fein politics, but not a member of the IRA, a fact corroborated by republican circles and security forces alike; he was part of a successful Provisional Sinn Fein strategy of street politics, and worked with the local community. The Provisionals were determined to become an essential community organisation by providing advice centres, thereby undermining government agencies as well as the opposition party, the SDLP. Brady was treasurer of his local community centre and a member of 11/E5 Branch of the Allied Transport and General Workers Union. Well respected and liked within his own community, he was a typical target for the blanket surveillance which the security agencies applied to republicans, both ordinary political sympathisers and Sinn Fein activists.

The means of surveillance were sophisticated, and computerised files exist on the majority of the population of Northern

Ireland, with the important files being those on terrorists, or people suspected of associating with, or supporting the aims of, the IRA. Very often, people came within the scope of surveillance simply because they had been seen talking to a suspect, or drinking with a former school-friend who was on file as a suspected activist. Files were constantly updated from information or observations made by police and Army patrols, or through the sophisticated surveillance of covert military groupings such as 14th Intelligence Company (sometimes known as the 14th Independent Company). Many files found their way into loyalist hands from the outset of the violence and grew into sufficient confirmation that a person 'deserved' to be assassinated. Dissident policemen, soldiers from the Ulster Defence Regiment and other regiments provided loyalists with a ready supply of this type of intelligence. The suspicion also existed that Special Branch and British intelligence permitted the leaking of such information to encourage the killing of people whom the agencies of law and order had proven unable to indict. Whatever the motivation or designation of the sources supplying files, the fact is that from 1970 onwards information on republican suspects was being made available to loyalist killer squads.

Several British Army commanders shared information with UDA/UVF leaders in East and West Belfast. A loyalist contact told me how it began:

It was 'our' police force, 'our' 'B' Specials and later 'our' Ulster Defence Regiment. We were helping them fight the IRA and that's why they saw us as friends. It is a small society and there was always someone in paramilitary ranks who had a brother, father or some relative within the security forces. There were people in the paramilitaries as well as the security forces. The UDA/UVF encouraged its people to join the UDR for free training plus access to weapons, ammunition and intelligence. We always reckoned that in a doomsday situation, if the Brits were going to pull out, or impose a solution, we could seize Ulster with the UDR and with elements from within the RUC. There were always some within the British Army willing to give us information, but even more so in the early days. Military Intelligence liaised with some of our people, mostly outside Belfast, and provided intelligence on IRA targets north and south of the border. I'm saying no more about that – it's too dodgy.

At 4.30 a.m. on 16 November Stone dressed quietly while Leigh-Anne and their baby slept. He wore blue overalls over his clothing and finally slipped on leather gloves.

I remember sneaking out of my flat. I left by the kitchen window as I didn't want anyone to hear me slamming the front door. The neighbours knew I was unemployed and would have wondered what I was doing leaving the place at that time. I was careful not to attract attention or suspicion.

He walked towards the Upper Newtownards Road and the Stormont Hotel which is opposite the obsolete parliament buildings. He planned to take a car from the hotel grounds rather than risk being caught stealing one in the Braniel, or on the heavily populated thoroughfares leading to the hotel; he was familiar with the hotel, and the large car-park at the rear of the premises. A single night-security man was on duty and Stone experienced 'some difficulty' avoiding him. Once in the car-park he chose a dark brown Ford Cortina, on loan to a Dr Sillitoe and his wife. Sillitoe worked for British Petroleum and was on a company visit to Belfast. All terrorists knew the Cortina to be a car easily burgled; it was also the favourite of joyriders. Stone gained entry to the vehicle through a rear passenger door, ripped the housing round the steering column and joined the appropriate wires to start the engine.

He drove the vehicle past the rear hotel entrance and sounded the horn to attract the attention of the security guard. Stone waved to him, and was greeted with a smile. The assassin's final gesture was indicative of his bravado and cunning. He sounded the horn to express familiarity and to lull the guard into believing a member of staff was leaving the grounds. It was also the action of a confident hitman relishing his own daring. Out on the Newtownards Road, he quickly navigated a route which included less conspicuous thoroughfares, until he reached Shaw's Bridge on the edge of the residential Malone district. From there, he drove along the upper Malone to the line of shops which marked his rendezvous.

Somewhere near the shops I bumped my horn and flashed my lights. Two youngish lads came out from my right and joined me. Both were walking tight together and concealing a shotgun between them. One had a revolver as well. I didn't know either of them. We all knew what the job was, and they only knew me by my alias, Tony May.

Stone drove his accomplices countrywards for a quarter of a mile until he reached a laneway where he stopped the car. He briefed them on the target and the escape route, pointing out he 'wanted no mistakes', and assured them that if they followed his instructions, the job would 'run smoothly'. Next, he ordered one of them to drive the car and the second accomplice to crouch on the floor between the front seat and the dashboard glove compartment. The second accomplice was responsible for the revolver and for making it quickly available if the shotgun jammed, or if Brady was accompanied by several people. In the latter event the accomplice was to provide covering fire while Stone stalked Brady. Stone laid the shotgun across the back seat, and lay on top of it. The two gunmen in the car were not visible to other drivers of passing vehicles unless, of course, a police landrover drove alongside them.

The car was driven down the Malone Road past an Ulster Defence Regiment base, to the Lisburn Road junctions with Tates Avenue. Stone said that if Brady ran into the dairy he would pursue him, and would expect covering fire from the armed accomplice. Stone's orders from McMichael were not only to kill Brady, but also his teenage assistant.

To this day, Stone says that the documentation on Brady alleged he was using his milk-round to acquire knowledge on where police and soldiers lived, and that Brady's helper was a member of the junior wing of the IRA, Na Fianna Eireann. The usual helper had no connection with terrorism, nor had 14-year-old Paul Anthony Hughes, who accompanied Brady on the morning of 16 November; he had been acting as a helper for only two weeks. Stone's accomplices were familiar with Brady and, unknown to Stone, had been briefed by UFF officers about the killing. Before meeting Stone, they were told that they would operate with someone unknown to them and accept his orders. They had also stalked Brady and knew every escape route from Boucher Road.

As they drove towards their target area, Stone was impressed by their knowledge, but was unconcerned that they had done the same groundwork. He was confident that they would not get him killed, because their knowledge of the geography of West and South Belfast was better than his. It showed that McMichael took no chances and, if Stone had not been available, there was a fallback position; two young men were trained for the hit. However, McMichael preferred Stone to do it, because he was a professional assassin and he was certain the accomplices would ensure that Stone was returned safely to a place of his choosing. On their way to the dairy they negotiated the roundabout at the entrance to the M1 motorway and they stopped for a moment to decide which route to take to Boucher Road.

A police car drove past them, and Stone says the driver of his car 'nodded at the policemen' who paid little attention to them. He reckoned the police were not suspicious, because they only saw Stone's driver; one man in a car did not constitute a murder bid. The three terrorists quickly proceeded to Boucher Road, made a pass of the dairy, did a U-turn and parked for twenty minutes at the entrance to a car sales showroom.

At 6.20 a.m. Brady collected his helper and drove to the M1 roundabout, towards Boucher Road. Paul Hughes was in the front passenger seat and provided this account of the journey:

Paddy drove up Boucher Road past Cregagh Foods. He then reversed his car and parked it just before you go into the dairy. When the car stopped I got out first. The passenger door didn't close properly and I slammed the door shut so that Paddy could lock it from inside. I saw him get out of the car. I walked over to the gates of Cregagh Foods and put on my two coats. I saw Paddy get out of the car. I saw him checking the doors and then he started fixing his wing mirror while standing on the road. Then I saw a car coming down Boucher Road.

Brady's preoccupation with the car mirrors probably cost him his life, because it distracted him from the approaching menace and from entering the dairy quickly. Stone saw Brady locking the car doors meticulously. The killers drove to within three feet of him; Stone, his passenger window half-lowered, placed the gun muzzle out of the window and levelled it at his victim. Using the window glass to steady and sight the weapon, he shot Brady once in the body and as he was falling a second shot struck his head. The accomplices shouted at Stone and told him to shoot the teenager. Stone refused and later told me he couldn't do it.

I looked at the kid but he was too young. I couldn't bring myself to shoot him. He looked like a wee boy. We sped off up Tates Avenue to the Lisburn Road, past a police station, to the Malone, and finally to the shops at Taughmonagh. They got out and took the gear with them. I drove back the way I came until I reached the Upper Braniel Road, where I drove through an open gate into a field. The wheels started to spin in the mud and I got out and left the vehicle.

He tramped through fields, across the Ballygowan Road and into the Braniel. At home he had a bath and washed out his ears with cotton wool to remove any traces of cordite or lead residue from the discharge of the gun. He washed his hair, scrubbed his body diligently, and burned his clothing, boots and gloves. It was a ritual he followed after all killings or when he fired a gun. He learned it in the early 1970s; it was a precaution which many terrorists ignored, but not Stone: he always ensured that no traces of cordite or lead residue could provide evidence against him if arrested after a 'sanction'. He lost no time in cleaning his body clinically and destroying every item of clothing, anticipating the type of police forensic tests applied to suspected terrorists: swabs taken from a person's hands, face, eyes, hair, ears, anywhere where traces of lead residue might reside after a weapon discharge; clothing removed and examined, particularly the sleeves of a jacket or shirt which might have been in contact with a gun or the minute particles which disperse on to any person firing a weapon. The Shankill Butchers' leader, Lenny Murphy, displayed a similar knowledge of forensic science. He frequently sat in the public gallery of Crumlin Road courthouse and listened intently to the forensic evidence used to convict terrorists; he later employed such knowledge to thwart the law. On one occasion, Murphy was arrested immediately after shooting two Catholic women, and while in custody in a police station he used a toilet visit to dispose of evidence. Constable Innes who was guarding him remembered the episode:

During the time I was guarding him he requested to go to the toilet. I went into the toilet with him but the urinal was blocked and he went into one of the cubicles. I heard the toilet being flushed and on hearing this I rushed over, looked into the cubicle and saw Murphy drying his hands which were still wet. He was also wiping the sleeves of his jacket with toilet paper.

While Stone was washing away the evidence he listened to the morning news bulletins and discovered that his victim was dead. He had left behind a witness in the person of the teenager but Stone was confident that his disguise and use of aliases would protect his real identity. Paul Anthony Hughes saw him fire two rounds into Brady and 'duck down' as the car sped away. Hughes did not see the third accomplice who was armed with the revolver.

Thomas Boyd, a security guard at Kennedy Bros, heard bangs

and assumed it was a car backfiring until Hughes ran towards him shouting 'Paddy's been shot'. Boyd ran to the front gate of the dairy and discovered Brady lying face-down in a pool of blood. At the RUC's Regional Control, Constable David Baird received a 999 call from the dairy and dispatched a mobile patrol to Boucher Road to cordon off the scene of the killing. There was little doubt that Brady was dead, as an ambulance crew quickly confirmed. Constable Trevor Prenter, accompanied by Constables Cosh, Fox and Kerr rushed to the scene. Brady was lying, his hands slightly raised above his head, about five feet from the pavement; a bunch of car keys lay in a pool of blood. He had been unaware of the killers' car until it was too late, and was standing with his back to the roadway, and his body slightly angled; Stone was positioned with the gun pointing towards Brady's left side and back. The first shot to the body lowered Brady who instinctively raised his hands after the second shotgun round struck his head. Stone's tactic, part of his mental planning before the killing, was to fire the first round to 'put Brady down'.

I knew his weight and that was one of the reasons I chose the shotgun. I reckoned he was so big that if I only got shots off from a pistol, and they were only body shots, he might survive. I was intending to do it all quickly. I planned to immobilise him with one round to the body, and then shoot him in the head as he was going down. The shotgun at close range from the car was the best weapon. With a revolver I would have been obliged to get out, thus losing time and the initiative, and taking too many risks. Fair enough, if he'd run, I would have had to go after him. He was big and I thought carefully about the most effective option. I opted for an automatic shotgun and size 4 cartridges. It wasn't simply because it was a good weapon, it was not easily traced.

Unlike a revolver or rifle, a shotgun does not possess the barrel rifling which leaves distinctive and traceable ballistics marks on bullets. A spent shotgun cartridge is similar to any other shotgun cartridge, whereas a bullet can be traced to an individual weapon by matching the rifling on a bullet with another discharged from the same weapon. Police have frequently been able to determine that several people have been killed by the same weapon on account of the similarity of characteristics in bullets removed from victims. A shotgun cartridge only has tell-tale signs to indicate whether it was fired from a pump-action or self-loading gun. The large number of legally held shotguns in Northern Ireland makes it impossible for police to examine forensically each weapon within twenty-four hours of a murder to discover if it was recently fired, or to ascertain the whereabouts of the owner at the time of a killing.

Young Paul Anthony Hughes said he saw the gun which killed Paddy Brady, and 'it had a magazine going up into it'. His description of the gun implied a stick magazine of the type used in rifles or submachine-gun. He may have used the word 'magazine' to define the rounded feed-container through which single cartridges are hand-fed into a gun from underneath the barrel. Most people use 'magazine' to describe a 'stick' magazine, whereas a gunsmith employs the word in respect of shotguns to indicate a rounded aspect beneath the barrel. Initially, I suspected that a 14-year-old would only use the word 'magazine' to mean the stick type. If this were so, what type of unusual weapon had Stone used? The only shotgun possessing a stick magazine was a Savage Stevens, a bolt-action weapon. The make of the weapon used by Stone (the RUC proved unable to determine it) was a Remington five-shot, self-loading, and there were two models of this gun, No. 17 and No. 1100. Neither model possessed a stick magazine, but were fed through a curved feed, a 'magazine'. Paul Hughes was after all an observant witness who defined 'magazine' with exactitude, if not technically correct in respect of the gun used by Stone. However, his evidence did not resolve the dilemma of identifying the shotgun type at the time of the shooting – a crucial matter, because the Remington may well have been a legally held gun, borrowed from its owner on the basis that if his gun was judged the murder weapon he would claim it was stolen without his knowledge. Many licensed gun-holders have been willing to 'lend' their guns to paramilitaries, particularly loyalist gangs; the majority of weapons held legally in Northern Ireland are in the hands of Protestants.

The Remington performed the task as Stone expected, and this became self-evident when Dr Thomas K. Marshall, one of the most eminent pathologists in the United Kingdom, examined the body of Patrick Brady. His post-mortem examination contained the following commentary:

Death was due to the discharge of a shotgun into the head. He had been shot twice. One discharge struck the left side of the head about three inches above and one and a half inches behind the top of the left ear. It had gone into the head fracturing extensively both the vault and the base of the skull. It had lacerated the brain from which were recovered the plastic wad of a shotgun cartridge and a number of small lead pellets. Blood from the skull base had run down into the mouth and the upper air passages. This would have proved immediately incapacitating, and rapidly fatal. Another discharge struck the left side of the trunk over the lower ribs about seven inches above the top of the left hip bone. Here there was a large hole, and a small hole in a ragged area of superficial laceration above it. The holes lead to a broad track which extended to the right beneath the skin into the muscle clothing the left side of the spine. A few small pellets were recovered from the tissues. This wound did not involve the chest or abdominal cavities nor the spine. It did not immediately endanger life.

The shot to the body represented a technique favoured by the SAS or 14th Intelligence operatives. In the killing of IRA volunteers Army undercover squads were trained to fire at the body to immobilise their targets before delivering fatal rounds to the head. (One interesting feature of Dr Marshall's post-mortem was his discovery that Brady was grossly overweight, had a large fatty liver and spleen and his heart was enlarged to twice its normal size. This, according to the pathologist, would have seriously reduced his life expectancy.)

Reaction to the murder was immediate, and republican groupings expressed concern: it was the third murder of a Catholic within a three-week period. The Irish Republican Socialist Party, which had links to the INLA, said they had warned the authorities of loyalist threats in the light of recent murders and attempted murders. They issued the following statement:

It seems that loyalists, British intelligence, or a combination of both are intent on murdering local community workers and leaders in an attempt to demoralise the nationalist people. We would ask: is this Thatcher's revenge for Brighton [*the bombing of a hotel during a Conservative Party Conference*], the murder of local milkmen.

Provisional Sinn Fein admitted that Brady was a member of their organisation, and suggested this would be used to justify his death. McMichael was in the process of drafting a public statement to that effect, adding that Brady was also an IRA intelligence officer. The murder led to calls from Sinn Fein for parole for the dead man's brother to allow him to attend the funeral. The Home Office rejected the request, giving as its reason the category-A prisoner status of Martin Brady. Patricia Brady, the dead man's widow, condemned the murder, and concentrated instead on the excellent work her husband had undertaken on behalf of his local community. The RUC reacted to the murder by arresting known loyalist paramilitaries and interrogating them. Stone and his accomplices were not on the arrest list.

Patrick Brady's funeral bore no paramilitary trappings and a requiem mass was celebrated by the Bishop of Down and Connor diocese, Dr Cathal Daly. He told the congregation he was appalled and asked:

Why should people like Paddy Brady be killed? Political differences provide no excuse for murder. Politics is about the peaceful solution of community differences, not about the killing of those who disagree with one's views. Justice will never come out of the barrel of a gun, be it loyalist or republican.

Dr Daly said the killers were loyalists. He had no intention – and too much respect for Protestants, for their beliefs – to speak of Protestant killers. He added it should be of great concern to all Christian leaders that the killers should claim evil deeds in the name of Protestant values. 'Sectarianism is a poison and we can never have a healthy society until it is exorcised from our midst,' he said.

Brady was laid to rest in Milltown Cemetery, overlooking the motorway and the scene of his death. The mourners included the President of Sinn Fein, Gerry Adams MP and his closest advisor, Danny Morrison. Bishop Daly's words struck no chords in Michael Stone and other loyalists. They were able to justify the murder, because Brady was a republican, whose membership of the IRA's political wing was sufficient for them to assert that he was a terrorist.

There were several aspects to the killing which were not immediately apparent. Stone possessed files on his victim, but embellished their contents by saying they contained a claim that the milkman was using his milk-round to find out the addresses of soldiers and policemen. That was simply not true; a loyalist source confirmed to me that the files contained suspicions about Brady's political allegiances and friendships, but nothing of the nature claimed by Stone. Proof that the files were unlikely to contain allegations of the nature outlined by Stone can be found in the type of work undertaken by Brady. His milk-round for over ten years was confined to the predominantly Catholic areas of Whiterock and Falls, not areas where any member of the security forces resided. Did Stone augment the file material further to justify the murder?

The car used by him was found where he left it three hours afterwards; a spent No. 4 12-bore cartridge was on the rear seat. To my puzzled enquiry, he replied that it was his 'calling card'. This act of bravado epitomised his attitude to violence. By leaving a round used to kill his victim, he was linking himself to the crime. It established a method of assassination which detectives would always recognise as the work of one man. It defined his *modus operandi*, and identified him without naming him. Thus, Stone was unable to walk away from the murder vehicle without leaving a trace, an imprint of his actions. Most loyalist killers used revolvers or pistols, but a shotgun cartridge would eventually closely point to the work of one operator, as if Stone was somehow subliminally anxious to impose his individualism on his actions by leaving a piece of evidence as testimony to his work: leaving a spent cartridge provided a personal identification. His accomplices were not aware he left a 'calling card'. It was his own secret – which he would later reveal to prove he killed an IRA intelligence officer.

8

Killing the Innocent

In 1985 Stone married Leigh-Anne and settled down in a house in the Braniel. He was constantly in touch with McMichael and John Bingham, and he made himself available when they required his services. At the beginning of October he was restless and contacted McMichael to enquire if he needed his expertise. The UFF leader presented him with a list of potential targets and Stone chose a Catholic taxi-driver.

It was a sectarian rather than republican hit, although Stone later claimed that the intended victim was an IRA intelligence officer. According to Stone, the taxi-driver regularly transported his son to the Newtownards Road and parked the taxi. The son left the vehicle and noted the movements of loyalist organisation personnel and vehicles. The information was passed to the IRA for the purpose of assassinating UDA activists. The truth is that the target and his son were not politically involved, but, like many people, had merely, by virtue of being Catholic, come to the attention of loyalists who lived near them.

Stone was now faced with a killing reminiscent of the sectarian warfare of 1972. The target and his son were not members of Sinn Fein but they were vulnerable because their taxi was registered to Bell Star Taxis of 172 Falls Road. That was sufficient for local loyalists to brand taxi-man Robert McAllister a republican. It is conceivable that his name had been noted at military roadchecks in republican West Belfast. Each day he drove his personal Ford Sierra 2.3 diesel from his home at 11 Ava Avenue, Ormeau Road across the city to the taxi depot. All cars entering republican ghettos were logged by military personnel in lookout posts on top of high-rise buildings, or by passing foot patrols. Roadchecks resulted in car numbers being fed into a computerised filing system which contributed to a detailed knowledge of traffic movements and pinpointed cars which were registered 'suspect' on the RUC computer.

If a rogue policeman or UDR soldier were present at several roadchecks, and noted McAllister's address and the frequency with which he entered the Falls area, that would have been sufficient to have led to UFF scrutiny of his life. Whatever the perverse reason for selecting him, and the complexities of life in Belfast can offer many, McMichael decreed that this man should be killed. This time there was no security file, merely a personal choice, and the killing was not an example of 'pre-emptive' violence.

McMichael's and Stone's motives were based on unfounded suspicion, and on naked prejudice of the type which led to the deaths of hundreds of people in Belfast. McAllister was a victim of the type of selection which loyalists knew to be indiscriminate terror. McMichael and Bingham, irrespective of their grand designs to change the nature of loyalist violence and assassinate IRA volunteers, were gradually resorting to the old methods. Security files on IRA personnel were useless if the intended targets were constantly in hiding, and thus out of reach of loyalist hit-squads: much easier to kill innocent Catholics on the basis of rumour. Brady, for example – there was a murder they could justify to their own people, irrespective of an RUC and/or republican denial that he was a terrorist. His political affiliations were enough to convince hardline Protestants he deserved to die.

In the case of McAllister they were prepared to invent evidence based on the fact he worked for a taxi company in a republican enclave. Such is the bitterness in Belfast that such a tenuous link with a community is sufficient justification for murder.

Stone was presented with the relevant detail on McAllister's movements and life-style. McMichael asked him to shoot his victim in the house he shared with his elderly mother, but Stone refused. As an assassin Stone possessed a personal code which he explained to me.

I never believed in shooting a man in front of his wife, kids, mother or girlfriend. I wouldn't have liked it to happen to me that way. I had a mother and I knew how she would have felt. I have a lot of respect for the family.

He told McMichael he would devise another means of killing McAllister, one which would not result in harm to others.

UFF personnel conducted surveillance on the taxi-driver's home. They discovered he often worked at nights, and parked his car in an alleyway at the rear of his house. When travelling to work he was required to reverse the vehicle into the street. Stone decided to construct an explosive device which could be placed under the car approximate to where the driver's seat was positioned. He asked McMichael to provide him with an accomplice driver, and requested a Mills grenade, coils of copper wire and nylon cord.

At 3.00 a.m. on 27 October, Stone left home and met his accomplice on the edge of the Braniel estate. They drove to a house off the Ormeau Road, where the accomplice gave Stone the bomb-making components from which he constructed a device. At 6.00 a.m. they drove past McAllister's house, and were pleased to see his car parked in the alley. Stone told his driver to park their car on the Ormeau Embankment overlooking the River Lagan. He ordered his accomplice to remain in the vehicle with the engine running. Stone placed the grenade and its attachments inside his clothing and began walking towards Ava Avenue. He was aware of workmen on their way to the Ormeau Bakery adjacent to McAllister's house and worried his operation might be compromised.

I walked down the entry beside McAllister's house and I could see men going to work in the bakery. I climbed over a fence, past a caravan to the blue Sierra. When I got to the car there were two workers passing and I pretended it was my car and wouldn't start.

Stone employed the tactic he used at the Stormont Hotel and displayed a familiarity with his surroundings by telling strangers 'the sodden car won't start'. He gestured hopelessly at McAllister's vehicle and the two workmen smiled, expressed their recognition of his dilemma and walked away. Stone was confident his disguise was such that he would not be recognised if the strangers ever saw him at an identity parade. His hair was long, he was unshaven and resembled a gaunt, dishevelled figure. He knew he was capable of totally reversing that image by cutting his hair, slicking it back, growing a moustache and wearing expensive clothes. Furthermore, he was not on file as a terrorist suspect.

I knew that the police only showed witnesses terrorist files. A description of the person they saw that morning would not only bear no resemblance to me later that day, but such a photofit would not accord with police photos of me when I was a teenager. As such, I had no terrorist profile and police would not seek to relate a photofit to me. I looked different in my private life to my other life. Even my accomplice didn't know me. If he talked and described me it would have been useless. I could be one of several people – Colin Moffat, Holmes, Tony May, etc.

When the strangers were out of sight, he crawled under the car and attached the Mills grenade to the steering column. He passed a wire coil through the grenade pin, tied it to the nylon cord and secured the cord to the front wheel.

I knew that when the car was reversed the pin would be pulled setting off the grenade. I got up, looked around, nipped back over the hedge, through a few entries where I joined the fellow in the car. He drove me back to where he picked me up and I walked home.

Robert McAllister had been in bed for two hours when the grenade was fixed to his car, and he remained asleep until 1.00 p.m. After a light lunch, he decided to return to the taxi depot. He drove the Sierra to the Falls Road and reported for duty at 1.30. He was in the depot several minutes when a colleague, Jimmy Black, entered and said: 'There's a grenade under your car.' McAllister thought his friend was joking but agreed to accompany Black to examine the car.

Black says to me: 'Look under the car.' I thought he was joking but I looked anyway. I saw a round object which seemed to be sitting on the drive shaft under the driver's side. I put my hand underneath it to test the weight as I thought it might be plastic. It felt heavy and at this stage I realised it wasn't a joke. We told people to keep away and called the police.

There was something bizarre and comical about McAllister's behaviour and for a second time that day he was lucky to survive. Black told a slightly different version of events; he remembered McAllister arriving and complaining of a strange noise emanating from his car. Black looked under the vehicle, saw the grenade and its attachments, and warned McAllister. Dennis John Leadbeater, a senior ammunitions technician of the Royal Army Ordinance

Corps, was detailed to defuse the device. He made it safe and recovered a No. 36 Mills grenade but his task was hampered by a 200-strong mob who stoned police and soldiers maintaining a cordon to prevent the risk of civilian casualties. It was typical that violence should be directed at those preventing an explosion – the absurdity of political life on the streets of Belfast.

The attempt on McAllister's life happened during a period of increased political tension and amid threats of violence from loyalists. From July that year, sporadic violence broke out in Protestant areas, when police prevented Orangemen parading through Catholic streets in Portadown. The political climate had begun to change rapidly, with increased dialogue between the London/Dublin governments. Restrictions imposed on the routes of traditional Orange marches were seen as an attempt to portray a sensitive appreciation of Catholic fears, and Catholic resentment that for decades Orangemen had been free to walk through nationalist territory, playing anti-Catholic tunes. Protestants perceived the new restrictions as an affront to their 'right to march' wherever they wished. Their attitude symbolised a belief that Ulster was their country and it was their God-given right to parade anywhere and everywhere.

The late Irish Cardinal, Thomas O'Fiaich, exacerbated the tension by alleging that 90 per cent of religious bigotry in Northern Ireland 'was found among Protestants'. Margaret Thatcher and the Irish prime minister, Garret Fitzgerald, were secretly arranging behind the scenes to introduce a new political accord, the Anglo-Irish Agreement, while the Opposition leader in the Republic, Charles Haughey, warned that he would resist any attempt to deviate from the principle of Irish unity. On 30 October, the Unionist leaders Paisley and Molyneaux warned Thatcher of a loyalist 'backlash' if the Republic were given a consultative role in the affairs of Northern Ireland. Such a warning, dangerous and negative, provided the UDA/UVF with comfort and impetus. 'Backlash' was a word imbued with historical memories of violence, used recurrently during turbulent years of sectarian strife: 'the Loyalist Backlash' was a phrase employed by successive Unionist and loyalist leaders to warn or intimidate British governments when political changes did not appeal to Protestants – a dangerous phrase, capable of inciting paramilitaries with its double-edged usage; it could be employed as a genuine warning, as Paisley and Molyneaux intended, or as a blatant threat that any change unapproved by loyalists incurred violence. On 2 November, a new organisation emerged from within the Protestant community, and pledged to oppose the rerouting of traditional loyalist parades, and to combat the encroachment of Irish nationalism in the affairs of Ulster. It claimed a membership of thousands in forty-eight branches, and its real aim was to prepare for a doomsday situation in which the defence of Northern Ireland was the real issue: it sought to be an umbrella organisation, willing to reflect and represent all Protestant thought and resentment to change.

In such periods of tension, the loyalist paramilitaries resorted to reflex violence, and Stone was again provided with a 'sanction'. He asked for the opportunity to kill, and was given the name Kevin McPolin. Stone's agreement to undertake this assassination would eventually haunt him, and lead to a private denial of the part he played in it.

McPolin was a 26-year-old Catholic carpenter who lived with his parents at Katesbridge, a townland near the town of Banbridge in County Down. He was single and shared his working life with his brother, Gerard. They travelled wherever they found work, and from September 1984 to November 1985 they were employed in the construction of a new housing complex at Old Warren on the outskirts of the town of Lisburn. Kevin was non-political, and friendly with Protestant neighbours and Protestant workmates. However, someone in the workforce at Lisburn did not feel well disposed towards him, and 'fingered' him.

McMichael had a personal interest in Lisburn, where he lived and owned a pub, the Admiral Benbow, a thriving business situated in the centre of Lisburn, offering good 'pub grub'. McMichael also masterminded the activities of the UFF hit-squads in an area encompassing Lisburn, Ballynahinch and several other centres within a fifteen-mile radius of his home. In October 1985 he was active politically in drafting the UDA's political policy and appeared frequently on television and radio programmes. Secretly, he was busy planning the military strategy of the UFF. In that month, the IRA was pressurising Protestant contractors in Northern Ireland. For several years the Provisionals had been engaged in targeting any contractors undertaking government-funded work, the objective being to prevent the building of police and RUC stations, or repairs to them. Many contractors, mostly Protestant, were murdered, and their deaths incensed loyalists. In

October, threats were made against contractors in the Lisburn area, and rumours circulated that Catholic workmen were responsible for passing information about Protestant contractors to the IRA and INLA. According to the Revd. William Beattie, a member of Ian Paisley's Democratic Unionist Party, a police commander in Lisburn claimed that contractors in the area were coming under heavy paramilitary pressure in October. Beattie later alleged that the IRA and INLA were 'using Catholics as a cover to gather intelligence on members of the security forces living in Protestant areas of Lisburn'. These allegations provided a blanket condemnation of Catholics and defined them as the eyes and ears of republican terrorists.

The Beattie allegation was made on 12 November, but it is fair to assume it was based on a belief in place before then; and if true, loyalist paramilitaries would have perceived a justification for the killing of any Catholic. The allegations also had the effect of narrowly defining any Catholics who were in a position to spy on Protestant homes – such as the McPolins, who had been employed for fourteen months in a predominantly Protestant housing estate. Beattie would not have intended to convey support for terrorism, but like so many political statements his careless wording could permit of a sinister interpretation. McMichael, with his own political and security contacts, also became convinced that many Catholics were secret republicans, who assisted the IRA and INLA. When Kevin McPolin's name was given to him as one of those providing lethal intelligence for the IRA, he questioned neither the source nor the accuracy of the allegation. Stone says he was told the target was a member of a 'Provie active-service unit'.

Thus, Kevin McPolin's fate was decided on the basis of an unfounded claim – which illustrates the cheapness of life in Northern Ireland. McMichael chose Stone both because he was efficient, and because he was not a native of Lisburn; McMichael judged that the police would react to the killing by concentrating their efforts on known paramilitaries in the Lisburn area, while Stone would be far removed from the crime. He was also determined to use an assassin unknown in the ranks of the UFF in his home town. If accomplices were arrested and admitted involvement, they would be unable to identify the 'trigger-man'. By such means, McMichael could distance himself from murder by giving Stone 'sanctions', and by encouraging him to liaise with accomplices. McMichael always made it possible for a third party to enter negotiations with Stone once the planning of a murder had been activated. From the moment that Stone accepted a 'sanction', other people assumed responsibility for handling the logistics and the assassin's requirements. This ensured that McMichael's participation could not be traced – an ideal arrangement, similar in character to the manner in which Mafia leaders contracted hitmen from 'out of town'.

The assassination of McPolin was planned with meticulous attention to detail. Several UFF volunteers from the Lisburn units were assigned to compile a dossier on the daily work routine of the victim. McMichael could have asked the UDA or UVF in Banbridge to commit the murder in the victim's neighbourhood, or on his route to work, but he chose Lisburn: the territory was familiar to him, and he could influence the way in which the 'hit' would be successfully executed.

He told one of his henchmen he was bringing a 'hitman' into Lisburn and two cars should be used, one to transport the gunman to the killing zone, and a second placed outside the town to take him to safety. McMichael wanted Stone quickly removed from the area after the murder. To achieve this, he took account of the possibility that the first car would be identified by eyewitnesses, and relayed to mobile police and army patrols. He advised that it should be abandoned without delay, and his hitman transferred to the second vehicle. It was important to ensure that the second car be a legitimately registered motor vehicle which, if stopped at a roadblock, would not attract attention, or scrutiny of its occupants. McMichael was well aware that when a car was stopped at a police or Army roadblock, the registration number was relayed by radio to the mainframe computer at Army/police HQ. If the vehicle was owned by a person with a criminal record, or suspected of paramilitary affiliations, this was conveyed to the personnel on the roadcheck within 15–30 seconds. Such a communication determined that the car be searched, its occupants questioned and their names placed on file. This tactic assisted the legal authorities in keeping an account of the movements of suspects and those who accompanied them. McMichael knew that a cordon would be placed around Lisburn after the killing, and roadblocks set up on routes leading to Belfast, or across country to Comber, and for Stone, thence easily to Ballygowan and the Braniel. Nevertheless, a possibility existed of a police or Army presence on that route and the safest way to deal with it was to use a car which would not attract attention. It was not possible to use a 'legit' motor for the initial stage of the assassination because the owner would come under police pressure to identify those who used it. A car would therefore be stolen a short time before the murder, to limit the time police would have to trace it. McMichael was determined that planning, and not chance, would guarantee a successful hit.

Towards the end of the first week of November, Stone was briefed on the arrangements and asked which weapon he preferred. He chose a shotgun because he intended to 'work close' to the victim. The date selected was 8 November, the time 8.30–45 a.m., and the place of execution a row of houses for the elderly in which McPolin was working. Stone said he did not wish to be collected at the Braniel on the day of the 'sanction'. McMichael told him to make his way to a house in the Village near Boucher Road, from where a 'legit' car would drive him along back roads to Lisburn, and he would be transferred to the car to be used for the killing. Unlike the Brady murder, more detailed planning took place this time, with the involvement of a full UFF active-service unit of six men. The 'legit' car would be parked one mile from the scene of the murder.

On the night of 7 November Stone arrived at the house in the Village area and remained there overnight. The following morning, at 8.00 a.m., a car arrived for him: the driver was unknown to Stone. 'I didn't know him, he didn't know me and that was the way I liked it.'

They avoided the direct M1 motorway route and reached Lisburn via minor roads. Stone transferred to a blue Vauxhall Cavalier which had been stolen from the premises of a car dealer, Derek Crawford, of 49 Waterloo Road, in Lisburn. He discovered the car missing at noon on 7 November and informed the RUC. They were unable to trace it because the UFF unit in Lisburn concealed it overnight in a lock-up garage.

When Stone got into the vehicle he found his killing weapon, a double-barrelled shotgun, partly concealed by a blanket and positioned along the rear seat as he requested. The position of the gun resembled the circumstances of the Brady killing. Stone gave the following account of what happened:

I asked the driver did he know what he was doing and he said 'aye'. He drove into the Old Warren estate for a while and spotted the target sitting parked at a footpath near houses being built. We cruised him for a couple of times and I could see he was on his own. There was a school near by and I could see a wee patrolman beating about. We stopped near the target.

Barry Flemming, a teenage pupil of Lisnagarvey High School, says he will never forget the events of that morning. He was walking to school with his friend, Stephen McCutcheon, both of them Protestants: he knew Kevin McPolin as a friendly workman with whom he exchanged pleasantries each morning. McPolin was habitually a punctual person who sat in his car every morning waiting for the arrival of his fellow workers. Barry Flemming saw the blue Vauxhall drive past and park in front of McPolin's vehicle.

A man jumped out of this car, ran to the driver's side of the worker's car, shot at the worker's car and got back into the other car and drove away.

Stephen McCutcheon saw the gun which he described as two-foot long and the gunman as 5ft 7ins, stocky build. He was wearing 'a blue woollen hat like a monkey hat and a long jacket'.

Alexander Gray, who worked as a window-cleaner, was sitting in his flat overlooking the scene when he heard two loud bangs with a five-second delay between them. He instinctively knew a gun had been discharged and rushed to his phone to contact police. As he dialled 999 he pulled his extended telephone lead to allow him to reach a window from where he could view the street and provide police with an eyewitness account.

I saw a man at a quick pace walk from the driver's side of a metallic blue Toyota car. He was carrying a double-barrelled shotgun in his right hand. The shotgun was closed and the barrels appeared to me to be of normal length. This man with a shotgun walked around a dark blue-coloured Cavalier car which was parked very close to the front of the Toyota car and facing in the same direction as the Toyota with its rear next to the front of it. I noticed another person in the driver's seat of the Cavalier. When the man with the shotgun walked round the front of the Cavalier, the rear nearside door of the car sprung open. The man with the shotgun seemed to throw the shotgun into the rear of the car. The Cavalier was driven off at speed down Drumbeg Drive in the direction of the Moira Road. Simultaneous to this I saw a man stumble out of the Toyota with his hands up to his face. His face and hands were covered in blood. If it had not been for the blood he would have reminded me of a very drunk man as he attempted to get out of his car.

Alexander Gray was watching the final moments of a tragedy being witnessed by others including the two schoolboys.

Another observer, an elderly patrolman, Joseph Acker Oliver, started work at 8.20 a.m. each morning, and he was positioned at Drumbeg Drive to escort schoolchildren across Avonmore Park. Little traffic went by when at 8.30 he saw Kevin McPolin parked thirty yards away. He next heard two bangs, and thought they had been caused by a car backfiring; he looked towards Drumbeg Drive and saw a gunman.

He had a long gun like a rifle. He was only about 5ft 7ins and well built. He was dark-haired and wearing blue clothes.

He watched the killers drive away and moments later was faced with horror.

I saw the workman's car door open and the workman got out. He was running and half-staggering and when he reached me he fell on to his knees and turned over on to his side.

McPolin, in a state of shock, his life ebbing away, tried to grasp the patrolman's hand.

Many victims of violence are killed instantly, whereas McPolin was left to cling desperately to life. He was barely alive when Maurice McCarthy arrived ten minutes later in an ambulance from the Lagan Valley Hospital. He saw the injured man lying face downwards in a recovery position.

I noticed the patient had chest and facial injuries and two fingers and a thumb were missing from his left hand. I kept his airway clear, gave him oxygen, and with my partner, Andy Spratt, we rushed him to hospital.

At the Lagan Valley the Senior Casualty Officer, Elisha Frances Brown, gave the injured man an intravenous infusion of saline, sedation and an endotracheal tube was placed into his trachea. Her efforts to save his life were to no avail and he died at 9.00 a.m. The State Pathologist, Dr Robert Marshall, determined the exact cause of death.

Death was due to shotgun pellet wounds of the head and chest. Numerous small abrasions, as made by broken glass, were scattered on the face. The region of the left eye and cheek were the sites of more extensive bruising and abrasions. A large pellet had passed downwards across the left cheek causing a deep laceration. It had then burrowed beneath the skin and had been arrested on the left side of the lower jaw which it fractured. A second large pellet struck the centre of the left cheek. It went downwards into the lower lip and fractured the lower jaw. A third pellet entered the cheek and lodged in the neck. A fourth caused a vertical laceration across the front of the chin. This pellet could have been one of five which struck the front of the chest close together over the inner end of the right collar bone. From one of these holes the plastic wad of a cartridge was removed. Three pieces of shot perforated and lacerated the right lung. They fractured two right ribs. Another was found in a large quantity of blood which lodged in the chest cavity. Four more pieces of shot struck the region of the left upper chest. Other pellets perforated the left lung and fractured the back of the seventh left rib. There had been massive haemhorrage in the chest cavity. Another pellet struck the left arm and one struck the upper abdomen. The forefinger of the left hand was mangled and the finger was attached only by a tendon. The hand had been raised in front of the chest. His death was due to massive bleeding into the chest cavities.

By the time news of this killing reached newspaper offices, Stone was sitting in a house in the Village listening to news reports of his handiwork. His own account of the manner he killed McPolin was laconic.

He watched me raise the shotgun and point it at him. I fired one at his chin and as he slumped over I blasted him with the other.

But there had been, as Alexander Gray recalled, a 5–6-second delay between the two shots. Stone watched the effects of the first blast which shattered the driver's window, and then he waited while McPolin placed a hand across his chest in anticipation of the next discharge. When he later learned the way in which his victim died, and when he was then faced with incontrovertible evidence that Kevin McPolin, a quiet young man, had no political affiliation, the killing preoccupied Stone. The victim's innocence, coupled with the description of how he staggered from the car, led Stone to make the following observation.

I heard later on the news that day that the boy McPolin had got out of his car and staggered up the street. I felt bad about this because I hadn't done the job quickly without causing him to suffer any further.

Stone took immense pride in his ability to dispatch his victims quickly, and when I first met him he expressed regret that he had not 'finished off' McPolin with two rounds. In subsequent meetings with me, he began to distance himself from the murder by refusing to discuss it. It did not fit neatly into his self-image of a hitman who only killed known republicans, and then with a clinical ferocity which demanded the minimum of suffering from victims.

Stone's consistent attention to detail, in respect of his own security, was a feature in this murder also. When he reached the Village an hour after the shooting, he washed and changed clothes. The garments worn for the 'sanction' were dumped in an industrial bin at the rear of a bar in the Village.

In the aftermath, the Revd. William Beattie, while condemning the murder of Kevin McPolin, said it had happened because the government and RUC proved unable to restore order throughout Northern Ireland. They had failed to give proper protection to Protestant firms, and in Lisburn it had long been well known that the IRA and INLA were using Catholics 'as a cover to gather intelligence on loyalists and security forces living in Protestant housing estates'. 'We have a very explosive situation where this is just the tip of the iceberg,' he added. Beattie's condemnation of the killing was not echoed by his party leader, Ian Paisley, nor by Unionist leader James Molyneaux; both remained silent.

The Catholic bishop, the Right Reverend Francis Brooks, responded swiftly to Beattie, though without directly naming him. Bishop Brooks said 'Irresponsible people in positions of power and authority can too easily stir up fears and tension.' This comment was read to mourners at McPolin's funeral but it did not deal fully with the heated nature of a public statement Beattie released twenty-four hours after the killing.

I deplore and repudiate the futile killing of the Roman Catholic workman in Lisburn. It is a dastardly act. This killing is a direct result of the intolerable situation in the construction industry whereby Catholic firms and Catholic workers can work in Protestant areas but Protestant firms and Protestant workers cannot work in hard-line republican areas. They have been intimidated out of republican ghettoes and now no longer attempt, for security reasons, to work in republican areas. This killing is the inevitable outcome of the government's failure to restore law and order in republican areas and the senseless insistence in such circumstances of bodies such as the Housing Executive [*government body for building public housing*] that Catholic firms must be awarded the contracts in Protestant areas irrespective of the consequences. The Sinn Fein councillors on the Lisburn Borough Council, Damien Gibney and Patrick Rice, have put themselves in the firing line by pouring fuel on the flames in that they blamed loyalist politicians. Their statement puts the lives of local loyalist politicians at risk. I warn Sinn Fein that they are putting their own lives at risk. They should remember that they are known and identified and can be hunted down and can be eliminated in the final analysis, if we have to defend ourselves, and we are capable of doing so. I would remind the government, the RUC, the Army, Sinn Fein and the IRA that there is a pool of able-bodied and trained men – trained by the Army, the RUC, UDR and the 'B' Specials – capable of mobilisation at short notice. If we are pushed to the brink by the IRA, Sinn Fein or the government, we will mobilise within the law in our own defence and in the defence of our right to retain full British citizenship within the United Kingdom.

Aside from the flawed logic about the background to the killing, Beattie's claim about Housing Executive allocation of contracts misrepresented government policy. The statement symptomatised loyalist thinking, and bore similarities to the views of loyalist paramilitaries. The response to Beattie included queries as to his use of language, of phrases such as 'known and identified'; the words, 'can be hunted down'; 'can be eliminated', evoked a 1972 statement by another loyalist politician, William Craig, who warned that loyalists possessed assassination lists of republicans. To the surprise of some, Beattie's statement was never tested at law. However, the political climate of Northern Ireland was then redolent with such linguistic imagery on both sides, and perhaps government chose to ignore it as an acceptable part of the whole bizarre political process.

One dimension to Beattie's statement, although reminiscent of loyalist history, was the reminder to everyone, including the British, that there existed 'a pool' of thousands of fighting men capable of immediate mobilisation. Beattie was reiterating a widely held belief that thousands of RUC/UDR personnel, and people trained by them, were prepared to answer a call to arms – even though the suggestion that such a grouping could 'mobilise within the law' bore little recognition to the legalities of British jurisprudence regarding unofficial armies or treasonable offences. Although Beattie's revelation of a potential 'army' waiting in the wings was dismissed by some as a typical loyalist threat, it may well have been intended as a reference to a grouping then being formed by other loyalist leaders. Meetings held in secret throughout loyalist areas in 1986 intended to establish a new force which would emerge one year later as Ulster Resistance. According to the UFF leader, John McMichael, a member of the Democratic Unionist Party, not the Reverend Beattie, approached him in late autumn 1986 requesting weapons.

He came along to us with a shopping list for armaments. I mean, he was looking for heavy gear, and he had the money. He was representing certain political figures and I thought – these guys are gonna start some helluva war. I told him to fuck off. I had no respect for him or the people he represented. They were the types walked away from us when the going got hot but they were the mouthpieces who helped start it all. There was no way I was gonna hand over our gear. I told him to go find his own contacts. That was a time when certain people were trying to put together Ulster Resistance to defend Ulster if the Anglo-Irish Agreement moved us towards a united Ireland. Some of these people were well known for threatening the use of force and using us as canon fodder. I resented that because when our volunteers did the job and were caught, these self-same people disowned them. They didn't visit our volunteers in prison.

At this point Stone had no awareness of the gradual emergence of Ulster Resistance, although he would later feature within its ranks. While he reflected on the McPolin killing, the year ended without his participation in any further acts of violence. The McPolin family were left with their grief but no malice; the victim's brother Gerard publicly appealed in vain to the UFF to admit they killed the wrong man.

I want peace of mind for my parents who are elderly. They are simple country folk and can't understand why anyone would want to kill their son. It is upsetting for them that the killers have not come out and said they made a mistake. Kevin was not in the IRA. He wasn't even in the local darts team. He was the most innocent person I have ever known. It is hurting my mother and father desperately. They want people to know Kevin wasn't in the IRA and I am begging the UFF to make a statement. I would also appeal to the man who pulled the trigger to meet me anywhere at anytime without his gun so that I could talk to him. I have to ask him why he killed Kevin. I want to know if he has a family and why he feels he has to take someone else's life for his country. I don't bear him any malice. I would like him to see the state of my parents and the grief he has left behind him in our home. I want to ask him what motivates him. I want to tell him what kind of person Kevin was. Kevin had no political views. He just worked to get his wages at the end of each week.

Stone knew he had killed the wrong man – even though McMichael lied to newspapers that McPolin had been arrested four times under the Prevention of Terrorism Act. The RUC defended the dead man's reputation by publicly refuting the UFF claim and asserting that 'Kevin McPolin was a respected member of the community'.

Stone maintained a low profile after the murder and the subsequent seventeen months of his life remain a mystery. I learned that he was involved in the Unionist strike or 'Day of Action', a protest against the Anglo-Irish Agreement on 3 March 1986. Commerce and industry throughout Northern Ireland ground to a standstill. Air travel was disrupted and the loyalists in the power stations reduced output. In images resembling the 1974 'workers'' strike, masked men manned barricades throughout the Province and shots were fired at policemen. The British government came under severe criticism for not confronting the open displays of paramilitarism, and for not keeping roads open. In the town of Bangor, armed loyalists sprinted across a dual carriageway in front of my car, and began stopping traffic – an example of the blatant intimidation which forced ordinary people to vacate the streets, thereby enhancing the loyalist claim that everyone stayed at home in support of the 'strike'. Stone manned a barricade in East Belfast, masked to hide his identity.

Later in 1986, on 16 October, police investigated a double murder. In due course, long after his arrest, they questioned Stone: informants pointed to Stone's involvement; features of the crime were later compared to his other offences and their *modus operandi*. The victims were a 76-year-old Catholic mother and her 31-year-old adopted son, Terry.

Stone denied the crime, argues now that he did not kill women, and therefore could not have been responsible for the crime. The UFF admitted responsibility but made no mention of the death of the mother, claiming the man had been a field intelligence officer for the IRA.

Kathleen Mullan, and her adopted son, Terry, lived in a remote farmhouse on the Dromore Road between Lisburn and the town of Ballynahinch – in an area for which John McMichael assumed direct UFF responsibility. Kathleen and her 75-year-old husband, Tommy, had spent the forty years of their married life there, regarded as quiet, decent, friendly, and respected by Protestant neighbours. In nearby Ballynahinch, relations between the two communities had been strained by sectarian violence aimed at the smaller Catholic population of the town; in July, loyalists rampaged through a Catholic enclave, smashing windows and daubing slogans on houses. Homes were petrol-bombed and twenty Catholic families fled from the intimidation. On the Lisburn Road off Main Street a huge wall slogan read: 'Ulster says death to all Jesuit bastards'.

Terry Mullan knew the area but had lived apart from his parents when he married. Shortly before his death, after a separation from his wife, Bernadette, and his sons aged 11 and 6 years, he returned to his parents' home.

In July the IRA had killed 22-year-old Robert Hill, a member of the Ulster Defence Regiment, on the outskirts of Ballynahinch and McMichael ordered the revenge killing of a Catholic. Terry Mullan was the chosen victim, because he was a Catholic and an easy target owing to the remote location of his house. His sudden reappearance in the area may have motivated loyalists to suspect him of being in the IRA. He led a quiet life, and it was suggested that his refusal to associate with many people attracted the attention of rumour-mongers.

In the early morning of 16 October, Kathleen Mullan and her son were having breakfast while Tommy Mullan was getting dressed in an upstairs bedroom. At 8.00 a.m. a car with three men in it drove into the yard of the farmhouse. Tommy Mullan's first thought was that someone was there to talk business to Terry who bought and sold second-hand cars. As Tommy walked from the bedroom, Terry said 'there were boys in the yard who were no good, and he didn't wish to see them'. In the light of what happened, the reference to 'boys' indicated to police that Terry Mullan recognised a person or persons from the locality, whom he knew to be extremist, or criminally minded. Alternatively, their appearance and demeanour may have struck him as sinister.

No one knows exactly what he saw from the downstairs window of the house – but it was enough to discourage him from responding to the doorbell. While accomplices remained in the car, a gunman entered the house through a rear kitchen door and chased Terry Mullan. Forensic evidence later offered the conclusion that one round was fired from a pistol in the kitchen, another in the living room and three in the front porch where he collapsed and died. His elderly mother was shot once in the chest with a bullet which passed through her son's arm. Evidence pointed to her death resulting from an attempt to shield her son as he ran into the front porch where he was given the *coup de grâce* by his killer. Both bodies were found lying side by side. Tommy Mullan was in an upstairs bedroom when the shooting started. He found the bodies and phoned the police. The UFF issued a statement alleging Terry Mullan was involved in the murder of the UDR man, Robert Hill, in July, but made no mention of Kathleen Mullan. The RUC responded by repudiating the claim. A year later an RUC inspector told an inquest the outrage 'was perpetrated against a totally innocent party on the basis of rumour and hearsay'.

Three weeks after the killing, the formation of Ulster Resistance was formally announced after a massive rally in the Ulster Hall in Belfast city centre. The media was denied access to the event, but BBC journalists later acquired a private video which was taken inside the hall. It showed Ian Paisley and his deputy Peter Robinson standing on a platform surrounded by several thousand men. Paisley wore a red beret to identify the newly created organisation and delivered a speech. Ulster Resistance was in place to 'take direct action as and when required' to defeat the Anglo-Irish Agreement. The event was symbolised by paramilitary trappings as men paraded with banners commemorating the origins of the Ulster Volunteer Force.

Rallies were subsequently held in towns throughout Northern Ireland and leading members of the organisation claimed it was comprised of nine battalions. The day after the inaugural meeting, Ian Paisley arrived at the BBC studios in Belfast for a lunchtime radio programme of which I was editor. On his way to the studio he heard a radio announcement that 'Ian Paisley would explain the origins of Ulster Resistance on the lunchtime radio programme, Talkback', and he became furious: he had earlier refused to talk to journalists, promising he would explain the nature of the Ulster Hall rally in an event sponsored by him and scheduled for later that day. The announcement that his self-imposed embargo was about to be breached displeased him greatly, and in the studio, throughout the live programme, he was heated and expressive. Public reaction, telephoned after this chaotic broadcast, largely criticised his behaviour.

Paisley's association with Ulster Resistance, like that of his party, did not last long. It was believed that many Ulster Resistance commanders favoured an aggressive line against the Anglo-Irish Agreement – whereas Paisley was moving along a road designed for political dialogue. The split between these factions did not deter leaders of the new body from establishing close links with McMichael's UFF and the UVF. Together, these three groupings, without the involvement of Paisley, forged terrorist links.

McMichael became amenable to the new leadership, and together with the UVF, planned large acquisitions of weapons. Ulster Resistance had the ready cash which its partners needed, and had also established links with the South African intelligence community. The South African defence industry desperately needed 'hi-tech' weapons but were prevented from buying them because of an international embargo. They were particularly interested in missile development at Short's Aircraft Establishment in East Belfast. Ulster Resistance was in a position to assist; many of its members, as well as people connected with the UFF/UVF, were employed by Short's. The South Africans were prepared to provide weapons in return for Short's plans for its latest missile, or for parts, or a replica of the weapon, a computerised surface-to-air missile; furthermore, they were keen to use their friendship with the Israelis – and an arms dealer – to acquire weapons which could not be traced to either country. The Israelis had a ready supply of AK47 assault rifles, grenades and pistols, recovered from their campaign in Lebanon.

When Ulster Resistance finally received a large supply of guns from the South African deal it was part of a consignment shared with its UVF/UFF partners. John Bingham of the UVF and John McMichael handled all the dealings with Ulster Resistance. Inevitably, they also employed the skills of Michael Stone, who was tasked to train Ulster Resistance units in rural areas, and make them familiar with weapons. Using his aliases, he travelled throughout Northern Ireland undertaking this role, and became familiar with parts of the countryside hitherto unknown to him. In the spring of 1987, he decided to put his new knowledge to use.

A few months earlier, in the autumn of 1986, he had lost one of his most important contacts within the UVF: John Bingham was shot dead by a Provisional IRA Active Service Unit. In an operation similar to the killing of Bunting, gunmen burst into his house and clinically executed him. The IRA planned the murder with the aid of UDA leader Jim Craig, who regularly supplied them with information in return for immunity from IRA hitmen. Bingham lived in a loyalist district in North Belfast where he was safe from IRA surveillance. The collusion between the IRA and Craig enabled the IRA to monitor Bingham's movements, as well as the lives of other loyalist leaders. That bizarre relationship permitted the IRA and other republican activists to kill three of Bingham's associates, Lenny Murphy, leader of the Shankill Butchers, William 'Frenchie' Marchant, and a firebrand Scots preacher, George Seawright. Bingham's death served to reinforce Stone's preoccupation with personal security, and a willingness to operate in rural areas, far from the scrutiny of members of the Belfast brigades of the UVF and UFF. The deaths of leading loyalists created fear and paranoia in loyalist paramilitary ranks in Belfast, and the UVF and UFF set up individual investigations to try and pinpoint the person providing the IRA and INLA with information. Craig maintained close links with the latter grouping – he shared with them the proceeds from racketeering. Stone and McMichael rightly suspected that the informer in their midst must be based in West Belfast, and felt inclined to point the finger at Craig – but without conclusive evidence they were powerless to act against him.

McMichael assumed personal responsibility for the UFF inquiry, and made it known that he would be relentless in pursuit of the culprit. He heard rumours that the West Belfast UDA commander, Jim Craig, led a flashy life-style, and had close relations with known republicans. Craig, an unscrupulous and powerful figure, with responsibility for one of the largest and most violent areas of Belfast, was preoccupied with racketeering, and, thus, less concerned with McMichael's UFF strategy. In a meeting with members of the INLA, Craig agreed to the carving-up of large areas of the city for the purpose of racketeering. He would control parts of the city without interference from the INLA and they would do likewise in a marriage of convenience, bizarre in the context of a conflict in which the UDA/INLA, loyalists versus Catholic nationalists, were implacable enemies.

Craig's relationship with the Provisionals had a different slant. They were not interested in his racketeering exploits, but in the knowledge that he possessed about the organisers of terror within his community. The Provisionals presented him with an ultimatum – to the effect 'you assist us or we'll kill you'. Craig knew they would realise their threat or, at the very least, interrupt his opportunities for racketeering. Once they had enlisted his support in the killing of Lenny Murphy, he was caught in a web of collusion from which he could not extricate himself. He knew the IRA to be capable of blackmailing him, of making him a target for his own people. McMichael was high on the IRA murder list: they knew he was the UFF leader responsible for the killing of several republicans. When McMichael then began investigating the murder of loyalist terrorists, and singled out Craig for special attention, he did not know the danger presented by such a course of action. Meanwhile Stone, on McMichael's advice, concentrated his effort in establishing contact with the UFF, UVF and Ulster Resistance in the Ulster countryside.

9

Murder Incorporated

Stone's work with Ulster Resistance was not simply to train some of its members in the use of guns but to blood them. Alternatively, they were a source of intelligence about their localities and were capable of providing logistical support for him. McMichael knew that Ulster Resistance would assist Stone and other members of the UFF operating in rural districts. Ulster Resistance units were capable of conducting surveillance on Catholics and providing safe houses and transport for loyalist killers. McMichael was pleased that Stone was operating with the new organisation, and would offer them the kind of service he provided for the UFF and UVF. Stone was anxious to display his talent to his new associates and in April 1987 they told him they knew the identity of an IRA intelligence officer. Unlike McMichael, they were unaware of the arrangements whereby Stone examined lists of potential targets, chose one or was offered a 'sanction'.

Stone says he decided, 'in his own mind', that the information given to him by Ulster Resistance, constituted a 'sanction'. It was provided by members of a unit who lived and worked in Counties Tyrone and Fermanagh. Both areas were close to the Irish border and were also major operational districts for IRA units who targeted members of the Ulster Defence Regiment, many of whom lived on remote farms. Both counties housed large Protestant populations and were subject to an intense security presence. The RUC and UDR constantly patrolled these roads, checked vehicles and questioned their occupants. Catholic Church leaders and politicians frequently condemned the behaviour of the police and reserved their severest criticism for full and part-time members of the UDR for the brutal manner in which they questioned and detained Catholics. Many part-time members of the UDR were residents of the areas and knew the history and politics of most of their Catholic neighbours.

The Ulster Defence Regiment possesses a dubious and torrid history. Since its inception, several hundred of its men have been charged with offences such as sectarian killings, possession of guns and explosives, and membership of terrorist organisations. The Regiment believed that Catholics harboured the IRA men who murdered their colleagues. In this climate of conflict, hatred and suspicion, the opportunity for harassment of individual Catholics was exploited by some policemen and UDR soldiers embittered by the deaths of colleagues.

The Catholic Bishop of Derry, Edward Daly, consistently accused, in particular, the RUC of 'harassing innocent Catholics'. He was long concerned that constant roadchecks contributed to a process whereby files were maintained on the whole Catholic population. A local priest explained to me the serious nature of harassment.

One of my parishioners was a quiet fellow who suddenly found himself being stopped, searched and questioned when his car was stopped at a roadcheck. He had once attended a rally in support of republican hunger-strikers, which many people did who were neither republican nor IRA. Shortly afterwards, he was told at a roadcheck that he was at the rally, so he assumed he had been photographed. After that, he was constantly stopped, any time he ventured out of doors, sometimes while on foot. Now the procedure gets worse, because each occasion is recorded by the police or UDR and eventually suspicion increases as well as the recorded number of times he is questioned. Anyone unauthorised who examined his file would think he was a major target for surveillance. Some of those who were responsible for the many occasions he was questioned on the road were members of the security forces who lived in the neighbourhood and knew him personally. On my advice he eventually moved house for his own safety.

One subject of constant scrutiny was 37-year-old Dermott Hackett, from the town of Castlederg in County Tyrone. Married with a 9-year-old daughter, he worked for a bread delivery firm, which necessitated travelling to outlying rural areas. In his spare time he did voluntary charity work with the St Vincent de Paul Society, which assisted deprived families and the elderly. He took little interest in politics, though related to Stephen McKenna who was the leader of the SDLP on Omagh Council.

Early in 1987, a UDR soldier was shot dead by the IRA in Tyrone. In the aftermath of the murder, the security forces threw a cordon of a quarter-mile radius, and everyone stopped within the cordon was questioned about their movements and searched. Hackett was driving to an area known as Spamount when the killing took place; in his private car he was detained at a roadcheck.

Within a short time of the incident he felt he was subject to constant harassment. Increasingly, security personnel stopped his van at roadblocks, and questioned him about his movements. He became increasingly concerned that he was becoming the victim of suspicion and a revenge campaign by local members of the RUC and the UDR. Hackett had no connections with the IRA or Sinn Fein, but felt that this deliberate attention being paid to him would result in loyalists targeting him. He visited his local constituency representative, Dennis Haughey of the SDLP, complained about harassment, and suggested that it was bringing him to the attention of loyalist paramilitaries. Haughey investigated the original incident and discovered that Hackett was engaged in charity work when the murder happened. Both Haughey and the local chairman of the St Vincent de Paul Society made represent-ation to the RUC, and the harassment ceased. Haughey was told by the police that Hackett had 'fully co-operated' with them when questioned on the day of the murder. Now, Haughey says he fears that the treatment of Hackett was 'unreasonable' and that public knowledge of it 'may have made him a target'.

There can be little doubt that the unceasing attention paid to Hackett by the security forces brought him to the attention of Ulster Resistance, which was using its contacts within the UDR to obtain intelligence on the IRA. Many members of Resistance, and other loyalist paramilitaries, found the Regiment a valuable intelligence source for maintaining surveillance on republicans. Loyalist paramilitaries were encouraged by their respective organisations to join the UDR; the Regiment provided weapons training, and access to security files on republican suspects. UDR soldiers, full-time and part-time, by virtue of their membership, were entitled to personal firearms – which made many Protestants in border areas feel secure against IRA threats.

The penetration of the Ulster Defence Regiment by loyalist paramilitaries had begun when it was formed. Dual membership – of both the UDA and UDR – was encouraged, and not considered incompatible by the Regiment's leadership: in 1972 the Regiment's commander, Denis Ormerod, accepted the right of UDA volunteers to join the Regiment.

The decision to allow a terrorist yet legal organisation access to a British Army regiment thenceforth proved disastrous in sectarian relationships. Dermott Hackett came to the attention of Ulster Resistance, and subsequently of Michael Stone, owing to the natural collusion between members of the UDR and loyalist paramilitaries.

While Ulster Resistance and Stone plotted to kill Hackett, the IRA planned the murder of a Protestant. The IRA target was Charles Watson, a former prison warder, and part-time member of the UDR. Watson, a prominent loyalist, had been dismissed from the prison service. He served for several years in the UDR, and later joined Ulster Resistance. In January 1984 he was convicted of assault, fined, and received a suspended two-year prison sentence. The conviction led to the withdrawal of his firearms certificate, which permitted him to have a shotgun and pistol. Prominent loyalists campaigned publicly against the removal of the firearms, because, they argued, it left Watson defenceless to IRA attack.

On the night of 22 May 1987, an IRA unit approached the Watson home in the village of Clough in County Down. They used a sledgehammer to flatten the back door, and pursued Charles Watson through his house while his wife, Doreen, and four children watched helplessly. The gunmen trapped him in the bathroom and murdered him.

The ferocity and speed of the killers exactly resembled the manner in which Catholics had been killed by loyalist hit-squads. This tragedy epitomised the cruelty and absurdity of the policy of the IRA, who killed their victims with the same inhuman indifference which they so frequently attributed to assassinations by the UFF or UVF. The IRA issued a statement claiming Watson had been murdered because he had been involved in sectarian killings – they offered no substantive proof.

Watson's death accelerated the Ulster Resistance plot to kill Dermott Hackett in retaliation. Stone was contacted and told 'the job was on'. He arranged for a car to pick him up and drive him to Enniskillen, where he met his Ulster Resistance contacts. Leaving Belfast immediately after midnight, he arrived at a 'safe house' in Enniskillen within two hours. At the safe house he changed clothes and was briefed about Hackett; Resistance officers told him that Hackett was due to drive his bread delivery van in the townland of Drumquin. Stone was then transported to another safe house, in the town of Omagh, close to his 'kill zone'. In the Omagh residence he met two other members of Resistance.

I was briefed on the said target, Dermott Hackett. They showed me photographs of Hackett with known Provisional IRA men. The story was that he was carrying information and gathering arms for PIRA.

The security file Stone saw had been created owing to the frequency with which Hackett was stopped and questioned; it contained photographs of Hackett alone, and in the company of other people. Stone's casual acceptance of the claim that Hackett was an IRA member suggests that Resistance relied on a rather basic file. A security force source confirmed to me that surveillance on Hackett would have resulted in many photographs in his file. Hackett did charity work, and came into contact with many people with whom he had little acquaintance. In the course of his work he may well have been seen in dubious company. Stone's evidence regarding the file tends to support the view that Hackett was the victim of unfounded allegations based on spurious evidence; it confirms that security files were made available to terrorists. Stone never questioned that type of testimony.

I had a good look at the information and I was happy he was a proper target to be shot. The information I had read was torched.

While he waited for dawn Stone examined his weaponry; a 9mm submachine-gun with two magazines, each containing thirty rounds; and an automatic shotgun, his favourite weapon. Although the submachine-gun was a much more lethal weapon, his knowledge of guns may have convinced him that there was a risk of the submachine-gun jamming and in those circumstances he would need a second weapon. In his experience, automatic shotguns had proven more reliable than pistols or machine-guns.

When dawn broke, a car arrived and took him to a laneway in the countryside outside Omagh, where another vehicle, an Opel Manta, was already parked with its engine running. Stone transferred to the Opel with another man and was driven along the route Hackett was expected to use. He was doing 'a dry run' for the actual killing so that he could select a stretch of road suitable for an ambush.

At 7.40 a.m. Police Sergeant Reuben James Black, travelling along the Castlederg Road in Drumquin townland, saw Hackett driving the bread van. Sgt. Black did not see the Opel Manta car cruising behind Hackett's vehicle. Sometime between 7.40 and 7.50 a.m. Hackett slowed his van to negotiate a difficult bend. Stone chose that as the moment to act. He wound a rear window down to enable him to use the submachine-gun.

We drew alongside of him and slightly ahead of him. The rear window of the car was down. I cocked the SMG [*submachine-gun or letters used to describe a Sterling 9mm submachine-gun*] and gave him a burst to the door and windscreen. The bread van shuddered to a stop.

Stone saw Hackett fall sideways with his body straddling the two front seats. He told the driver to manoeuvre the Opel alongside the driver's door of the van. Stone pushed himself out of the window of the car until he 'was standing level with the shattered window of the van'.

I held the SMG at head level and fired down into the van. I fired all the SMG rounds until the clip was empty. I saw the rounds enter Hackett's body. We then drove off.

One mile from the scene of the shooting, a car waited to transport Stone to the Enniskillen 'safe house', where he burned the clothes he wore during the 'hit'. He replaced them with his own clothes, and was then taken by car to Londonderry where he caught a train for Belfast. The route chosen for his trip home had been astutely planned to distance him from the murder scene, and to avoid public highways on the return leg of the journey to Belfast.

Ten minutes after the shooting, Dermott Lynch, on his way to work in a supermarket in Omagh, drove past the bread van and saw Hackett slumped. He did not stop to investigate, and later offered an explanation that he assumed Hackett was searching for something in the van. A local farmer, passing by a short time later, stopped, looked into the van and saw Hackett lying with his head on the passenger seat. Mrs Sarah Ellen Pollock, who next arrived on the scene, drove to the home of Dr Gordon Frazer Gervais who lived near by. He later recalled her being 'in a state of panic': she explained that there had been a shooting, medical assistance was urgent.

Dr Gervais drove to the scene to discover the glass of the driver's door shattered, with Hackett's body sprawled across the front seats. The time, approximately 9.40: Hackett was dead.

Hackett's death was rapid – struck by eleven bullets on the right flank and buttock. One round lodged in his skull, another in his chin, four in the region of his left shoulder; he was struck by sixteen rounds, every major organ in his body lacerated.

The Bishop of Derry, Dr Edward Daly, reacted to the murder of Hackett by again accusing the RUC of 'harassing innocent Catholics'. He said the 'special attention by police left Catholics open to murderous attack'. The RUC responded by denying the bishop's allegations, and calling on the community to unite to defeat terrorism.

An interesting fact of Hackett's murder went unnoticed. When police found the Opel Manta car they recovered several spent 9mm rounds fired from the submachine-gun – and a shotgun cartridge: Stone's calling card. No one understood its significance.

Two days after the Hackett murder, Stone was informed by McMichael that he was required for another 'shoot'. The target – a Catholic taxi-driver who lived and worked in Ballynahinch. A UFF unit under McMichael's control had been planning the killing for two months. In April, they met Stone and requested his assistance. They agreed to carry out surveillance on the taxi-driver and contact Stone when a date and time was chosen for the 'hit'. McMichael hurriedly ordered the operation after Watson was murdered. Watson and McMichael were friends, and Watson's home was in an area under the UFF leader's control.

The taxi-driver was singled out for 'special attention' because McMichael believed there should always be a target available to his units when he ordered a retaliatory strike against Catholics. Unconcerned when an intended victim was non-political, he simply preferred to have a prominent Catholic killed. McMichael was constantly offered lists of victims by his units, and he personally selected the targets. Politicised Catholics, such as IRA and Sinn Fein personnel, lived in nationalist ghettoes, which made it difficult for the UFF to target them. McMichael, unperturbed, sanctioned the murder of innocent, uninvolved Catholics, who lived in vulnerable areas such as Ballynahinch, where fewer risks attended.

This policy of McMichael's illuminates the sectarian view of Northern Ireland Republicans in heavily populated areas, such as the Falls in West Belfast, remained relatively safe from sectarian assassination. Firstly they kept vigil; the IRA had a presence on the ground; the police and Army moved around in strength. Therefore, a loyalist hit-squad entering a nationalist stronghold ran the risk of being apprehended, or shot on sight, by Army personnel in the mistaken belief that they were IRA. An additional problem for would-be loyalist killers was the geographical size of areas like the Falls, and the time required to enter and escape. This explains why so many innocent Catholics were seized while walking along thoroughfares on the edge of the city centre late at night, or targeted because they lived in predominantly Protestant districts. Catholic taxi-drivers provided easy targets – they could be lured to remote destinations, or to a Protestant neighbourhood. Their jobs demanded that they answer all telephone requests, but without being able to check accurately the identity of passengers.

The taxi-driver in Ballynahinch was John James Bloomfield who owned J.J. Taxis which he operated from his home at 63 Windmill Gardens in the town: willing to answer any call, he was obvious and vulnerable to Stone's associates. In order to 'hit' Bloomfield, the UFF established a 'safe house' in Ballynahinch, and selected the night of 27 May for the operation. That afternoon, Stone met UFF personnel at a prearranged Belfast venue; they drove him to the 'safe house'. A change of clothes waited there – at his request – and documents related to the means which should be employed. When dressed, Stone was taken in a car to the proposed 'kill zone', and to the road which bypassed Bloomfield's house. The trip was intended to permit him to express an opinion on the murder arrangements, and to decide which area was most suitable to unleash his violence. Years later Stone could still remember Bloomfield's address – a testimony to his retention of significant detail.

Stone returned to the safe house and discussed the operation with the intelligence officer of the UFF unit. They planned to lure Bloomfield from his home to a hotel on the outskirts of the town. A bogus phone call would be made by a woman – and Bloomfield would be shot on his way from his house, or when he arrived in the grounds of the hotel. Stone preferred the hotel site because of its remoteness and, particularly, the driveway which connected it to the main road. He requested a submachine-gun and a shotgun as his 'back-up' weapon, and recommended that a UFF volunteer should use the shotgun, both weapons to be fired simultaneously. Stone considered that time to undertake the 'hit' would prove scarce, and that shooting would alert the security forces in the town. He emphasised the need to act with speed and pointed out that Bloomfield's photograph showed him to be a large-bodied man. The greater the firepower, he added, the greater the chance of killing him. Thus, Stone chose to use two weapons: it was his intention to shoot Bloomfield as he drove towards him in the hotel laneway, and there might not be sufficient time to get close to him to deliver a *coup de grâce*. Having delivered his lecture to the unit, Stone retired to a back room and, in his words, 'kept himself to himself'. He was a loner who was there to kill and preferred to avoid conversation which might reveal something about his identity; therefore he always took care to distance himself from idle chatter, or to allow accomplices familiarity with him. Now, he remained in the room for several hours, his way of protecting himself, and of ensuring his security at the expense of friendliness.

While he waited, innocent people were unknowingly drawn into the web of murder. One of them, Robert Dickson, worked for Fast Taxis, a large company based in East Belfast. In his spare time, he earned extra money by undertaking journeys for friends or associates, and sometimes his wife, Agnes, assisted him in his extra-curricular work which he called 'homers'. The UFF singled him out for special attention because they needed a legitimate car to transport Stone and his accomplices to and from the murder scene. Robert Dickson's recollection of how he was drawn into the terrorists' plan was later contained in a statement to police:

On May 27 at 10.30 p.m. I answered the phone and a female said, 'Could I have a taxi to the Woodlands Hotel please?' I said, 'Is that Mary?', and she said 'yes'. I asked what time and she said 'twenty to twelve' and then added 'no, make it ten past eleven, I'm getting away early'. My wife has a friend called Mary and I automatically thought that was who was on the phone. I told my wife about the run and gave her the car keys. She left the house at 10.55 because she wasn't sure of the exact location of the Woodlands Hotel.

The most important aspect of the terrorists' strategy was to lure their victim to the hotel and that proved easy. Bloomfield also received a phone call from a female and logged her taxi request in his company logbook. She told him she lived at Carlisle Park in Ballynahinch and worked in the restaurant at the Woodlands; she said she finished working at 11.30 p.m. and, plausibly, required a taxi because her husband, Samuel, was using the family car.

Bloomfield agreed to pick her up shortly after 11.30 p.m.; it did not occur to him that the hotel restaurant closed each Wednesday.

Agnes Dickson remembers having a brief conversation with her husband before leaving for Ballynahinch. He told her: 'That's the wee girl from Saintfield. She wants a lift home.' Neither of them questioned whether the call was authentic and Agnes travelled out of Belfast towards the Spa, a townland on the outskirts of Ballynahinch where the hotel was situated in leafy grounds. In her haste to pick up the fare she stopped to ask a young man for directions.

I stopped and asked the fellow where the Woodlands was. He pointed up the road and I told him to jump in and he could show me where it was. I asked him where he lived and he told me Hillside Spa. Because I was early I drove him home. I don't know who he was. On my way back to Ballynahinch I missed the turning at Woodlands and I reversed back.

Agnes Dickson turned her car into the hotel driveway and was confronted by two masked gunmen who leapt from some under-growth. She stopped her car and rolled down the driver's window.

The gunmen told me to open the boot and I did so with a lever inside the car. I was told to get out of the car and was bundled into the boot. The lid was closed, the car doors were closed and I was driven off in the vehicle. It seemed to drive for miles on rough ground and round corners. While they were driving around the radio was turned up loud. The next thing the car stopped.

What she did not know was that the gunmen were killing time in anticipation of killing Bloomfield. They knew that it was too risky to remain parked in the hotel driveway: a passing police or Army patrol would investigate their reasons for being there late at night. They also knew the exact time Bloomfield would arrive at the Woodlands. With the radio on full volume to disguise their conversation, they drove over rough country lanes where no one would hear Agnes Dickson's screams for help.

At 11.40 John Bloomfield drove to the hotel and rang the front doorbell. An upstairs window was opened and the hotel owner, David Sandford, peered out and asked if he could assist. Bloom-field said he was there to collect a member of the hotel staff who worked in the restaurant: Sandford said the restaurant was closed every Wednesday, and Bloomfield suddenly realised he was dealing with a hoax call. Sandford says he retired to bed as Bloomfield drove away. Halfway down the driveway Bloomfield saw a car parked close to the main road. He says he 'thought it strange' because the vehicle was not there when he entered the Woodlands.

The car lights weren't on and as soon as I had it in my view there were shots and my windscreen shattered.

Bloomfield acted with speed and intelligence – and saved his life. He drove towards the gunmen, then accelerated to the main road, and only stopped his vehicle when he reached the nearest police station. The shooting had ended but the ordeal for Agnes Dickson continued. She heard the gunfire, then the gunmen getting back into her car, and driving away. A short time later, the gunmen transferred to another car, leaving her in the sealed boot of her taxi.

I had no idea where I was. After fifteen minutes I tried to force the back seats but couldn't manage it. Eventually I released the boot catch and freed myself. I got into the car and drove up a laneway but it was a dead end. I turned the car in a field but got stuck. I got out and was going to walk but changed my mind. I got the car out of the field, drove to the main road and saw a signpost, 'Ballynahinch ten miles'.

Instead of going to the police she drove home to Belfast and told her husband about her ordeal. He telephoned the police.
  Stone recollected his part in the attempted murder.

I lay down in the back of the car so that no one would recognise me as a stranger in the area. There were two men in the car. I lay across the back seat and found a home-made machine-pistol with a pistol grip. I cocked it a few times to make sure it worked. I saw what I believed were 9mm rounds in the magazine. The front passenger had a shotgun.

Stone says he fired at Bloomfield from the side passenger window and his accomplice with the shotgun fired several rounds from the driveway.
  When Stone returned to the safe house he completed his usual routine of destroying the clothes he wore during the shooting. He washed his hair and cleaned himself with lemon juice.

I always washed thoroughly but I completed the exercise by using lemon juice. It finds its way into the pores and in the event of police taking swabs there would be no lead residue. I made sure my clothes were torched so that there was never going to be forensic evidence. In Northern Ireland witnesses rarely give evidence. They know the risks. The police are left to rely on forensic evidence and I made sure I was never going to provide them with a scrap of evidence against me. I knew the rules of evidence and how many guys were caught simply because of tiny particles on their body or a fragment of clothing.

When Stone was later interviewed by detectives, he denied any knowledge of the kidnap of Agnes Dickson and her presence in the boot of the taxi. He claimed his accomplices did not tell him she was in the car, and then told police that he had transferred from the taxi to another vehicle before the shooting: he believed this would confirm that he had been unaware of Agnes Dickson's ordeal. She insisted that she had remained in her car from the moment she was kidnapped until it was abandoned. The only times the gunmen parked her car was, first, when they stopped to shoot Bloomfield, and then, when they eventually left the vehicle to transfer to their getaway car.

Stone's wish to distance himself from the imprisonment of the housewife in her car, again falls into line with his habitual tendency to portray himself as a man with respect for women, as a 'chivalrous' man with basic human values. Prepared to kill men for a 'cause', women were sacred, and he firmly believed that the killing of a woman, or violence towards them, stood in contradiction to his self-image as a man of honour. It may have related, not simply to his personal values, but in general to a society where killing was tolerated, provided women did not become targets. Throughout the history of the conflict, killer gangs rarely selected women. On both sides of the divide women represented motherhood. One Irish writer has remarked that men in Ireland love their mothers too much, and as a consequence find it impossible to love other women fully and well. Within Stone resided a preoccupation with motherhood, and, equally, a desire to represent himself as a man who loved and respected all women. To maintain that as part of his character he insisted that he would never kill women, even when they were known members of the IRA. During many of his conversations with me he emphasised his detestation of violence against women. Murder he could justify – but to retain the image of an ideologically committed hero did he need to demonstrate that he was a person with real human emotions, a family man who represented the integrity of family life and respected the role of the mother as the vehicle for procreation and love?

In general this view of women has pervaded the conflict. The Provisional IRA, likewise, was imbued with a desire to remove women from its target lists. Throughout IRA history, women who played a role were revered. The term 'Mother Ireland', which featured prominently in republican ideology and literature, testified to the thesis Stone propounded: in only a few instances have women been deliberately selected as targets. The killing of Mrs Mullen in Ballynahinch typified operations where a mother, wife or girlfriend died in the line of fire, or while trying to prevent murder.

Exceptions to the rule abound – such as the shootings of Susan Bunting, Bernadette McAliskey and murder of Miriam Daly, or the Provisionals' killing of female members of the security forces. On the loyalist side, hesitation existed concerning Catholic women who were prominent republicans; McMichael and Bingham considered such women legitimate targets, but Stone had always insisted that he never subscribed to that aspect of loyalist policy.

In the failed murder attempt, Bloomfield, the taxi-owner, received one hundred minor wounds to his left forearm caused by shattered glass from the windscreen of the car. Stone says he was disappointed with the operation and should have killed him. This was not his only such failure in 1987. McMichael asked whether he might be interested in undertaking the assassination of Martin McGuinness, a leading republican in Derry. McGuinness, one of the most prominent republicans in Ireland, had once been described by the authorities as a member of the IRA Army Council.

Stone says he examined a UFF file on McGuinness which contained security forces' documentation: photographs, details of the Derry man's life-style, his address, names of his associates, his regular daily movements, houses he visited, and the school to which he often accompanied his children. Stone accepted the 'sanction' and in his own words, 'decided he would be a target to be shot by himself'. McMichael arranged a back-up team in Derry to liaise with Stone, and to provide him with means of surveillance and weapons. Stone agreed to travel to Derry by train to avoid attracting attention, and to examine ways of assassinating McGuinness.

I was picked up at the station and taken to the area of McGuinness's house. When we got there I took a ball out of the car and kicked the ball about to have a closer look at his house. The house was in a cul-de-sac with about four houses in a row. The house was different from the rest. It gave the impression that it had bullet-proof glass, it had different-coloured frames round the windows. I didn't think McGuinness was at home, as his red Jetta car was not parked at the house. I took particular interest in the windows because I intended shooting him through the bathroom window.

Stone returned to Belfast and reported to McMichael, saying he would return in a fortnight and kill McGuinness. The reconnaissance in Derry illustrated Stone's daring and confidence – able to enter a republican stronghold and behave nonchalantly, suggesting to anyone who observed him that he had a right to be there, using a football to convey casualness.

When he returned to Derry, his accomplices told him the 'hit at the house was off'. They believed it attracted too much risk, and that escape from the area could prove costly in lives, or even result in capture by the security forces or local republicans. They further agreed that they had no fixed hope of McGuinness being in the house at any given time: therefore, undertaking the operation with such an uncertainty seemed futile. And if it failed, it would alert McGuinness to the risk to his life, and he would increase his personal security arrangements.

All of the arguments persuaded Stone to concur with his accomplices, but he refused to be diverted from his goal. He re-examined the files to seek an alternative means, and then singled out the school attended by McGuinness's children. He also found a police/Army observation on file that McGuinness habitually visited a newsagent after leaving his children at school. Stone drove to the school and decided not to kill him there. He says he was not prepared to endanger the lives of children. He visited the newsagent's in Bishop Street and chose it as the place for the hit.

It was decided that was the most convenient place to do it as he went there every morning.

A member of the Derry UFF unit drove Stone to Belfast after he agreed that the killing should take place one week later. During the journey the car-driver talked to him about weapons and the type of firearm he required. Stone replied that he needed two guns, 'one heavy piece and a small piece'. He suggested an Armalite, the favourite weapon among IRA hitmen, and a revolver, a choice in keeping with Stone's preference for a back-up gun. He knew that if an automatic weapon such as the Armalite rifle jammed, the revolver would prove reliable.

I liked to get close and an automatic makes an awful mess but it leaves no prisoners. I never took the risk of having only one piece, because if it jammed you were in serious trouble. For example, if I had decided on one weapon, an automatic, and it jammed, McGuinness could defend himself and maybe others come to his rescue. I had these things in mind. Now I knew that if that happened and I had a back-up weapon I could finish the job and take care of anybody else who prevented my escape.

Another reason why he selected the Armalite was that suspicion would immediately centre on the IRA and lead to speculation of an internal IRA feud. The Armalite was not a loyalist weapon and police forensic examination of McGuinness's wounds would quickly lead to identification of the type of murder weapon used by his killer.

To this day Stone will not reveal how his accomplices were able to acquire an Armalite. He says the UFF driver told him he would provide one, and that the back-up weapon would be 'something special'. One week later Stone phoned Derry, to be told 'the job was on'. Stone says he 'made arrangements at home'.

I travelled to Derry by train, was met by locals and taken to a safe house. I discussed the getaway route and all arrangements were made. I was given an Armalite rifle and two mags, with thirty rounds in each mag. I cleaned the weapon and made sure it was in working order.

He was also given the 'special weapon', an American .38 Special revolver, which he also cleaned: he took great delight in his comprehensive knowledge of guns, how each weapon behaved and the damage it was capable of inflicting. In our conversations, he enjoyed illustrating his attention to such detail, and describing the types of weapons best suited for killing. He says he was determined to make 'no mistakes' and intended 'to give McGuinness a head job' – one high-velocity bullet from an Armalite.

Stone remained overnight in the 'safe house' in Derry, was awakened early in the morning and dressed in clothes supplied by his accomplices, including 'a monkey hat', a rolled-up woollen cap which could be pulled down over his face. He cut three slits in it for his eyes and mouth so that it could be quickly converted to a face mask at the moment of killing. Round his neck he wore a red and white scarf. At 8.35 a.m. a car arrived at the house and he was driven to a rendezvous point where he transferred to another vehicle which was to be used in the murder. At 8.45 he was sitting in the back seat of the second vehicle outside the newsagent's premises, the automatic rifle concealed under a blanket alongside him, and the .38 Special revolver in his right-hand pocket. He waited for one hour but McGuinness failed to appear. Stone decided to abandon the mission and returned to the safe house where he changed into his own clothes and returned to Belfast.

I couldn't wait longer than an hour without incurring risks. Firstly an hour was really too long and you could say I was reckless. I later realised that. At the time I was wrapped up in the desire to kill McGuinness and ignored the risk. After an hour I knew that there was a chance someone had warned him. Somebody in that district might have spotted our car and suspected we were Army undercover or Special Branch. If that was conveyed to McGuinness he would have stayed away. Another risk was that the Army or police would come across us and search the car. Once the opportunity failed I decided that was it. There was too much danger for me remaining in Derry. Anyway, once a job like that fails it's best to leave it. We may have created too much activity and scrutiny. For me to go back was to take too many chances. There was always the possibility an IRA team would be waiting for us at a future date. Anyway I knew there would be other opportunities and I would find an alternative means of getting to McGuinness.

Another prime target for loyalist hitmen was 33-year-old Peter Joseph Bateson, one of the IRA's most feared and dedicated operatives. He was a native of Magherafelt in County Derry and a 'cradle to the grave' republican. In 1971 his 18-year-old brother, John, died while transporting a bomb. Peter Bateson, well known to the security forces, and high on their wanted lists, was finally caught in 1977 and charged with the attempted murder of three policemen three years earlier. In that incident, he had been prominent in an ambush on an RUC patrol car, and the occupants later identified him from wanted posters. Bateson received a twenty-year prison sentence, of which he served only ten years owing to a 50 per cent remission on sentences related to terrorist offences. When he was released in 1987, loyalist prisoners in the Maze sent a communication to all their paramilitaries. They knew he would soon return to IRA active service, and the UVF and UFF shared intelligence on him.

McMichael contacted Stone to ask whether he 'would do a hit'. Not yet naming Bateson, he suggested that Stone travel to the town of Ballymena where a UFF unit possessed detailed inform- ation on a target. Stone was provided with a return ticket and several days later, in Ballymena, he met a UFF intelligence officer and two accomplices.

In a safe house, they produced security forces' documents containing photographs of Bateson meeting IRA associates. Stone says he was told that Bateson worked as a salesman for a double- glazing firm and had a widely varied work schedule. The UFF officer claimed that the IRA man had recently been involved in the murder of a businessman's brother, in the Ballymena area and 'had to be taken out'.

Stone says:

I decided right away that he was a legitimate target and agreed I was interested in doing the hit. Arrangements were made for me to see this man. He was tallish with black hair and a Mexican moustache. I was taken to a pub he frequented on Monday nights and was shown where he parked his car. The plan was to wait in a parked car and hit him as he left the premises. I was happy about the arrangements and went back to Belfast.

Stone was assured that in his absence the local UFF unit would maintain surveillance on Bateson, particularly each Monday night at the pub. Three weeks later Stone returned to Ballymena and was taken to a safe house. Again, he says that he was supplied, at his own request, with overalls, and the ubiquitous 'monkey hat'. Two cars were borrowed, one to be used by Stone and the other as a getaway vehicle. One car would be driven to the pub car-park by Stone and the other would be parked a short distance away. When the shooting was over Stone would drive to the other car, transfer to it and be taken to the safe house.

He was given a Walther pistol with two magazines each containing nine rounds of ammunition. He dismantled the gun, cleaned it and ensured that it was fully operational. At 9.30 p.m. he drove to the pub with the getaway car travelling ahead of him.

The reason why I was fronted by the other car was a security precaution. It travelled ahead so that if there was a police or military roadcheck I would be warned. We had intelligence on all military and police movements for the area but we were not willing to take chances. There was always an outside possibility that an incident could occur and a roadcheck be put in place. You always have to allow for the element of chance and be prepared. The most unexpected things occur but with a car ahead and someone in it equipped with a two-way radio to me there was less risk. If something happened up ahead I could be warned and take evasive action such as dumping the weapon or taking a diversion. I placed my car in the larger car-park opposite the pub, slid down into the seat and waited half an hour. Bateson didn't turn up and the other car came back to my position and we decided to leave. There was too much risk in sitting around. I had to consider that Bateson had become aware of the surveillance on him and an IRA team might arrive at the pub and wipe me out. The next day I went back to Belfast.

In November, an event occurred which was to have a profound effect on Stone's life. On the morning of Sunday 8 November an IRA bomb exploded at a Remembrance Day service in the town of Enniskillen. Eleven people were killed, sixty-three injured, some of them children, and the tragedy shocked the world. The bomb had been hidden in a building adjacent to the town cenotaph, and it exploded as thousands gathered to remember the dead of two world wars. The IRA did not admit responsibility until twenty-four hours later, and then cynically expressed regret, claiming that the device exploded because it had been activated by RUC radio signals. The cenotaph symbolised the Britishness of the Protestant Unionist community, and the targeting of the event struck deep into the consciousness of every Protestant in Northern Ireland. Not the worst tragedy by numerical standards of atrocities, it proved the most shocking for Unionists and loyalists. Certainly sectarian, more significantly it was a blow to the body politic, the very ethos of the Unionist attachment to Britain through the blood ties established at the Somme and on the Normandy beaches.

Stone regarded the tragedy as creating the bitterest moments of his life. His claim to be British was unassailably confirmed by his English birthright, and the history of his own family was inextricably linked to the purpose of Remembrance Sunday. He says that from that moment he became ever more determined to exact revenge upon republicans. He was, he admits, determined to find the culprits, and enact a similar tragedy at a comparable commemoration or ceremony.

Initially, Stone and McMichael reacted to the Enniskillen tragedy by deciding to seek revenge in the town where it happened. McMichael claimed that the 'leading Provisional in the area', Owen Carron, should be their target. Carron, a prominent republican, also sat at Westminster as MP for Fermanagh/South Tyrone. McMichael said he would contact the UFF and Ulster Resistance in Enniskillen, and ask them to provide intelligence on Carron, plus a back-up service for Stone.

At the beginning of December Stone travelled by car to Enniskillen where he met the UFF contacts provided by McMichael.

I was later taken out of Enniskillen along country roads and shown a house and told it belonged to Carron. This was a chalet-type house with a lane up to it to my left as I looked at it. The house was protected by cameras and bullet-proof glass. There was a garage beside the house and a couple of cars outside. He had a black labrador and another dog, a collie, I think. I had no weapons with me. I looked at a house opposite which was owned by some old folk and I made up my mind I would take over this house and shoot Carron as he drove into his home. It was going to be a shoot job. I took note of everything in my mind and asked the boys with me to take me home. I was driven straight back to Belfast and I told them I would do the hit.

One week later Stone returned to Enniskillen, to be further briefed about Carron's movements. In mid-December he made yet another trip to the town: he felt uncertain regarding his original plan: it depended upon factors which had failed in the planned murder of McGuinness. He had no guarantee that Carron would arrive in the 'killing zone' at an exact time. Firing from a distance of 30–50 yards did not guarantee a successful operation. Men such as Carron, who knew they were potential targets, varied their daily routine and were often accompanied by bodyguards. Stone did not wish to face another failure through lack of planning, and therefore he involved himself directly in assessing alternative, more practical methods.

His contacts told him that Carron regularly visited the Provisional Sinn Fein advice centre in the town. Stone made several inspections of the neighbourhood surrounding the centre and decided upon it as a better operational zone. He discovered that Carron visited the Sinn Fein premises daily, always accompanied by associates, one of whom was 34-year-old James Joseph Murphy, nicknamed 'Mexican Joe' because of his moustache and dark complexion. Stone decided that he would shoot Carron and whoever was with him at the appointed time of the killing. Before he left Enniskillen, Stone completed necessary arrangements – such as date, weaponry and escape routes for the hit. The date: Christmas Eve; the weapons – a .45 semi-automatic Colt pistol and a sawn-off hammer-operated shotgun.

I instructed them to have concrete blocks and cover cushions ready for me when I returned. I intended to place the blocks in the boot of the car to be used in the hit, to fill the cushion covers with sand and place them on the back window. These were safety precautions to protect me if it all went wrong and I was fired at. It was the simplest method of bullet-proofing the getaway car. I wanted to make sure that when I went down on 24 December that everything was in place.

On 22 December, while Stone relaxed at home, an IRA Active Service Unit killed his mentor, John McMichael. Stone felt alone in the world. The last of his leading terrorist advisers was dead. All his mentors, Herron, McKeague, Bingham and McMichael, had died at the hands of IRA hit-squads.

McMichael was killed weeks before he was about to unmask Jim Craig as the informer in the loyalist midst. His inquiry had centred on the West Belfast UDA commander who, in the course of 1987, learned that the net had begun to close. Craig had to act quickly to prevent his own execution, and he offered the Provisionals the intelligence they needed to kill McMichael.

Craig already knew that UFF investigators were hot on his trail. They had uncovered letters exchanged between him and a leading republican prior to the killing of Lenny Murphy. The letters detailed the planning of Murphy's death and the fact that Craig had provided a safe house for an IRA hit-team in the heart of the loyalist Glencairn area where Murphy lived. The hitmen stayed overnight in the house, and shot Murphy as he stopped outside his home. UFF investigators also discovered a record of a telephone call to Craig after McMichael ordered the assassination of the Sinn Fein president, Gerry Adams. Adams, shot while travelling in a car through Belfast, sustained serious gunshot wounds, but survived. The IRA phone call to Craig sought reasons why the UDA/UFF were prepared to shoot a republican leader, contrary to an unspoken agreement between the terrorists on both sides that the leaders of all the groupings should never be targets. Craig gave the IRA McMichael's name as the person responsible for breaching the unwritten rule. From that moment, the IRA decided that McMichael be killed in retaliation for the attack on Adams, and for the UFF targeting of other well-known republicans. The telephone call from Craig had confirmed IRA suspicion that McMichael had acted with Bingham in planning the murders of Miriam Daly and others. Craig even offered to assist in setting up his loyalist colleague, once it had become clear that McMichael had begun unravelling his links with the other side: McMichael had made the mistake of warning Craig about his republican connections, the racketeering and suspicion which tied him to the murders of loyalist leaders. In a verbal confrontation several weeks before Christmas 1987, McMichael threatened Craig. Further details appear in a UFF inquiry document prepared after McMichael's death (several names have been blanked for legal reasons):

Despite McMichael's warning, Craig continued to meet PIRA/INLA/IPLO people. Although the row before Christmas probably hastened John McMichael's death, it in itself did not bring it about. McMichael had confided in close colleagues that he knew that Craig had warned the IRA that — was a UFF target. McMichael had also told UFF Intelligence to drop information that Craig could pick up —, the idea being to watch for the information coming back. There is no doubt that — and —, both members of the PIRA, were warned about the UFF targeting them. Last but not least, McMichael had opened the issue of alleged IRA/UDA collusion in Lenny Murphy's murder. Within two days of McMichael's murder, sources close to senior UDA officers indicated loyalist involvement. Rumour became rife, not least because his office in UDA HQ in Gawn Street in East Belfast was ransacked and orders issued that the office should be locked and no one allowed admittance. Inner Council members who were not happy about the affair decided to make their own enquiries. For obvious reasons these early enquiries had to be very discreet. The breakthrough came when a member of the UDA Inner Council was contacted by some UDA people in England who claimed to have information about McMichael's death. A meeting was arranged in England at which it became clear that what was being said came from Northern Ireland sources using the English people as a means of relaying vital information about McMichael's death.

By this stage it became clear that Craig supplied the colour, make and number of McMichael's car as well as information about a place (not his home) where it would be parked for a certain period. It was decided to watch Craig as closely as possible, not because we did not believe what we were told, but because we wished to catch him out ourselves. Within limits, Craig had been under almost constant surveillance since

Christmas. The results of this surveillance make interesting reading. All of Craig's taxi journeys were monitored and the drivers questioned. The areas he was dropped off included the Central Information Agency in Ormeau Avenue, and Apollo Road off Boucher Road, as meeting places with Provisional IRA people. He nearly always used taxis for these journeys, getting out of the taxis to sit in other cars, telling the taxi-drivers to wait for him as he was collecting money from builders. A short piece in the 'Who' column of the *Sunday World* newspaper asking how a leading Shankill Road loyalist was able to walk about freely in the Unity Flats complex [*a republican enclave close to Shankill*], came as no surprise to our investigators. They had twice observed Craig going into the flats, meeting a girl and being taken to two separate addresses.

In February 1988 Craig was in a car stopped by a security forces' patrol in Dunmurray. The other occupant was ——, a top Provo whom Craig had met in Crumlin Road jail. The Provo is the boyfriend of another leading Provo, —— of ——, Glen Road (telephone number ——). Craig was also observed meeting ——, of Moira Street in the Short Strand area who had Provo form. His other act of treachery was to tell leading Provo, —— (last known address ——), that a Protestant builder was carrying out work for the security forces. Craig had fallen out with the builder after he refused to pay him protection for a site in Templepatrick. The Provo, ——, let this slip to a source friendly to the UDA and Craig's meeting with the Provo was observed, and a warning was passed to the builder.

While the above report was being compiled, Stone now became concerned for his own safety. He knew that McMichael had been followed on the day of his death, from his Lisburn pub to his home. The IRA hit-team waited until he entered his house before attaching a bomb to the underside of his car. Several hours later, McMichael left his family to attend a UDA meeting, and as he started his car the bomb exploded beneath him, causing horrific injuries. He died on the way to hospital.

Stone knew that Craig had been responsible for providing the IRA with the details of McMichael's movements. Three days before the murder, Stone had had a meeting with his mentor, at which they discussed the killing of members of the republican movement, and/or the planning of an atrocity in revenge for Enniskillen. McMichael said they should try to kill members of the IRA leadership and Sinn Fein councillors. A plan was in place to hit a leading councillor, and he hoped that Stone would undertake the 'sanction'. He advised Stone to 'lie low', and to operate outside Belfast, until the investigation of Craig had been completed. A UFF source confirmed to me that McMichael told Stone Craig was probably preparing to kill him, and he named Craig's accomplices. When McMichael died, Stone was in possession of the names of those who helped the IRA plot his friend's assassination. Craig was still in command of West Belfast, and Stone was frightened that someone within Craig's circle might know of his last meeting with the UFF leader, and thus suspect Stone of knowing the identity of the plotters. A UFF source told me the following:

At that time Stone knew the names of those around Craig who were accomplices to his dealings with the IRA. Craig was unaware of Stone and his closeness to McMichael. If Craig had known about the meeting and the information Stone possessed, Craig would have had Stone hit. Jimmy Craig was ruthless in protecting his own operations.

Stone was determined to kill Craig, but was unable to get close to him without compromising his own security. Secondly, he required a UFF 'sanction' to execute a loyalist leader, and proof of Craig's guilt was only in the process of being assembled. He concentrated, instead, on fulfilling McMichael's request to kill Owen Carron.

Within twenty-four hours of McMichael's violent demise, Stone was taken by car to a safe house in Enniskillen. He was shown a blue Ford Cortina, legitimately owned by one of his accomplices.

I was told to use this for the hit, because it would not attract attention. The owner would later claim it was stolen without his knowledge. I was to drive this car to the advice centre myself and after the job to rendezvous two miles away where I would abandon the Cortina and be picked up by another car and taken to the safe house.

Stone supervised the placing of the concrete blocks in the boot of the Cortina and the sand-filled cushions on the rear window. Early on the morning of 24 December he drove the Cortina to a car-park opposite the Sinn Fein advice centre. It was one of the few occasions he chose to operate alone to avoid attracting attention. His plan was to approach Carron on foot and fire both barrels of the shotgun into him and kill his companion with the .45 pistol.

The shotgun was easily concealed under my coat and the pistol in a pocket. I was in a car which was legit. I knew that if someone in the advice centre was suspicious and phoned the police, they would be informed the vehicle was not stolen and was a privately registered car. I reckoned that one person such as myself in the car would not unduly worry anyone. Most people expect hit-squads to include at least two people. It was my intention to get out of the car as soon as I saw Carron and finish him off first. It was likely that he would be accompanied by one person and at most two. I knew that in situations where a gun is produced, people automatically freeze out of fear. I didn't need more than a few seconds to get the job done even if it meant killing the three of them. It was the best place to do it. I had recced Carron's house to examine if I could approach it on foot but was convinced there were trip wires round the perimeter to set off alarms. The ultimate way was to get close to him on the street when he was least expecting it.

Stone sat in the car for three hours until his getaway car drew alongside and one of his accomplices told him to abort the operation. He returned to the safe house and was told Carron had been arrested that morning and charged with possession of a rifle. Carron later absconded when released on bail and found sanctuary in the Irish Republic. Stone was again foiled in his attempt to exact revenge for the Enniskillen tragedy, but he remained determined to find another means of achieving his objective.

He spent Christmas and New Year with his family and his Staffordshire pit-bull terriers. The dogs were a hobby and a source of income; he bred them for sale and for dog-fighting, a clandestine, illegal sport steadily developing in loyalist estates in Belfast, and in towns such as Bangor. Throughout his married life, Stone habitually kept fearsome dogs, especially pit-bulls, his favourites, and he wallowed in the public attention he attracted when he walked them through East Belfast. In previous years, he took two of the pit-bulls with him when meeting Bingham, who shared a fondness for dogs, although Bingham preferred his own golden Labrador.

In the first week of January, Stone turned his attention from family and dogs to his pursuit of the IRA. During the holiday period, he devised new ways of assassinating republican leaders. Before McMichael died, he had suggested to Stone that if they could kill a prominent republican such as Carron they would be presented with the ultimate means of realising a greater ambition:

I was aware that if we could just get to a leading member of the Provos down country, his death would lead to an IRA funeral with all the military trappings and ceremony. There would be people present like Adams and McGuinness and in one operation we could hit several of them. It was felt that to undertake such an operation it was preferable in a rural district. Adams and McGuinness would be obliged to travel, on their way to a funeral, through areas controlled by our people and the same when they were leaving the event. There were several options in those circumstances. Firstly we could target them on the way to, or when they were leaving, the cemetery or we could booby-trap graves surrounding the republican plot.

Towards the end of the first week of January, a leading member of the UFF contacted Stone and told him that a unit in South Derry required his services. Stone knew the members of the unit, young men he had trained at McMichael's request. He travelled to South Derry to meet them, and with them, members of Ulster Resistance, with whom he had previously shared intelligence on republican suspects. The target – John Joe Davey, a leading republican. The prospect of killing him excited Stone – the perfect device for realising his plan of luring Provisional leaders to a rural cemetery.

Davey, 60 years old, married with three children, worked as a Sinn Fein councillor. He led a life steeped in republican tradition, not wholly confined to political activity. In the failed IRA campaign of the 1950s, he had been interned without trial, and re-interned in Long Kesh in 1971. In the 1980s he moved away from IRA operational requirements, and devoted his energies to the political strategy of the IRA's political wing, Sinn Fein. By 1988 he had become a well-known political figure in Magherafelt District Council. Loyalist paramilitaries and politicians took a different view of him. In 1987, one of Ian Paisley's political colleagues, the Revd. William McCrea MP used the privilege of the House of Commons to brand Davey 'an active IRA terrorist'. Did McCrea understand that by naming Davey publicly as an 'active terrorist', he thereby suggested him as a target for loyalist hit-squads? Kevin McNamara, Labour spokesman on Northern Ireland affairs, criticised McCrea's use of privilege and added that 'people should be very careful what they say in the Commons'. Obviously no proof exists that McCrea's comments led to the direct UFF targeting of Davey. It could be said in McCrea's defence that Davey was, *de facto*, a prominent republican, and would have been regarded by loyalists as a legitimate target irrespective of what was said in the Commons. Furthermore, the IRA's campaign of murder had touched his life in that some of his friends and constituents had died. Nevertheless, he was severely criticised for naming Davey without the proof necessary to support the allegation; for pre-empting the issue; for the fact that his comments could have prejudiced any legal proceedings which might later have been taken against Davey; and for behaving in an irresponsible way, that is, using the privilege of Parliament, knowing that a statement of that nature, if made elsewhere in public, could have been legally questionable, to say the least.

At the beginning of February, preparations for the murder of Davey were completed, and Stone was given 9 February as the ideal date. His accomplices said that Davey would be required to attend a council meeting that evening, and would be home around teatime. A family man, who maintained a regular pattern of travelling home for his daily meals, the local UFF unit reckoned he would leave his house before 7.00 p.m. to make the journey to Magherafelt. The Davey home, surrounded by fields, was situated at Gulladuff, a townland known to Stone. The UFF planned that Stone and another gunman would lie concealed in the bushes of the laneway leading to Davey's house. When he drove his car towards the main road the firing would begin – a plan which, in its detail, resembled the attempted murder of Bloomfield. Stone recommended that the telephone wires leading to the house be cut prior to the shooting, to render the Davey family unable to alert quickly the security forces, thereby allowing Stone and his accomplices valuable time in which to escape. At 6.30 p.m., in the dark, Stone and an accomplice were driven to a road several hundred yards from the Davey home. Stone believed that they should approach the house on foot, and then trek across several fields.

There was no sense in approaching the house in a car and leaving the vehicle near by. Someone was likely to spot it and remember the number plate. It was my intention to use a legit motor so that the escape was not hampered. Secondly, people like Davey or family friends would have been naturally suspicious of a strange car parked near the house. I believed that if we could get to the house by a different route and cut the telephone wires, an escape would be made easier. It would allow time for the journey back across the fields. Under darkness the plan was a good one.

Stone was given a Ruger pistol with six rounds in the magazine. He was also handed two speed-strips for the gun, and ten loose rounds of ammunition: the speed-strips facilitated a fast loading of the chambers. The handgun belonged to a member of the RUC and would feature in a later operation. Stone adored the Ruger, and made clear his admiration to his accomplices. At 6.00 p.m., a car took Stone and an accomplice armed with a submachine-gun to a minor road adjacent to the fields bordering the rear of Davey's home. Both gunmen made their way to the side of the house and Stone's accomplice severed the telephone wire under the eaves of the one-storey cottage. The two men crept stealthily down the laneway where they cut other telephone cables, and then hid in the bushes, Stone on one side of the lane, his accomplice on the other. I asked Stone why he did not attempt to gain entry to the house?

There was no guarantee that Davey did not have security doors on the inside of the wooden doors. He was the kind of guy who would have been naturally security-conscious, and would not have fallen for the trap of opening the doors to strangers. It was better to hit him when he least expected it. Anyway I didn't like the prospect of shooting a man in front of his wife and kids.

Again – the familiar ring, the chivalrous justification: at the same time, he preferred a plan which appeared flawless and did not depend on chance. He believed he was dealing with a wily, experienced IRA officer who might well be armed. Any attempt to kill Davey in the house presented an element of risk which Stone did not wish to contemplate. If such an attempt failed Stone and his accomplice would have to make their way across several fields, possibly with Davey or someone else in pursuit. Stone preferred calculated risks, and by February 1988, he had experienced several failed enterprises. He was convinced that he could successfully kill Davey in an ambush.

At 6.45 p.m. Davey left the cottage, went to his car and drove into the laneway.

He drove towards us and we both stepped out and his headlights picked us up. I waited for the other boy with the submachine-gun to open up but nothing happened and I knew his weapon was jammed.

Stone's plan was that his accomplice would use the superior firepower of the submachine-gun to stop the car and, at best, wound Davey. Stone intended to use the Ruger pistol to deliver the final death shots by firing into Davey's skull.

Davey later recalled driving from the house to make the 300-yard journey to the main road. Fifteen to twenty yards into the lane he saw two gunmen with black masks covering their faces.

The masks had eyeholes cut into them and both gunmen wore black coats down over their knees. I could see both of them clearly in the car headlights. The man who came out from the left seemed to be carrying a weapon with something across the barrel and seemed to have difficulty with the gun.

The Sterling submachine-gun had a magazine protruding horizontally from the middle of the weapon. Davey considered accelerating his car into the gunmen but stalled the vehicle. He next saw the gunman with a pistol begin firing.

The boy to the right appeared to be doing all the shooting. The one who was having difficulty only managed to fire one shot.

Davey's early IRA training may well have saved his life because he opened the car door and rolled out onto the ground. Stone saw him undertake that defensive manoeuvre and fired at him. Davey's own account illustrates the tenacity of Stone and his accomplice.

I ran back towards the house. I stayed close to the wall of the house, ran across the backyard, went over a ditch and into a laneway. As I went round the side of the house the whole place lit up for a few seconds and then went black again. The two gunmen followed me as I ran towards the yard and a shot was fired as I went round the side of the house. When I was in the laneway I heard footsteps coming after me so I crossed into a field and over several other fields. When I was in one of the fields I heard several whistles of the type used by duck-shooters.

The whistling signalled from Stone to those waiting to drive him from the scene. Davey was lucky to survive the murder bid: forensic examination of his car showed a bullet hole in the windscreen on the driver's side of the vehicle. The driver's side-window had been shattered by a second round. Stone says that after the shooting he returned to the safe house to change his clothing, again taking care to deny forensic experts any link between him and the scene of the crime.

The other boy and I wore thick, navy-issue socks over our boots to disguise any footprints. These were burned along with the gloves, overalls and masks.

Stone decided to return to Belfast without delay, and he expressed a desire to own the Ruger, telling his accomplices it was a 'nice wee piece'. As a reward for his services, they told him to keep the weapon and supplied him with suitable ammunition. He hid the ammunition inside his socks and the gun behind his back, and, notwithstanding his habitual caution, took the risk of transporting the gun and the bullets to Belfast. Although he is only willing to concede that he did so because he 'liked the gun', he had other, more sound reasons. It did not possess a forensic history linking it to other acts of terrorism; and it permitted him the luxury of a personal firearm with no police history beyond the fact it was an official RUC weapon belonging to a serving police officer.

The failed attempt on Davey's life deterred Stone from considering a proposal from his UFF accomplices to return 'and finish the job', a decision, he claims, based on the premise that Davey would increase his personal security, in order not to be lured into a similar trap. However, Stone agreed to an alternative course of action – a murder bid on Davey's brother-in-law, John Augustin O'Kane. O'Kane, a farmer from County Derry, had no involvement in terrorism. Stone later told police that he undertook the 'sanction' because 'O'Kane was a republican activist'. His justification for that allegation related to photographs of O'Kane taken at a republican funeral, Stone's suspicions being again based on the narrow loyalist premise that everyone attending a republican funeral was by definition republican. This belief resided firmly within the loyalist political equation that 'all Catholics were nationalists, all nationalists were republicans and all republicans were IRA activists'. It did not occur to Stone or his loyalist accomplices that many nationalists abhorred or disagreed with republican values, or that many republicans were content to subscribe to the ideal of a united Ireland, but not at the expense of human life. Within Stone's reasoning also dwelt the firm conviction that any Catholic who appeared on a security forces' list was, by definition, a legitimate target. Predictably and unfortunately, the penetration by loyalists of the UDR and RUC intelligence-gathering apparatus did not easily discriminate in its targeting of individuals: its basic information procedures were easily misunderstood with devastating consequences for those on the lists. A former intelligence officer explained the problem to me in the following confession:

Intelligence gathering is by definition indiscriminate because anyone has to be regarded as a potential subversive. In a society where terrorism is rife and where it has been in place for such a long time there is no guarantee who may emerge. Files are kept on the whole population. In Northern Ireland which is not much larger than Yorkshire that is feasible. No one would believe the extent of phone-tapping or phone surveillance. It is very sophisticated but that dimension is kept very tight, extremely secret and well away from the normal security personnel. Now the real problem is general intelligence-gathering which is undertaken by large numbers of personnel within the Army and police. It consists of photographic surveillance of large gatherings of people passing check-points etc. That provides a basic assessment of the political motivation of people, the company they keep and sometimes the places they visit. IRA funerals are photographed to inform us of people whom we might otherwise overlook in our general calculations. Remember that a teenager who wasn't even born when the conflict began may suddenly be emerging into IRA ranks. We also depend on gossip, on the use of the confidential phone service, or on informers. Of course there is always the risk that neighbours may act vindictively against each other and provide information, but we have to take it at face value until we know otherwise. Sometimes we will decide to target particular individuals for a period of time out of curiosity or a hunch. When we do that, a file is prepared on the person giving details of his address, car registration, possible associates, etc. Roadchecks are valuable for logging the movements of a targeted person and for recording the identity of those who travel with him or her, or whom he or she chooses to visit. Of necessity, these files are passed to normal security personnel and that is where the breakdown occurs. Equally there will be photographs of potential suspects on the walls of police stations or military barracks which can be viewed by a large number of people. It is difficult to prevent access to what is in reality low-grade intelligence. If there are people who wish to use that intelligence for malicious reasons there is little which can be done to prevent it.

Stone says his contacts told him that Joseph O'Kane's movements were unpredictable and 'he could not be tied down to a particular place at a particular time'.

I decided a shoot was out of the question, and I made up my mind to plant a booby-trap bomb. When you cannot determine the exact movements of a target it is a waste of time and energy to prepare an ambush. It requires too much risk hanging around hoping he will turn up at a particular place. There is always the risk that when you remain static for too long, you bring too much attention to yourself. I made up my mind to booby-trap some place where he was likely to be on at least one occasion in any week.

Stone's accomplices possessed a general outline of O'Kane's weekly routine. He lived at 76 Coleraine Street in Kilrea with his common-law wife, Annalena, a retired nurse. His farm lay a short distance from Kilrea at Drumsarragh Road, and consisted of twenty-seven acres with a dwelling house and shed: he owned a further twenty-four acres one mile away on the Drumsarragh Road. O'Kane only occupied the farmhouse during the lambing season, and preferred to make the journey from Kilrea when it was demanded of him. The laneway to the farmhouse offered a view of two sheds, one with a single wooden door which opened outwards and housed eight hens and a cock. The second shed contained feed for his sheep and kennels for two dogs. Alongside the farmhouse stood another shed used for rearing chickens. Every Saturday, Annalena took her two grandsons, Jonathan and Ryan, to the farm to feed the hens and chickens. Aged 12 and 9 respectively, they had grown to love the weekly trip, and regarded the hens and chickens as their possessions. On the afternoon of Friday 4 March Annalena drove to the farm with livestock feed, and fed the hens. She did not notice unusual activity, but examined the sheds to assure herself they were secure.

Simultaneously Stone prepared the booby-trap device.

I made up a bomb in Belfast and hid it in a hedge near my home. It was a percussion cap grenade. I collected it, was picked up by some people and taken up country somewhere in County Derry. It was early Saturday morning. I was taken in a legit motor deep into the country and across fields to the old farmhouse. I knew Farmer O'Kane visited the farm at some stage during that day.

From the intelligence provided by his accomplices and a layout of the farm, Stone knew where to plant the booby-trap. He knew that O'Kane was typically accompanied to the premises by his wife and grandsons every Saturday; nevertheless, he elected to booby-trap the henhouse and examined its interior. On the inside of the door frame, he screwed a small hook into the wood. To this, he attached a wire to a bolt on the back of the door to the fly-off lever of the grenade. With meticulous attention to detail, he tested the amount of wire required to ensure that the grenade would activate as soon as the bolt was slid backwards. The device, concealed from the person opening the door, had an 8–9-second fuse, and would therefore not explode until O'Kane actually entered the shed. The confined area of the building would concentrate the power of the explosion with fatal consequences.

I left everything set for Farmer O'Kane so that he would be killed or at least seriously injured. I was led to the legit motor and driven straight back to Belfast, dropped off, and I made my own way home. Before I left the countryside, I torched a pair of gloves and also a pair of thick navy socks which I had worn over my boots to disguise the shape of my feet.

Just after midday Annalena and John O'Kane placed food scraps and egg shells in a plastic bag and prepared for their journey to the farm. Annalena's nephew, Stephen Kennedy, decided to accompany them and the three drove the short distance to Drumsarragh Road. On the way they met Annalena's daughter, Pattie, who told them she had just left Jonathan and Ryan beside the shed adjacent to the farmhouse, and they were busy feeding game fowl. Stephen Kennedy says he joined the boys, and remained with them for five minutes. John O'Kane suggested they all make their way to the two sheds in the laneway, and Annalena handed Stephen Kennedy the food scraps for the hens. Kennedy, unaware of the danger, proceeded to the henhouse while O'Kane and his wife's grandsons entered the other shed. Kennedy vividly remembers the following events:

When I got to the deep-litter henhouse, John and the boys went into the shed beside me. I pulled back the bolt of the deep-litter henhouse and pulled the door open. As I did so I think I saw wires or a wire down near where the bolt was. At the same time I heard a bang followed by an explosion a few seconds later.

He was blown across the farmyard and his screams brought O'Kane rushing to his assistance. Kennedy's sight was badly impaired but he scrambled to his feet and shouted a warning to everyone to stay away from the henhouse. His injuries consisted of shrapnel wounds and cuts caused by hundreds of wood fragments from the doorway. He recovered well but was later told by medical experts that he would eventually be blind in his right eye.

His life was saved because Stone miscalculated the timing of the percussion cap on the grenade. It was part of a new batch of explosives provided by South African intelligence – grenades called 'RGD-5', an anti-personnel device designed for use in an offensive role. The fragmentation produced upon initiation of the explosive filling (approximately 110 grams of TNT) was known to be most effective at close range, but the potential for destruction diminished rapidly with any increased distance from the seat of the explosion. Stone believed that the grenade possessed an 8–9-second delay-timer to allow for his target to enter the shed – at which point, the intended victim's proximity to the seat of the explosion, and the compression caused by the walls of the building, would concentrate its lethal potential, causing death or serious injury. In fact the grenade had only a three-second delay, which probably saved Kennedy's life: the outward blast threw him back into the yard, thereby protecting him from the full force of the grenade. Not only that, if the grenade had continued on an eight-second delay-fuse, Kennedy might have been uninjured: alerted by the wires he saw attached to the bolt, he might just have had sufficient time to escape the blast.

By now, Stone's accomplices had begun to wonder at his failure to fulfil his 'sanctions' successfully: he felt equally unhappy. So far, he had not succeeded in realising his and McMichael's ambition to exact revenge for the Enniskillen bombing.

10

The Milltown Massacre

On Sunday 6 March 1988 SAS operatives killed three members of an IRA active-service unit in Gibraltar. The three, Sean Savage, Daniel McCann and Mairead Farrell were shot as they walked towards the Spanish border. The three were unarmed, and the character of the triple killing bore similarities to many covert military operations in Northern Ireland: they were individually shot dead in a style of execution which Michael Stone admired – first, immobilised with bullets to their torsos, and then finally dispatched with rounds to the head, fired at very close range.

Their deaths possessed an additional significance for a jubilant Stone: at last he could contemplate the prospect of a major republican funeral, which would be attended by the IRA and Sinn Fein leaderships – the moment for which he had been waiting, and which he had personally failed to create. This would realise the plan by the late UFF leader, McMichael, to attack the IRA at its cenotaph.

Inevitably, the funerals would be held at Milltown Cemetery in Belfast, the three IRA dead being natives of the city. The manner of their dying, and the attendant publicity, had provided the IRA with a propaganda exercise: a major funeral with paramilitary trappings. Within days of the killings, condemnation of the actions of the SAS soldiers spread wide and heatedly – especially when it soon became clear that a car which they had left parked in Gibraltar before attempting to make their way from the colony did not contain explosives (as official accounts had suggested). The three had gone to Gibraltar on a reconnaissance mission, intending to organise an Enniskillen-type massacre at a planned ceremonial changing of the guard by British troops. A bomb containing 500 pounds of Semtex explosive lay hidden in Spain, waiting to be transported to Gibraltar, and then driven to the parking space provided by the car abandoned by the trio on the day of their deaths. The explosives came from a consignment supplied to the IRA by Col. Gadaffi, and had been unloaded off the coast of Spain at Marbella several months earlier. In Belfast and in Dublin, the IRA was quick to exploit public anger at the killing of its unarmed members; an indication of public disquiet at their deaths was summarised by the fact that sixty Labour MPs denounced the killings as 'capital punishment without trial'.

One week after the shootings, the bodies of the three left Malaga for Dublin airport on a privately chartered flight, for burial in the republican plot at Milltown Cemetery. Days before the return of the bodies, Stone acted quickly to examine ways of gaining access to Milltown on the day of the funerals; his intention – to assassinate Adams, McGuinness and other leading republicans who were certain to be there. When he approached members of the UFF who had been close to McMichael, they considered the plan 'suicidal', but they 'would consider it'. Stone then approached several loyalist freelance killers, but they all argued that an escape from Milltown Cemetery could never be successfully negotiated from such a crowd. The UVF agreed to assist with the provision of weapons, but they refused to provide manpower: they suggested that, instead, he gain entry to the cemetery prior to the funerals, and booby-trap the ground surrounding the republican plot. Stone has never revealed any of the planning detail which preceded the Milltown incident but other loyalists had been privy to paramilitary discussions of Stone's request for assistance. In the words of one:

The UDA leadership was consulted but they were scared of Stone's idea. You have to take into account that many of them were individually concerned about their own safety. They liked the idea about wiping out IRA chiefs in the very heartland of West Belfast, and particularly while they were commemorating their own dead, just as our people were massacred at the cenotaph in Enniskillen. As I say, the problem was personal. There was no collective view beyond the fact that many members of the UDA/UFF were thrilled to think something like that could be achieved. The UDA had a major problem in that its leaders were known, and could be easily targeted in a retaliatory strike by the Provos. The killing of McMichael frightened a lot of guys in the public eye, and the Provos had made it clear after the attempted murder of Adams that any attempt at killing their leadership would be met with the wholesale assassination of UDA leaders. Now you might think that was the kind of threat which would have been part of the order of things, but not within the UDA. It was able to operate as a legal body while privately ordering UFF operations. Its leaders were well known and, as such, felt vulnerable. A small core of prominent UFF activists who were previously attached to the late John McMichael supported Stone's concept. They were in favour of the UVF plan to booby-trap the cemetery and Stone initially agreed with them.

It was possible to acquire anti-personnel mines which could be placed under the surface of the ground or to manufacture several bombs which could be remotely detonated. Two nights before the funerals were due to take place, Stone and two others were detailed to examine the layout of the cemetery. They were firstly provided with British military surveillance photos and maps of the cemetery. The photographs were of the type taken from a British Army helicopter and were acquired from UFF sources within the military. Under cover of darkness they entered the cemetery and went to the republican plot and examined its surroundings. It was felt by Stone that the plot was the IRA's cenotaph where the killing should take place. The three-man team managed to complete the recce without interference. There was always heavy security in West Belfast, but the risk of them being caught was minimised by the fact that our people were in a position to know the schedule of all security forces' activity in the area at that time. When they returned to East Belfast, a meeting was held at which Stone vetoed the booby-trap plan. He argued that the bombs might not go off at the correct time or find the right targets. He was very single-minded and said it was a 'haphazard way of operating'. He believed it was important to make sure that the right people were assassinated, and the risk of using booby-traps was that a lot of women and kids might get hit instead of the real targets. He was insistent on putting forward his original idea of getting close to people like Adams and McGuinness and killing them. It seemed like madness but he was convinced he could do it. He said he would do the killing if two operatives acted as back-up. He was obsessed with a wish to kill McGuinness and Adams, not only for Enniskillen but as revenge for the death of McMichael. Two guys agreed to act as a getaway team, but were not prepared to enter the cemetery. Stone was the kind of guy who oozed confidence. He believed he could get in, do the job and get out again. He had operated for so long without getting caught, that he almost saw himself as invincible. He said no one would know him and, if someone later offered a description of him, there was nothing on security files to identify him. After all he was seen operating on other occasions but the description given to the police never led to his capture. It was agreed that he could go ahead. I suppose it was a case of people saying if he is crazy enough to think he can succeed, maybe he will.

Stone spent hours examining UFF files containing confidential police and Army photographs of known IRA activists and suspects. He knew the geography of republican West Belfast – he had made 'several runs' through the Falls and Andersonstown areas in the 1970s. Those 'runs', as he calls them, journeys by car, formed part of the planning of sectarian murders. He reckoned he could mingle with mourners at Milltown, pull a mask over his face and fire at republican leaders, and he believed that in the confusion, he could then escape towards the M1 motorway where his back-up team would be waiting. In assessing the risk to himself, he believed he had a fifty-fifty chance of surviving. To his mind, that was similar in risk analysis to all the other operations he had carried out. One further piece of information heightened his conviction that a clear escape from the cemetery might prove possible; UFF contacts within the security forces confirmed that the police and Army presence would be considerably reduced. This would be in marked contrast to previous security policy, which authorised large numbers of police and soldiers to surround IRA funerals and seize people in paramilitary dress. Angry Catholic politicians and clergy claimed it led to violence and to distressing scenes, as coffins were being carried from homes or churches. In IRA tradition, a coffin bears a tricolour, and volunteers, dressed in military uniform, fire volleys of shots over the grave. Funerals had long been propaganda events at which the IRA determined to parade military hardware and other symbols of defiance. The British government viewed such public displays as provocative and the Catholic Church eventually felt obliged to deny the use of immediate church grounds to such expression of IRA traditions. RUC chiefs were convinced that the IRA exploited the presence of the security forces at funerals in order to create violence and generate Catholic antagonism towards the forces of law and order. The IRA then resorted to organising paramilitary maneouvres outside the homes of the dead, or in the cemeteries.

At the beginning of March, nasty scenes had occurred when mourners and police clashed during the funeral of an IRA man in South Armagh. Catholic bishops and politicians condemned RUC policy as deliberately provocative, and demanded restraint. Prior to the planned funerals of the Gibraltar Three, the SDLP leadership asked the Chief Constable to reduce the security-force presence at Milltown. They argued that tensions ran high in West Belfast owing to the manner in which the three had been executed. The

Catholic Bishop of Down and Connor, Dr Cahal Daly, told the security authorities that they could be assured no illegality would arise at the funerals, and that no attempt would be made by the IRA to exploit the situation. He appealed for a major reduction in the number of police and Army personnel detailed to funeral duties. Dr Daly's assurances were given after priests in West Belfast had consulted the IRA, and received guarantees that they would hold no displays of paramilitarism.

Several days before the funerals, a meeting was held by security chiefs, at which it was felt that Catholic requests for a change in security policy were acceptable. Knowledge of the outcome of the security meeting was leaked to the UFF, and to Michael Stone. An example of Stone's personal ability to acquire classified intelligence is to be found in an incident which occurred prior to the death of UVF leader, John Bingham. Stone was approached by a Special Branch source and warned about a surveillance operation. According to loyalist sources, Stone later conveyed details of his meeting with the Special Branch officer to Bingham and McMichael.

Stone was told there was an Interpol file on Bingham, which contained photographs showing him meeting people in Paris and Brussels. It was a warning passed through Stone to Bingham, to let Bingham know he was under surveillance. Bingham made several trips to Europe in relation to arms deals. Stone's contact told him the Interpol file was very detailed, and passed to British intelligence who allowed Special Branch to view it. Obviously the British had hoped Special Branch could add to the file from their knowledge of Bingham.

The Special Branch source also issued a personal warning to Stone that MI5 possessed photos of Bingham, one of them taken in the grounds of Belfast Castle. One particular snapshot was of Stone and Bingham walking through the public grounds of the castle. Both were walking their dogs, Stone his two Staffordshire bull terriers and Bingham, a golden Labrador. This photograph therefore indicates that a file existed on Stone: yet – and amazingly – why was he never made a target for security surveillance? It transpires that MI5 possessed other photographs of Stone, some taken while he sat with McMichael in his car outside a restaurant in Comber. Several photographs exist, taken by MI5 and British Military Intelligence, which show McMichael driving through rural areas of Northern Ireland. One of the pictures was taken in

South Derry, as McMichael drove along a country road: the person in the passenger seat was Michael Stone, although his facial image was slightly blurred by rain on the passenger-door window. None the less, his presence on file in the company of two terrorist leaders does not seem to have led to greater scrutiny. No action was ever taken to discover the precise nature of his relationship with two men who were known, if not proveably so, to be masterminding a murder campaign.

Stone's ability to acquire classified information further made it possible for him to assess the risk of his proposed Milltown operation. He knew the cemetery layout, and the security measures planned for the vicinity of Milltown on 16 March. To accomplices, he indicated that he would attack the funeral cortège once it arrived in the cemetery, and then, in the confusion, escape towards the M1 motorway. His getaway car should be parked there, on the hard shoulder facing citywards. From the motorway they could then drive to the loyalist Village area in 2–3 minutes.

On the evening of 16 March 1988 Stone met members of the UVF, who supplied him with a Browning 9mm pistol (serial no: L44788), ammunition and seven grenades. He hid these in a shed at the rear of his house where he had also concealed the police-owned Ruger pistol and ammunition speed-strips. The following morning he awoke at 8.30, went to the shed and examined the weapons. His equipment included a crudely made double holster, consisting of two pockets secured to each side of a substantial pouch which measured 11" x 15"; red and black straps allowed the arrangement to be hung around his neck, with a holster then roughly positioned under each arm, and the pouch placed across the chest, stomach area. Each holster was capable of holding either the Browning, or the Ruger, and the pouch was designed for grenades. The complete kit had been fashioned from an old pair of denim jeans, and gave him an effective means of containing his weaponry.

At 9.00 a.m., Stone returned to the shed to dress himself for his mission. He wore black boots, denims, a black tee-shirt and blue pullover. He carried a denim jacket, a cap, a pair of imitation leather gloves, an anorak with a hood and a woollen cap which could be pulled over his face with eye slits cut into it. In the shed, he donned his holster arrangement, placed the guns, grenades and ammunition in it, and a handful of loose rounds for the Ruger in the pocket of his anorak. He stowed the cap and woollen hat inside his clothing. At 9.15 he walked into the house and kissed his wife goodbye. He says she looked at him, puzzled by the kiss – not a customary gesture – and he walked to a nearby bus-stop, to board the No. 24 for Belfast city centre. A friend, Stephen Ritchie Lorrimer, later remembered seeing him on the bus.

I was going to Belfast to catch a bus for Newtownards where I was appearing at court on a speeding charge. I sat down on a seat from the rear on the driver's side. The bus stopped at a primary school and Flint got on. I have known Michael Stone whom I call Flint for a number of years. I thought he was going to sit beside me but he sat in the back seat. I asked him where he was going and he replied: 'Into town to do a bit of shopping.' I had a general conversation with Stone but I can't remember the details. The funerals of the IRA men at Milltown were mentioned but I can't remember in what context other than he said he hoped it rained on the bastards.

Stone left the bus in central Belfast and walked towards Castle Street, where Catholic taxi-drivers offered free trips to Milltown Cemetery. He considered waiting for a taxi ride, but too many people were queuing for the free one-mile journey. He walked towards the Falls Road, and his mission could have ended at that point. At Divis Street, RUC Constable Robert Smith, on foot-patrol duties with Constable Pengelly, saw Stone.

I was at Divis Street at approximately 10.15 a.m. when I observed a number of people walking towards me. These people were in small groups of two or three and individually one of these persons I observed was a male of stout build with long black hair and a beard. He was wearing a royal blue rain jacket with white strings, a blue jacket underneath the rain jacket and a grey cap. My attention was drawn to him by the way in which he turned his head slightly to his left away from me and appeared to have a nervous twitch. He was unaccompanied.

Constable Smith did not act on his observation, and Stone proceeded along the Falls Road. Minutes later he saw a taxi stopping to pick up several young men, hitched a ride with them to the Andersonstown Road, and left the taxi outside St Agnes's Church. Two hearses had parked in front of the building, and, as Stone watched, a third hearse arrived, carrying the remains of Mairead Farrell, the third member of the IRA's Gibraltar trio.

Stone says he mingled with the crowds going into the church for a requiem service, and found himself standing behind the

President of Sinn Fein, Gerry Adams and one of his associates, Joe Austin. 'I was going to do them but I didn't,' says Stone; he 'wanted to finish the job on McGuinness, and other top people, who would be standing together at the graveside', the symbolic place where he intended the killings to take place in revenge for Enniskillen. While the requiem service was in progress, he was approached by a girl who said 'hello Stoner'. He recognised her as a barmaid who once worked in Drury Lane, a Belfast city-centre bar.

I suddenly realised I was close to being exposed but thankfully she didn't know anything about me. She remembered me drinking in a bar beside the college in Amelia Street. I ignored her but I felt that whatever happened I was suddenly compromised. As I walked into the cemetery I spotted surveillance in one of the sangars [*lookout posts*] at Andersonstown police station and wondered if I'd been photographed. I had the cap pulled down, and the anorak hood over it, and reckoned I was reasonably secure. I thought, they will never recognise me from photographs, because it was easy to change my appearance. I looked older, bulkier and the beard and long hair was a disguise easily removed later. As I walked into the cemetery, I saw about forty Provos, three of them armed. They were searching the area around the republican plot and scrutinising people.

On his way into Milltown he was again recognised, but this time it was someone who knew his true identity. He says a man turned towards him saying 'hey Stoner'.

I looked quickly at him and walked on. He was a former member of the Hole in the Wall gang who was later on the fringes of the IRA. I thought 'if that bastard makes a move I'll blow him away'. Maybe he sensed that, or maybe he wasn't so sure it was me, because I paid no attention to him.

Stone says he knew at that moment that whatever transpired he was 'in the cemetery to do a job and was going to see it through'.

I thought, here I am, two people have seen me, and what the hell, there's no point disguising myself with the woollen cap. I'll operate as I am. Maybe they know me and maybe they don't. Either way they might be too scared to admit it after I've finished.

Stone walked through the cemetery and rehearsed his escape

route, through lines of headstones, and a long laneway leading to the motorway. The lane was bordered by a ditch and open field; access to the motorway was alongside a high fence. Stone returned to the IRA graveside to await the arrival of the cortège, and on his way noticed a white transit van parked citywards on the motorway exactly at the spot where he expected his back-up team to arrive. He says he knew the van was a police vehicle, probably used by the RUC's undercover unit E4A, and was engaged in surveillance.

I reckoned the van was positioned there to record events in the cemetery. There was a general lack of security presence, and the van was a means of providing one, or linking with helicopter surveillance in the event that there was a paramilitary display, and there could be a coordination of photographic images of the mourners, and in particular of Provos who fired weapons. I was not too concerned because I was prepared to deal with them if and when I reached the motorway.

Stone's awareness of the van, and his surmise that it contained an undercover unit, did not deter him from continuing his operation. It could be that he believed they would not remain in position for long, or even that they would not seek to prevent his escape. After all, he had enough weaponry in his possession to deter anyone from capturing him. The presence of the van later became a contentious political issue, but the RUC claimed it contained members of police traffic branch. According to the RUC the traffic branch personnel in the van were in position from 0700 hours to prevent people using the motorway as a route to the cemetery. Their claim, vaguely absurd at the time, became, as subsequent events will show, a complex issue, difficult to unravel. That morning, Stone saw a policeman alight from the van and speak to children who were hurling abuse in the direction of the vehicle.

As Stone walked to the graveside he encountered members of Provisional Sinn Fein with walkie-talkies, and one of them spoke to him in Gaelic.

I answered 'our day will come' in Irish, and we both raised our hands in salute. That satisfied him.

Stone chose a Gaelic phrase – known to any enquiring Provisional – common parlance in West Belfast.

The funeral cortège left St Agnes' Church at noon. The crowd swelled to thousands, lining the route from the church to

Milltown; the event, unlike other IRA funerals, bore the hallmarks of a well-organised peaceful display of grief.

Members of the police and military monitored the passage of the cortège, unaware of the killer lurking in the cemetery. Police Inspector Keith Russell watched proceedings from the heavily fortified Andersonstown police station opposite the cemetery gates:

I was in the temporary command room staffed by Assistant Chief Constable Steenson, Chief Superintendent Scullion, Superintendent Donnan and Sub-Divisional Commander, Woodbourne. Inspector White, staff officer to Assistant Chief Belfast, was also present. My role was to monitor the movement of the funerals. I was initially in the front sangar when the funerals went to the church but at twelve noon the coffins accompanied by a crowd of 8–10,000 moved into Milltown Cemetery. At this stage, ACC Steenson, C/Super Scullion and Super. Donnan were in the top area of the 'super sangar'. Once the main body of mourners entered the cemetery we returned to the command room. The time was 1320 hours.

Stone, now within sight of the cortège, and among the thousands of mourners, moved into the cemetery. In discussions with him, I pieced together his feelings.

I saw the cortège and I was fascinated. There was something about it which struck me as familiar. I have to admit I regarded myself as a soldier, as had the three about to be buried. I was more interested in Mairead Farrell, a woman who was prepared to die for the cause. I don't know what happened. I was so preoccupied I almost forgot why I was there. It was as if everything had stopped and I was observing something which was close to me. I knew that if I was killed on active service I would like to know I would be given all the trappings they were receiving.

Stone was left feeling absorbed by the public display of admiration granted to heroes in the other community. He saw the event as a mirror image of his desire to be elevated to a similar status in death, and was captivated momentarily, sufficient to distract him from his purpose; so preoccupied that he allowed the burial service to take place, including the prayers, and the lowering of the coffins into the graves.

By now, Stone was surrounded by mourners, many of them women and children.

There was a kid who kept coming up to me and I kept telling her to go away. I gave her fifty pence. The main thing was I did not want her hurt or harmed. She reminded me of my own kids and I had no intention of killing children.

In which case – he was in the wrong place, and armed with weapons designed for indiscriminate violence: the assertion that he did not wish to harm children rings hollow in the light of the violence he subsequently unleashed.

Most of those in the cemetery had never been members of the Provisional movement, nor even supporters of violence. The manner of the killing of the Gibraltar trio had angered many Catholics, who displayed their resentment of SAS methods by attending the funeral. Typical of many mourners, Theresa Keenan, her sister Kathleen Morgan and husband Philip had travelled across Belfast to attend the requiem mass and burial service. Theresa Keenan later remembered her sister talking to a man in the cemetery. She says he wore a cap, had dark bushy hair and a moustache. This, she learned later, was Michael Stone.

Stone waited until the third coffin was lowered into the grave, and leading republicans prepared to deliver customary orations. Ahead of him, the graveside was surrounded by mourners; close to the grave stood Gerry Adams, Danny Morrison, Martin McGuinness, the leaders of Provisional Sinn Fein. Stone unbuttoned his anorak and denim jacket and removed two RGD-5 grenades from the pouch straddling his chest. He might not have known with certainty the exact time-fuses in each grenade, but later he admitted that he knew some contained seven- and nine-second fuses and at least one, ten seconds.

The two grenades he removed from his pouch had seven-second delays, permitting him time to remove his guns from their holsters. He intended to throw the two grenades over the heads of mourners, and into the very centre of the republican plot. As they landed, he would withdraw his guns and wait for the explosions. He expected that the blasts would force people to lie low, thereby providing clearance for him to approach the graveside and shoot Adams, Morrison and McGuinness. Stone knew that the grenades would cause devastation in a tightly packed crowd – a fact which conflicts with his claim that he wished to avoid harming innocent people. Perhaps he underestimated, or failed to consider the danger, and the suffering he would undoubtedly cause. It may well be that his fascination with the scene before him goaded him into action; this was the final stage where he had the opportunity to increase his self-esteem, and become a hero to his community as Mairead Farrell had become to her people. Irrespective of his desire to survive, he admits that he decided 'there was no going back on his purpose'.

I was there and I knew that it had to be done. I suddenly realised I had blown it and should have taken out Adams and the others as they walked into the cemetery. That would have proved the best course but my mind was elsewhere. It was as if I had to see it all take place – the burial, the trappings and all that. I was in a daydream when I suddenly came out of it and thought if I'm here I may as well get on with it.

He did exactly that and lobbed two grenades towards the graveside. Jeannette McCabe was struck on the head by a grenade and knocked unconscious. Another mourner, Damien Glenholmes, later testified to the inaccuracy of Stone's throwing arm:

I was forty yards from the republican plot when I saw a black object flying through the air towards me. It landed close to me and I heard a loud bang and smoke. I was thrown to the ground and a fella with blond hair fell into me. He was holding his left side and I think he was bleeding. I heard another bang. There were people shouting and screaming.

The two grenades sent shrapnel tearing into the crowd and ripped marble from headstones creating a lethal storm of vicious objects. Stone says he aimed the grenades at 'the boys with berets and flags' and when the grenades exploded the crowd turned towards him. He aimed his Browning pistol towards them and claims he fired above their heads to kill Adams and his Sinn Fein colleagues. Stone told me he shouted to Adams and McGuinness 'to come to him' but they refused.

I did not want to kill women and children. I mean that I walked on. I didn't run. Everything started. I wanted to get more grenades into them.

His claim about women and children is absurd; only luck prevented their deaths, and scores of women were injured by shrapnel or ragged fragments of marble. What is not in doubt is the coolness Stone displayed, as he slowly left the scene of the first explosions. Theresa Keenan, whose sister had spoken to Stone during the burial service, remembers seeing him after the grenades exploded. She was propelled over a headstone by the force of a blast and injured by shrapnel. As she lay on top of a grave, she saw Stone fire several shots into the crowd, and then stroll towards the motorway. He left a scene of carnage with people lying injured in pathways and on graves surrounding the republican plot.

John Jordan, a self-employed taxi-driver, has reason to feel he was lucky to survive. He began the day as a contract driver for the American television network ABC, to ferry a film crew and correspondent to the funeral; having driven his minibus and the ABC film team to the Falls area, he parked his vehicle in Milltown between the republican plot and the motorway. As the cortège entered Milltown, his attention was drawn to three men and a woman entering the cemetery from the motorway. He thought they were a film crew but was puzzled as they 'were a bit late to cover the funeral. They were cutting it a bit fine.' Then his attention was quickly drawn to other events:

I heard about five or six shots and a couple of explosions. At first I thought they were shooting over the coffins but the next thing I heard people shouting 'lie down, lie down'. I saw this fellow come running from the direction of the grave. He was wearing a blue anorak. He ran past my van towards the fence linking the motorway, jumping over the grass. He was about twelve yards from me when he turned in my direction. I could see his arm come up.

Stone saw Jordan's van and says he decided to shoot 'the fat boy in the driver's seat'. His account differs from Jordan's:

I took out the Ruger. There was a parked beige van. This skinny fella jumped out to tackle me. I fired at him, not aiming, just to keep him down. I was being stoned and walked round the front of the van. I was going to shoot the fat boy in the driver's seat but the crowd was closing in on me and I left it.

The discrepancy in the two accounts may relate to the fact there were other vans but whatever the disparity, a bullet shattered the windscreen of John Jordan's vehicle.

Stone's journey from the graveside remained casual, until young mourners began to pursue him regardless of the risks. He pulled out a grenade and threw it at them, but it only deterred them momentarily, and their pursuit began again. Moving quickly now, he turned to fire at his pursuers, and to throw more grenades. He says what angered him was they shouted 'Orange bastard', but offers no reason as to why a typical sectarian slogan offended him while he was trying to kill people at random. The epithet may have triggered the secret worry he was illegitimate. 'Bastard', he says, was the offending word and not 'Orange' which denoted his Protestantism, and in one of my many conversations with him, he expressed the residual fear that he might discover his natural parents were never married. He knew I was researching his family history and asked me to promise to reveal it to him, and he hoped my research would not confirm his suspicion of illegitimacy. His reaction to the taunt 'Orange bastard' was to kill at least two if not three of his pursuers at that moment. He later said that as they shouted at him he fired his Ruger at 'the cunts coming for him'.

As he made his escape, Stone sank into marshy ground and was temporarily out of sight of those in pursuit. It provided him with a temporary respite to check the Browning pistol which was jamming. He reloaded a full magazine, rose to his feet and fired again.

I fired two shots and she jammed again. My hands were soaking and covered in muck. The crowd shouted 'he's out of ammo, kill the bastard'. I threw the last-but-one grenade. It slipped out of my hand and went only about ten feet exploding and throwing up a large spray of water.

One of those pursuing him was 20-year-old Thomas McErlean who earlier that day left his wife at home, collected unemployment benefit and went to the church and cemetery. He watched a large crowd follow Stone but decided to take a shorter route to prevent him reaching the motorway. McErlean ran along the cemetery perimeter fencing, the route Stone was taking. John Patrick McCaffrey was a witness to McErlean's fatal behaviour:

I ran down behind two boys along the perimeter fence. They appeared to be trying to cut off the escape of the guy who threw the grenades. The next thing he turned and pointed a gun at the two boys. He had been pointing the gun at the main crowd chasing him but he turned to point it at the first of the two fellows in front of me. I heard only one shot and the gunman turned and ran. It was then I noticed the guy in front tried to get up off the ground and then slumped down again. He half-rose with his hand on the ground and the other hand stretching out to try to grab hold of something. He was Thomas McErlean, though I didn't know at the time. I knelt down beside him and loosened his tie and shirt. There was blood coming from his mouth and nose. His eyes and mouth were wide open. I checked for his heartbeat and pulse but there was nothing. I started pumping his heart and another fellow gave him mouth-to-mouth resuscitation. When I was pumping his heart I heard him gasp and thought to myself 'fuck – this guy's died'.

McErlean was hit by one bullet which entered his right shoulder, passed through his right lung, lacerated the aorta artery and bowel, and lodged in his left thigh. The track of the bullet suggested he was bending down, possibly in anticipation of Stone firing. He was small and in bending the bullet tracked downwards through his body. If he had remained standing he might have suffered a shoulder wound. Before Stone exited the cemetery, two other young men were dying from gunshot wounds: 30-year-old Kevin Brady, a member of the IRA; and 26-year-old John Murray, father of two young children. Brady was shot in the buttock but the bullet travelled upwards damaging organs and he died from haemhorrage to lacerated arteries. John Murray was shot in the neck: cause of death – massive internal bleeding. No one has clearly established where they were shot, but the evidence points to them pursuing Stone from the graveside. It is also possible that one of them was the person referred to by Stone as the man who 'tried to tackle him' near John Jordan's minibus.

Stone's journey through the cemetery was closely observed by Police Inspector Russell in Andersonstown station. When he heard the first two grenades explode he left the command room for the 'super sangar'. With the aid of binoculars he was able to view most of the cemetery ground. He saw a large number of injured being taken in taxis from the cemetery. His attention was drawn to Stone who was running along the pathway which bordered the perimeter fence. Russell says one of twenty youths pursuing him 'could have been carrying a firearm', although his suspicion was not confirmed by journalists, photographers and film cameramen who recorded the violence. He watched the pursuers reach fifty in number, and Stone throw a grenade at them. The crowd swelled to at least one hundred teenagers before another grenade was hurled at them. Stone was seen to walk nonchalantly as he reached the motorway.

Stone claims he fired towards the police van on the motorway forcing its driver to leave the scene. There is no proof that he did, although the van sped away as Stone reached the motorway.

According to him he 'put a round through the windscreen'. By now he knew that his two associates had abandoned him. As he walked on to the citybound lanes of the M1, his pursuers drew closer behind him, undaunted by grenades or bullets. Stone's guns were temporarily empty and he had one grenade. The Browning pistol was jammed but he had ample rounds for the powerful Ruger.

11

Captured

Stone says he was aware that some of his pursuers were IRA, because they counted each round he fired, and knew each time he needed to reload. He heard them shout to each other when the sixth round was fired from the Ruger. When he reached the motorway he pointed his empty pistols at oncoming cars in the hope of hijacking one. When none stopped, Stone walked slowly along the motorway his pursuers slowly edging closer to him, increasingly aware of his reduced potential to kill. Paul Tohill was in the crowd and followed Stone as he crossed the central reservation and proceeded in the direction of the countryside.

We were about twenty yards from him. He was waving both his hands as if beckoning us towards him and shouting abuse. He then turned his back and slowly walked away. The crowd started to get closer to him. He walked closer to the grass embankment and the next thing I saw a grenade hit the road about 10–15 feet in front of me. I turned away from it and the next thing there was a loud bang and I was lying in the road. There was a lot of pain in both my feet. Other people who were injured were lying beside me.

The grenade was Stone's last attempt to halt the approach of the crowd. He knew he could not use the Browning, and he did not have time to put a speed strip into the Ruger, or feed single rounds into its barrel: his hands were too wet and muddy to permit such a careful exercise. In acknowledgement of approaching capture, he threw the two guns into the grass verges of the motorway and continued walking; he gave the appearance of a man who knew what was about to happen, but was not prepared to exhibit cowardice. Even at that moment Stone's ego rather than instinct for survival conditioned his actions. His exploits were captured on film, and to the end he seemed determined to portray himself as a man without fear, even at the moment when the crowd looked about to tear him to pieces. Later, he would revel in the story of how he ignored his pursuers and refused to be intimidated by them. His admirers regarded his actions on the motorway as those of a man without fear, prepared to accept his fate. Stone's account of what transpired illustrates his bravado even when he felt he faced death.

I threw the two shooters down the bank. They were useless. A boy hit me on the head with a piece of wood and as I went down I flicked the last grenade at them. I went down and the crowd gathered round me shouting 'get the Orange bastard'. They were fighting to get at me. The cunts were mad to get me. I was dragged along and bundled into a car. The only man I remember was a ginger-haired man in his 30s who wore a black 'bomber' jacket. They were shouting 'put one in his head'. Someone shouted about using pliers on my balls. They were mad.

Stone was spreadeagled across the rear seat of the car with men sitting on top of him. One of them remarked they should take him to a garage and find out where he acquired his weapons. Another suggested they take him away and 'nut him', a euphemism for shooting him in the head. As the car drove away, one of the occupants saw police landrovers approaching and shouted, 'Fuck – there's the rovers.' Stone kicked and struggled and managed to open a rear door. His feet were dragging along the road as his captors tried to secure him in the car. The approaching police forced the captors to turn their car and return to where the crowd was assembled. Fearing they would be arrested and charged with his abduction, they flung him to the crowd and sped away shouting 'citizen's arrest' to the oncoming police.

The crowd surrounded Stone and began beating him. Inspector Keith Russell watched the proceedings through binoculars and relayed details to the RUC operations room. He saw Stone in the middle of a crowd which 'swayed in all directions' with people jumping up and down. Others were trying to keep at bay two police officers who appeared on the scene. The policemen were Constables Williamson and McKnight. They had been operating a vehicle checkpoint at a motorway junction, and saw a crowd spilling on to the citybound carriageway. The crowd numbered 200, they guessed, and the constables saw a grenade explode in their midst. A section of the crowd pursued Stone while others, believing McKnight and Williamson posed a threat, ran towards the constables.

The policemen drew their own Ruger revolvers and stopped the advance, but came under attack from stones and bottles. McKnight radioed for police assistance and an ambulance. Williamson was aware of two youths lying injured a short distance from him and observed that one had been hit by shrapnel and the other by a bullet.

Meanwhile, Stone was at the mercy of scores of people, all trying to bludgeon him to death with fists, feet and pieces of wood. Inspector Robert Verner was on duty at Grosvenor Road station when he received a communication about the Milltown explosions from the command room at Andersonstown. He reacted quickly and selected a landrover crew to drive him to the motorway; he was joined by Sergeants William Hamill and Jeffrey McClatchey. As they drove from their base, they received several radio transmissions to the effect that a gunman was being pursued through the cemetery towards the M1. Inspector Verner later compiled the following report which illustrated the courage of the three policemen, and how their swift and determined action saved the day:

We travelled to the motorway and observed a scene of chaos. A large crowd of some 300 persons had spilled on to the motorway, and traffic was in a state of panic, with vehicles reversing and turning to get away from the crowd, which was in full riot. A number of heavy vehicles deliberately crashed through the central reservation to avoid the throwing of missiles. We drove countrywards towards the crowd which was mostly on the city lane. From a distance of 150 yards I saw a car near the crowd. The crowd appeared to be surging towards the vehicle which was parked on the hard shoulder in the city lane but facing countrywards. As we approached within 50 yards of the crowd I heard McClatchey shout 'There he is – there.' I looked through the windscreen, and saw a commotion at the front of the car. We drove to a position directly opposite this commotion and we dismounted. I saw a person in a blue jacket being viciously attacked on the ground from kicks and punches. He appeared to have received a severe beating. His clothes, face and body were smeared with blood and mud. He was in an apparently semi-conscious state.

There were six men attacking Stone, with the crowd observing, but Verner was not deterred by the threat to his life. He ran across the country lane, jumped over the central reservation and confronted Stone's attackers. He says uppermost in his mind was a radio transmission several minutes earlier informing him that a firearm and possibly grenades were in the possession of the crowd. As he stood facing the six men, his Ruger pistol still holstered, he caught sight of the 300-strong crowd edging closer to him. They were in a vicious mood and were 'screaming hatred at him' – a classic Northern Ireland situation, with policemen doing their duty caught in the middle. The crowd wanted Stone; some, or many, of them probably believed the police were acting in collusion with the Milltown gunman. Political conditioning in Northern Ireland led many Catholics to regard the RUC as a partisan force which conspired with loyalist terrorists in the assassination of Catholics. The immediate carnage perpetrated by Stone on hallowed ground exacerbated the mood generated by the SAS 'execution' of the IRA trio in Gibraltar, an event still fresh in the minds of those who attended the funerals. At the burial service that morning the officiating priest, Fr. Tom Toner, articulated the anger of many Catholics:

The use of the word murder has been questioned. Let me put it like this: if there is a war on, if the rules of war apply, then murder is not the right word. But where Christian rules apply, where the commandments of God apply, these killings were murder, just as the killing of soldiers and policemen is murder, and every murder draws a chorus of condemnation. We gathered last Sunday as angry people, angry that three Irish people, whatever their plans, had been needlessly gunned down in the street. We were angry that we were initially told lies, angry at people in high places gloating, and angry in the treatment of Irish people over the past months.

Fr. Toner's words reiterated the thoughts of those attending the funerals and, when mixed with the anger and revenge unleashed by Stone's actions, left the policemen who had arrived to do their duty in a highly volatile situation. Constables Williamson and McKnight prevented the crowd and Stone's captors from proceeding countrywards towards Andersonstown, while Inspector Verner and his sergeants blocked the route citywards.

The presence of the Ford Transit van prior to the shooting, and then its departure when Stone approached the motorway, did not go unnoticed. Provisional IRA marshals at the funeral had been aware of the van and its occupants, and when the shooting began they spread the rumour that RUC officers were involved in the massacre. Some people present in the cemetery that day told me that the crowd did not expect a loyalist killer to undertake such a mission. The ferocity of his attack, the clinical methods he used and his array of weaponry all implied an SAS or E4-type operation. To an outsider it would appear absurd that people should have suspected undercover military involvement, but an understanding of the daily events in Northern Ireland makes such suspicions inevitable. One is obliged to take into consideration the Gibraltar method of execution used by the SAS, and many other such killings in Northern Ireland, which are rarely examined, and more or less mundanely accepted. Incontrovertible evidence exists that the SAS and other covert military groupings seem provided with licence to kill unarmed terrorists, and to employ methods which go far beyond the scrutiny of law officers or the media. Increasingly, the term 'undercover operations' obscures a policy which some have termed 'shoot-to-kill'. The RUC's investigative arm, CID, has long been frustrated in its pursuit of the truth of many controversial shootings. Detectives have found their enquiries blocked, and access to secret military establishments denied, or thwarted. The intelligence community, mainly MI5, Special Branch and Military Intelligence, have used dubious and unacceptable methods to defeat the IRA – *agents-provocateurs*, the sacrifice of agents/informers; and when told about the planned killing of prominent republicans, have permitted loyalist gangs to find and eliminate their targets. One source now retired from the intelligence community, offers this analysis of the way his former colleagues operated:

From the outset of the Troubles we found it easier to penetrate the loyalist groups. The reason is simple, but not always obvious. The loyalist community is by definition supportive of the arm of the State which combats their enemy, the IRA and other republican groups. Loyalists are also part of a community which contains the vast majority of policemen and UDR personnel in Ulster. Most policemen and UDR men derive from working-class backgrounds, and represent collectively a vast amount of intelligence on working-class areas where loyalist terrorists are based. A policeman may have a brother, cousin or whatever who still lives in a loyalist area or is maybe on the fringes of a paramilitary group. When you put all this together and you know the allegiance of loyalists to the Crown it becomes easier for the forces of the Crown to penetrate loyalist organisations. They see the forces of law and order as their forces defending their State. Now none of those factors exist in the Catholic/republican community. They have an overt or subliminal antagonism towards the forces of law and order and the British. It is a historical thing which is deep-rooted. The notion of an informer is unthinkable in republican ideology. That makes the notion of an informer unthinkable in republican ideology. That makes it difficult, and so, many informers who are recruited within the IRA are blackmailed into becoming agents. They can also prove unreliable, though when they're tightly controlled they are more frightened of the IRA than us. That adds an edge to a handler's sense of security for his agent. Republican informers will do it for money or because we have something on them which they know breached IRA rules. The IRA has a history which makes it very professional and its Internal Security apparatus is always ferreting out informers/agents. That makes for a difficult cat-and-mouse game. We all have to be aware of the double agent. They could discover one of ours and turn him, or offer us someone they will continue to control. Its a dirty, dangerous game. The loyalists are easier to manipulate. We have recruited some of their top leaders. We have recruited people in loyalist groups who were traditionally police informers. There is nothing which happens within the UDA or UVF which the intelligence community does not know about even from its planning stage. Loyalists are always keen to assist the war against the IRA and that makes them ideal recruits.

Within the Catholic community an awareness of the collusion between the security forces and loyalist terrorists has been more of a suspicion than conclusive evidence. The IRA constantly exploited any opportunity to show such a connection and pointed the finger at the RUC. Ironically they were correct in assuming a connection, but were wrongly accusing the RUC uniformed branch and CID.

So, when Verner and his colleagues confronted the crowd to deny them Stone, they were facing a personal hostility, rooted in the complexities of the war, the effects of rumours, and unfounded suspicion.

Verner, aware that the crowd attacking Stone could also cost him his life, acted with coolness and authority.

I drew my police-issue Ruger and moved towards the six men and challenged them to hand over the male they were holding. I covered the six with my revolver. Sgt. McClatchey was to my left and alongside him Sgt. Hamill. I challenged the group and moved closer. They released the male and moved back a few paces. Sgt. Hamill and I moved forward. One man still had his hand on the male. I moved my revolver to my left hand

and Sgt. Hamill moved forward and grabbed the male. I again challenged the group to move back and stay back. They did move back a pace and I grabbed the male by my right hand, still covering the crowd which was surging towards us. We moved the limp body of the person across the carriageway and I assisted Sgt. Hamill to roll him over the central reservation towards our landrover. I moved back to face the crowd which was then a matter of yards from us. Sgt. McClatchey was to my left. I pointed my Ruger at them and ordered them to move back. They halted and retreated some paces but their mood was ugly. Some of the crowd broke away and tried to attack us and the male we detained. I challenged these people on several occasions during a 4–5-minute stand-off. We were the target of verbal abuse, threats and stoning without injury. I was aware of police crews of Blue 3, 4 and BW 82, 83 arriving and deploying behind me. The crowd retreated and I noticed several prone persons at the fence at the bottom of Milltown and several others lying on the grass verge of the motorway. They required first aid. I had already asked for an ambulance for them.

Verner was in an exposed position, and he further feared that the IRA in West Belfast might have tasked a unit to attack his position and retrieve Stone. Little did he know that several IRA active-service units were on their way to his position. Verner reckoned an IRA attack would only be undertaken to recover the cemetery gunman. The inspector knew if IRA gunmen reached the scene his position would be untenable and a gunbattle would leave scores of civilians dead or injured. To cancel the source of his difficulty, he had to remove the gunman from the scene. He ordered patrols BW 82, 83 to transport the killer to Belfast City Hospital, not the Royal Victoria Hospital, in the heart of Catholic West Belfast. If the gunman were taken there, without proper security procedures, IRA active-service units would storm the building and snatch him. The City Hospital was both nearer, and easier to protect, adjacent to loyalist districts, the IRA would not be capable of a swift operation at that site, and yet be sure of escaping from it to the Falls or Andersonstown districts. Verner was determined to defuse the situation but knew that if he returned the gunman to a Catholic neighbourhood for medical treatment, the IRA would encourage rioting and perhaps use it as a cover to invade the Royal Victoria. His course of action, designed to prevent further chaos in the area, succeeded. Stone's departure encouraged the crowd to disperse, and the IRA active-service units were recalled to the 1st Battalion area.

While Verner held the crowd at bay during the critical moments of the confrontation Sgt. Hamill found an opportunity to frisk Stone who had recovered consciousness. He asked Stone if he had a weapon and Stone replied he was 'clean'. 'The fucking thing jammed or I'd have got more of the bastards.'

Stone's defiance was not limited to those comments and his preoccupation with his handiwork was expressed with virulence when he was placed in the landrover. Between lapses of consciousness he addressed himself to Constable Pollin and Reserve Constable Pollin who were tending his injuries. 'How many of the bastards did I get?' he asked.

While Stone was en route to hospital, police HQ tasked Verner to guard the entrances and exits to the building; Verner and his colleagues were unable to identify Stone and there followed a frantic attempt at police and Army HQ to put a name to the lone gunman.

Two detectives, Sgt. Gerard Gibbons and Constable Shaw, were assigned to interview the captive: the authorities were puzzled by the unexpected and clinical style of the killer. Detective Gibbons was ordered to go to the casualty department, and he arrived there at 1.45 p.m. Within fifteen minutes the doctor examining Stone gave the two detectives permission to talk to the suspect. Detective Gibbons took notes of the interview:

Q.   What's your name?
A.   On aye. Dead on, big lad. I said it's John Gregg.
Q.   What were you at?
A.   Would you fuckin' believe it? My mate fucked off and left me.
Q.   Who's he?
A.   Aye, dead on. Do you think I'm stupid?
Q.   We'll find out anyway. Your wife will have to be told.
A.   My wife knows nothing about my business, God love her.
Q.   Do you know what you've done?
A.   How many did I get?
Q.   There's at least two dead.
A.   Fuckin' brilliant. I'm game for anything, big lad. Aren't I? I got some of the fuckers anyway. Hey big lad, don't be so serious. That's a good piece you're carrying. Those fuckin' automatic pistols aren't worth a fuck. Mine jammed before I could kill a lot of the cunts.
Q.   What's your name?
A.   Aye. Dead on. Do you think I'm stupid? You's were very slow in gettin' me. Where were you's?

Gibbons terminated the interview and radioed the text of his conversation. Police HQ fed the name John Gregg into the computer but it proved worthless. The police/military computer system contains data on the whole population and, unlike Great Britain, the data on individuals is extensive, on a system devised during the conflict to provide intelligence profiles on the political, social and religious character of each person living in Northern Ireland.

At 1.55 Gibbon's colleague, Det. Constable James Craig, was requested by his HQ to interview Stone and, if possible, discover his identity, which might lead to further arrests. If he were listed on the computer, his file would contain names of associates, or the organisation to which he belonged. The name of the organisation would be sufficient to enable CID and Special Branch to target an informer in the relevant terror group and ask him for information on the gunman, and the names of people with whom he operated. Film footage of the Milltown massacre taken at Andersonstown barracks and from a military helicopter, was scrutinised by detectives, and by members of the intelligence community while Stone was in the cemetery, and later while he lay in the casualty department. No one in the RUC, Army or MI5 was able to identify him.

Neither Special Branch, MI5 or Military Intelligence revealed that they possessed surveillance photographs of him conspiring with McMichael and Bingham. MI5, in particular, had an agent within the UDA leadership and he could have informed them it was Stone. The MI5 agent was recruited by the agency because he was a long-term police informer. In 1990 he came to the attention of the Stevens Inquiry, set up by the government to examine the leaking of police and Army documents to loyalist terrorists. The MI5 agent was prominent in trying to compromise the RUC by privately informing selected members of the Northern Ireland media that the leaking of intelligence files on IRA suspects was mainly the work of policemen. In fact, since the beginning of the conflict, security files on republicans or suspected republicans were supplied to loyalists by some policemen only – but mostly by members of the Ulster Defence Regiment, by a small number of British soldiers and by the British intelligence community. The motivation of the MI5 agent in blackening the RUC is difficult to analyse. I suspect that the RUC uniformed branch, and the CID had been pressurising the UDA in an unprecedented fashion at that time, and that the motive was one of revenge.

The subsequent Stevens Inquiry Report cleared the RUC, but reserved little criticism for the UDR, considering the extent of its collusion with terrorism. A decision twelve months later merged the UDR with an Irish regiment of the British Army to accord it respectability, and provide tighter control of its activities. Stevens had a difficult investigation, and on at least one occasion, received a phone call from MI5 telling him to reverse a particular course of action. Officially, he was strictly forbidden to exceed, in any way, the terms of reference set for him, particularly when his inquiry looked like encroaching on matters sensitive to the intelligence community. Aside from the MI5 agent who came to his attention, although Stevens may not have known his connection to the agency, the inquiry leader scrutinised another significant figure – a UDA operative, who was also a Military Intelligence agent, and whose activities were outside the law. He provided information on loyalist assassination plans but his handlers did not warn the RUC, and thereby permitted killings of republicans to take place.

This figure was quick to act in denying UDA involvement with the Milltown gunman, and he made private calls to selected members of the media, informing them that neither the UDA nor UFF played a part in the massacre. He made it clear that he could not speak for the UVF, but by doing so he pointed an accusing finger directly at them. The agent knew about Stone, about the planning of the Milltown operation, and he knew that the UVF supplied some of the weaponry. He was now seeking to protect the UDA from being proscribed, and to avoid the assassination of UDA leaders by the Provisional IRA. Like many UDA figures, he himself was known to the IRA and was an easy target. He was able to lead a relatively normal life and had bought immunity from the Provos by occasionally providing them with information and appearing publicly as a reasonable man.

The murder of John McMichael had been sufficient to convince him that if the Provos selected a target, they proved relentless in their pursuit of that person. If the UDA were to be linked with Milltown, his own life would certainly be in jeopardy. He made the telephone calls before the UDA leadership had time to publicly disassociate itself from Stone.

While the RUC detectives were probing their files for information on the gunman, Det. James Craig tried to discover the killer's identity, and, on orders from above, anticipating Stone's refusal to reveal his name, he tried a different form of questioning. Craig surmised that if he could discover the organisation to which he was attached, the HQ staff could begin to search the files on relevant terrorist organisations.

Q.   What are you?
A.   I'm a freelance.

The reply only deepened the mystery surrounding the gunman, and Craig, whether on orders from his superiors, or as an orthodox tactic, asked if he was a member of the security forces, namely the RUC or UDR? The question embodied the character and complexity of Northern Ireland. Why should a policeman pose such a question? It would be an unlikely question to be put to someone who went on the rampage in a cemetery in Great Britain or in many other European cities.

Stone replied 'no' to the question, and further resisted Craig's attempts to discover his name. Craig noticed him peering uneasily at other people in the room, and suspected that the gunman did not wish to talk in the presence of hospital staff. The detective asked where he lived but was refused a reply. He enquired if he knew what he had done? Stone was willing to respond to any question which highlighted his actions in the cemetery and responded to a series of questions. He said he threw grenades, fired a Ruger and a 'Browning High-Power' and the Browning jammed. 'It was no use – those automatics,' he remarked.

He repeated an earlier claim that 'his driver fucked off on him'. As he became more lucid and voluble, Craig slipped a question into their dialogue: 'What is your proper name and address?'

Stone from a prone position beckoned Craig to him and whispered: 'I don't want the wee woman messed about.'

Craig assured him the police would not frighten his wife but they would search his house. Stone appeared content with the detective's promise and revealed his full name and address. He said there was nothing illegal at his home at 48 Ravenswood Park in the Braniel but a combat jacket was in the shed at the rear of the building. Craig walked from the room to inform his superiors of his good fortune but turned momentarily to deliver a final question. He asked Stone the name of his accomplice. Stone laughed and replied: 'Don't be stupid.'

Once Craig had informed HQ of the gunman's identity, a search party was tasked to Stone's home; the police military computers were scanned for information; and a decision was taken to remove Stone to more secure surroundings. The computers provided a file which categorized Stone as a criminal who was occasionally seen in the company of known paramilitaries; no hard evidence connected him to any terrorist offences or organisations. The RUC were puzzled and mystified. They were also concerned that the City Hospital would not remain safe from IRA attack, and until they had established Stone's connections and motivation, the risk also existed that loyalist groupings might snatch him, and spirit him to safety. The police could not be sure who had an interest in his survival or demise. A team led by Det. Constable Kenneth Shannon was dispatched to the hospital with orders to remove Stone to a secure unit, where a structured interrogation would be undertaken away from the prying eyes of regular hospital staff. The RUC knew from experience that the IRA, UVF and UDA had volunteers employed in hospitals who provided intelligence enabling active-service units to penetrate hospital security. In one instance, loyalist gunmen had entered the Mater Hospital on Belfast's Crumlin Road and murdered a patient, Maire Drumm, a leader of Provisional Sinn Fein.

The only reliable hospital unit was at Musgrave Park where a section of the grounds was under Army control. Stone was transferred to Ward 18 at 1555 hrs, and placed under the control of the ward security officer, Det. Sgt. Robert James Barr.

At 2000 hrs, Barr entered Stone's room to check his medical condition. Stone said he had no complaints and added: 'I am ready to talk to detectives any time. I might as well tell them everything.' It was exactly what Belfast CID wanted to hear: Dr Glenn Rowan at the hospital had declared Stone medically fit to be interviewed.

The officer given the task of interrogating Stone, Superintendent Derek Thomas Waites, selected a team of officers to provide a rotating interrogation plan in the days which followed. He chose men with considerable experience in the questioning of terrorists: Det. Chief Inspector David Russell, Det. Superintendent Harry Colgan, Det. Chief Inspector Robert Wilson, Det. Constable Henry Nixon and Det. Constable James Cunningham – a high-powered team, schooled in the art of evidence gathering, and of subtle questioning techniques.

While the RUC concentrated on unravelling the Stone mystery, large-scale rioting broke out in Catholic districts of Belfast, Newry and Derry. Police and Army patrols came under fire and terrorists threw blast bombs. Mobs rampaged through streets, hijacking vehicles and setting them alight. The President of Sinn Fein, Gerry Adams, issued a statement alleging police collusion in the massacre. He argued that the killer and accomplices had been informed of the intended low-security profile at the funerals.

The two gunmen involved alighted from a transit van in full view of two British Army helicopters. They carried holdalls and approached the republican plot. We assert they had prior notice from the Crown Forces that the RUC presence in the cemetery would be minimal.

A priest officiating at another funeral in the cemetery told an *Irish News* reporter he saw the van and assumed it was an RUC surveillance vehicle because it was parked at a point often used by the RUC for such a purpose. As speculation mounted and rioting increased, the RUC issued a press statement denying Adams's allegations and admitting the van was theirs. They said it was a traffic patrol vehicle. An RUC spokesman was asked why the van hastily departed the scene and he replied: 'If you were a policeman in uniform and a horde of people came rushing towards you from a republican funeral what would you do?'

The explanation seemed perfectly reasonable if the thesis were true. Stone believed the vehicle belonged to E4A, the controversial RUC undercover unit, which had been the subject of many enquiries by John Stalker, the English policeman who investigated allegations that members of E4A had been involved in a 'shoot-to-kill' policy against republicans. E4A managed to disguise many of its activities from Stalker, its connections with MI5, and its methods. After one controversial shooting, members of E4A held a drinks party and carried their commanding officer on their shoulders. As they paraded him in a drunken ritual they called themselves '—'s Commandos'.

Whatever the nature and purpose of the transit van the police version of its purpose and identity remains open to question. Stone claims he fired through the windscreen but that remains un-proven. One – unofficial – police source has indicated to me that the van was there for intelligence duties, and was therefore not stopped at a police cordon as it exited the motorway. It would be natural practice for the RUC undercover unit E4A to undertake surveillance of the cemetery at a discreet distance. After all, cameras operated in the sangars at Andersonstown Station, and

Military Intelligence had two helicopters in the air with sophisticated photographic equipment. The security authorities needed all
the photographic surveillance they could reasonably muster,
owing to their decision to maintain a low personnel profile at the
funerals. Intelligence analysts knew that the funerals would attract
large numbers of people, thereby providing wanted terrorists with
perfect cover to attend the burial service and, in respect of general
intelligence gathering on all republican suspects, it seemed
sensible to have an extensive photographic record of many of the
mourners.

Adams reacted to the RUC's description of the vehicle by asking
why it had taken the police almost eight hours to admit ownership
of it. He claimed that the van left the cemetery, and drove to the
British Army Barracks at Holywood on the outskirts of Belfast.
Martin Cowley, a reporter with the *Irish Times*, sent a story to his
news desk outlining eyewitness accounts of the van, and an
episode involving two cars parked close to it. The eyewitnesses
said they saw a Ford Sierra and red hatchback car park next to the
van.

The front passenger door of the van and the sliding door opened. One
person got out of the side door and one from the passenger door. The
person from the passenger door put an official-looking peaked cap on his
head. He was dressed in a uniform of sorts, of dark green or black. The
person who emerged from the sliding door was similarly dressed. They
both went to the red car. The occupants of the red car were already out.
The boot of the red car was already open. They did something there. They
were taking something out in the presence of the occupants. One of the
figures went to the blue Sierra and said something to the occupants.

The figure with the peaked cap then returned to his vehicle. Later three
people seemed to come from the red car, crossing waste ground at the
side of the motorway and up by the perimeter fence. We looked at them
and there seemed to be two men and a woman. The man in the middle
was dressed in a grey anorak or jacket and was carrying a holdhall. The
lady seemed to be carrying a bag over her shoulder.

When I first examined this evidence I was reminded of John Jordan
the taxi-driver who drove for the ABC film crew and almost became
one of Stone's victims. He told police he saw three men and a
woman walk into the cemetery from the M1 and remarked:

I thought they were a film crew and I remember thinking to myself they were a bit late to cover the funeral. You know what I mean, they were cutting it a bit fine.

Although Jordan's testimony differed numerically – he saw a fourth person – from the eyewitness accounts written by reporter Martin Cowley; it therefore was reasonable to assume that the strangers were a camera crew who were stopped by traffic officers in the transit van, told to remove their vehicle and make their way on foot through the cemetery. Anomalies materialise: camera crews rush to a scene, cameramen prepare the camera, carrying it, or shouldering it as soon as they remove it from the boot of a car; the archetypal image of a cameraman is of him moving with the camera on his shoulder, secured by his right hand. If the strangers were members of a *bona fide* film crew, they would have seen the mourners assembled at the plot and would have hurried to their task, and the cameraman would have looked like other members of his profession: anxious to get the job done. This reasoning does not rule out the possibility that they were members of a film crew, or that one of them was a stills photographer. But it is further strange that the subsequent publicity did not encourage a film crew or photographer to acknowledge publicly their, or his, presence in respect of the van controversy.

At Stone's subsequent trial, the van story did not feature. The van and its occupants were more significant than the strangers. One could easily argue that the strangers were a foreign film crew, or journalists who left the country the following day, unaware of the necessity for them to clarify their purpose and position in the cemetery.

But – in the course of researching this book, in matters related to tragic events which took place some days after the Milltown massacre, I uncovered the existence of a secret counter-insurgency unit which has operated in Northern Ireland for several years *without the knowledge of the RUC, politicians or the media* – of which more later; but at this stage I tentatively suggest the transit van may not have belonged to the RUC. The vehicle may have been part of this ultra-secret taskforce, and Provisional Sinn Fein President Gerry Adams may indeed have been correct in asserting that it travelled from Milltown to the military establishment at Holywood. It is conceivable the RUC was told to claim public responsibility for the van in order to prevent exposure of the secret unit.

While controversy raged over the Milltown massacre, mobs rampaged, and politicians issued familiar denunciations of violence, the RUC interrogation team, led by Det. Superintendent Derek Waites, began probing Michael Stone's history. They needed answers quickly to allay public opinion, and to lower the sectarian temperature on the streets. A confession would enable them to charge the killer, and demonstrate the nature of the RUC's professionalism and impartiality. While they debated their tactics, several men entered Stone's room, scrutinised him and talked in whispers. Stone did not know them, and the hospital has no records of their visits. They came from MI5 and Military Intelligence. Waites and his colleagues were not the only people interested in the lone gunman.

Stone had time to reflect and he says he felt angry that he failed in his plan to kill Adams and McGuinness. He regretted that he didn't kill more people, and that his Browning failed him when he most needed it, and he expressed bitterness that his two accomplices did not appear to spirit him to safety. One of them fled to England, and the other was court-martialled by the UFF but Stone requested that he should not be punished. The man who fled was later contacted by relatives, and advised that he could return safely to Belfast. As Stone lay nursing his wounds, particularly the swelling which made speech a painful exercise, he was faced with the prospect of life imprisonment – a killer caught red-handed. The question now – would his ego, his insatiable appetite for self-esteem, spur him to admit to other crimes?

12

Interrogation and Trial

Stone felt no remorse about the killings and maimings at Milltown. The presence of so many people, however innocent, at the IRA funerals was sufficient to warrant his hatred. He expressed his views with clarity when he was captured, regretting that he only killed three people, and thus regarding his operation as a failure. In one of his letters to me, he said that he often sat in his cell and relived the Milltown experience.

Do I have any regrets? Of course I do. Any man who says he doesn't is full of it. I regret this war has not ended, and that my last operation was a failure in that I failed to achieve the military objective, i.e. the termination of the President and Vice-President of Provisional Sinn Fein (PIRA). My greatest regret is that my children will never really know me and I them. I had hoped this war would have ended – that they would have had a chance to grow up in a normal integrated society – free from bigotry or sectarian strife. I fear that this is now an impossibility as the political and religious gulf has widened. The abnormal has become the normal. After some twenty-one years of conflict, today's teenagers, our war babies, have been indoctrinated from birth.

Within all Stone's letters is an element of revisionist thinking, typifying the mind of a man who prefers to be seen as a thinking ideologue, not one motivated by hatred of the other community. In his many conversations with me he constantly revised his history in an attempt to portray himself as a soldier of conscience. When he threw the grenades into the midst of so many funeral-goers, his intention was to kill as many as possible, as witness his remarks to the policemen who saved his life: 'How many of the cunts did I get?'

His regret that he failed to commit more murders in the cemetery hardly accorded with his professed concern for today's teenagers. Stone's actions helped to fan the hatred and sectarian aggression which provided fertile recruiting ground for paramilitaries on both sides, and dragged many young men into the spiral of revenge violence.

I have never been a threat to society, i.e. the law-abiding nationalist population. I was most certainly a threat to those PIRA terrorists who wage unjustifiable war against Ulster's innocent mixed population.

The above remarks, made by Stone in a letter to me on 13 November 1990, again reflect his desire to be seen as a non-sectarian soldier. He frequently reminded me that he did not harbour hatred of Catholics, yet his killing career did not support his contention. Since then, life in prison has permitted him time to refashion his image, and seek to erase the tabloid view of him as a mad sectarian killer. His preference for a reasoned logic rooted in a 'just war' ethos also exemplified a man concerned about the way others viewed him. Remorse has never come across as central to his thinking; a preoccupation with self-image has appeared repeatedly.

For instance (albeit a small detail), Stone has constantly reminded me that I should not assume that the clothing he wore on the day of the Milltown operation offered sound evidence of his dress sense. Frequently he pointed out that his language when arrested did not exemplify his normal choice of words. He did not, he argued, use words like 'cunt' in his day-to-day conversations.

I hope when you research my dealings with the police you don't think I normally spoke that way. I was highly charged and when I talked to police I was in pain, my mouth was sore.

In one of his letters from the prison he ended by asking me to excuse misspelling and added:

my usual apologies not forgetting the scribble, well its a case of horses for courses, I know its my excuse and I'm sticking to it.

(Until late 1991, when he suddenly began to employ an elaborate handwriting style, all his correspondence with me was written in capital letters.)

If Michael Stone learned anything from the Milltown massacre it was to be found in his growing appreciation for the policemen who saved his life. Their actions prompted him to admit that the RUC played a valuable role in society. He referred to them as 'the official forces' and told me it was important they 'survived' to protect society from 'rapists, thieves and other such criminal parasites'. All loyalist prisoners' families, he said, needed police protection.

The RUC have never done me any favours in the past but on 16.3.88 they not only arrested me after the Milltown operation but they saved my life. They risked their lives to save mine. Granted they were carrying out their duty but what can one say except 'thank you'.

His gratitude towards the RUC was not reciprocated confessionally when Superintendent Derek Waites arrived at Musgrave Park Hospital to interrogate him at 9.45 p.m. on 16 March 1988. When Waites cautioned him that anything he said would be noted and maybe used in evidence, Stone asked whether police had recovered his guns and remarked that his injuries had left him sore.

He did, however, identify the weapons as a Ruger .357 pistol and a 9mm Browning automatic, and promised he would 'tell them all about Milltown and some other jobs', then told Waites he was 'tired and wanted to sleep'. Waites tried to probe him with further questions, but found Stone too uncooperative, and reckoned it preferable to return the following morning.

At 10.30 a.m. on 17 March, Waites, accompanied by Det. Chief Inspector Russell, visited Stone and again cautioned him. Stone, in a lively mood, appeared willing to confess to his crimes. He told the police that he would tell them 'the score', and added that he knew he was facing life imprisonment.

Waites asked him to begin his story with an outline of how he acquired the weaponry used in Milltown, but Stone replied that he was 'a loner', and stole the weaponry from an arms dump belonging to a loyalist paramilitary organisation. He reinforced his assertion that he was not a member of any grouping, and emphasised his commitment to withhold the names of his associates. Waites pointed out a previous comment by Stone in which he said 'his mate fucked off on him' at Milltown. Stone stared down his interrogators, saying he had acted alone the previous day.

Waites refused to be diverted from his own line of thought and reminded Stone of his promise of the previous day to 'tell them the score'. Stone retorted that he undertook operations for 'the UDA, UFF, UVF, everybody' and added: 'Look lads, let's talk about yesterday. I'll maybe talk about other jobs later, we'll see.'

Determined to discuss the events in Milltown, he made it obvious that he revelled in his cemetery exploits, and with gleeful anticipation waited for the detectives to relive the experience with him. Waites chose to control the conversation with an examination of events, beginning with Stone's procurement of the weapons. 'Where was the arms dump you referred to?' he asked.

Stone replied it was in the grounds of Shandon Park golf course adjacent to the Braniel estate. This revelation was immediately conveyed to RUC HQ and search teams were detached to a section of the course identified by Stone.

The information was bogus, and police time was wasted tearing up sections of the golf course in search of an arms cache.

In one of my meetings with Stone I enquired why he chose to send police on a 'wild goose chase', and pointed to his praise for the RUC in one of his letters; did his actions conflict with his words? His answer gave an insight into his working-class roots, and resentment of people socially his betters.

I didn't do it to annoy the cops. It was my way of sickening the snobs who used Shandon Park Golf Club. I knew the police would go there and tear the place up and when that got into the papers it would wreck their clean-cut image. The bastards who used the place thought they were better than the rest of us.

Shandon Park Club, a respectable institution with a good reputation, has a mostly Protestant and middle-class membership; Stone lived near by.

While the police were searching Shandon grounds, Stone talked to Waites, and persisted in his determination to discuss the Milltown massacre. He began by discussing the clothes he wore during the operation and he spared no detail, informing Waites his anorak cost £7, his boots were 'black dealer-type'. Occasionally Stone punctuated his observations with questions about newspaper reaction to his exploits, anxious to know how the world viewed his killing spree.

The Times of 17 March referred, in its leader column, to 'Ulster's vicious circle', and described the images of Milltown as eloquent portraits of the psychological effects of terrorism: the circle of murder and injury, followed by fear and terror, followed in turn by revenge taken on the instigators of violence. The leader-writer defined three lessons to be learned from the event:

First and most obviously, the police have to show eternal vigilance; they now have to act on the assumption that nothing is sacred any longer. The second lesson takes the form of a question for those who have presumed that the shooting of the Provisional IRA bombers in Gibraltar cannot be justified. Suppose, for argument's sake, that the Royal Ulster Constabulary had known of the planned attack on the crowd in advance. Suppose there existed a possibility that the attacker carried, or controlled, primed explosives. Suppose that he could be intercepted only close to the edge of the crowd. Should a normal arrest have been made; or should he have been shot with or without warning?

Should *The Times* leader-writer have posed further questions? Why were the firepower and sophisticated weapon sights available at Andersonstown barracks not used to eliminate the gunman, for a long period a clear target in open ground? Why did those in the transit van, assuming them to be police, not shoot the gunman as he reached their position? After all, he was still armed, and dangerous, and only moments from causing more casualties? The third lesson outlined by the leader-writer, addressed –

the Roman Catholic clergy. Those in Northern Ireland have issued general condemnations of violence with great frequency in the past twenty years. But there are those among them who have also yielded to the temptation to paint a romantic picture of terrorists. There were innocent people among the dead yesterday. But the priest who compared Ms Mairead Farrell to Jesus and who described her death as the barbarous assassination of someone out for a walk on a sunny afternoon went far beyond what was necessary or appropriate.

Such distortions of moral reality, whatever their provenance, can never justify violence of any kind, but in current circumstances they make their own contribution to the heightening of communal tension. Everyone in Northern Ireland now has a contribution to make to the reduction of tension and mistrust.

The Times leader, a blinkered piece of writing, nevertheless contained lessons for the Catholic population, its politicians and clergy; yet bore too distinctive a mark of someone ignorant of the complexities of Northern Ireland and without the sophistication to understand that there were lessons for the whole community. Since the loyalist section of society would shortly revere Michael Stone, the Milltown killings also demonstrated with shocking clarity that violence did not emanate only from within the Catholic community.

The tabloid press reacted to the story by calling the Milltown gunman a 'loner', a 'psychopathic killer', a 'madman', a 'Rambo'. Their coverage accorded with the television news images of Stone running, firing and throwing grenades.

In the *Independent* the New York correspondent, Leonard Doyle, worried that the incident would 'set back British efforts to stop Irish Americans supporting the IRA'. He quoted a publisher of Irish-American periodicals:

This is the latest in a series of events that will ensure the Noraid collection boxes will be bulging on St Patrick's Day. I think the callousness of the British approach on Gibraltar, the Birmingham Six, Stalker . . . is the best recruiting agent for IRA supporters in America since the death of the hunger striker, Bobby Sands. I foresee a very emotional reaction to recent events. It is like Enniskillen never happened.

Ironically, given Stone's original purpose for such a simple large-scale act of revenge, his actions detracted from the universal condemnation of the IRA's barbarity at the Enniskillen cenotaph. The Milltown massacre now erased that carnage in the minds of those vulnerable to IRA propaganda; it temporarily obliterated the need to be reminded constantly of the suffering and compassion of those who survived Enniskillen. None of the papers sought to link the tragedies, other than by the very fact they happened, and the latter possibly took place in revenge for the first. Milltown was no more than a reminder of Enniskillen, of the futility of violence and the savagery lurking within both communities.

Several newspapers continued to search for answers to the presence and role of those in the transit van, while politicians engaged in a futile debate about whether the RUC role at the funerals was designed to allow for such a chain of events – to which the RUC responded by clarifying its position in a statement to the media:

The Roman Catholic Church had confidently expressed its belief that no illegality would occur. The Church was deeply convinced that the families wanted the funerals to be quiet, peaceful and dignified. And the

Church believed there was a strong public desire that there should be no exploitation of the funerals for political or paramilitary purposes. SDLP politicians having castigated the RUC for their presence at previous funerals made strong representations to the police to change their stance on this occasion. Being aware from previous experience that paramilitary elements would exploit the presence of the police and create situations for their propaganda purposes, and in the trust there would be no breaches of the law, a decision was taken not to breach these funerals as in the past. This was done in the hope that this whole distasteful problem of paramilitary funerals would be resolved now and for the future.

Support for the RUC policy at the funerals came from the Catholic bishop, Dr Cahal Daly, who said they 'got it right'. He reckoned the killings would have taken place irrespective of the police decision to maintain a low profile.

The Belfast *Irish News* devoted part of its editorial to the Secretary of State, Tom King's, continued refusal to ban the UDA.

It is not good enough for the British Secretary of State to use his vocabulary of outrage and sit back and wait for the next atrocity. He could have a look at the absurd existence of legal paramilitaries. He could consider telling the British Army and RUC that they exist – and are generally paid to work – within the law and to apply that law with equal courtesy to every person they come into contact with. He could urge his colleagues at Westminster to remember that if you prick the Irish they also bleed. He could remember the dead of Milltown as he remembered the dead at Enniskillen.

Suddenly, many issues, peripheral to the events at Milltown, surfaced in newspapers that morning. Tom King was also pressed by politicians to clarify his attitude to the UDA. The question of whether it was tactically possible or judicious to proscribe the UDA was irrelevant; the intelligence community constantly argued privately there was nothing to be gained from proscription. They believed while the UDA remained a legal body it was possible to maintain surveillance on its leaders and its recruits. Once it was made illegal, it would become an underground terrorist organisation more difficult to penetrate. The argument possessed some logic, but they would not propose that the IRA should be made legal. But can society function according to democratic principles, when the principles are not embodied in equilateral action; permitting *any* terrorists any legality erodes the very fabric of democracy. The expedient arguments of the intelligence community, *per se*, present contradictions dangerous in a divided community, where the rule of law must apply equally.

The UDA recognised the risks to its status and issued its own statement denying any association with Stone. In a further attempt to distance itself from the atrocity, a member of the organisation's leadership, the Inner Council, provided off-the-record press briefings, similar to one later given to Deric Henderson of the *Belfast Telegraph*:

Stone approached us [*said the UDA spokesman*] and said he wanted to join, but we took the view he was too extreme. He had all these hare-brained ideas. He would offer to strap himself full of explosives and go into Sinn Fein headquarters. But some people felt he could be useful and he had an association with people who are now former members of the organisation. I think it is only proper to point out that he had associations with loyalist organisations. He was a freelance, a mercenary.

The person who gave some of the briefings was the Inner Council member to whom I referred, in a previous chapter, as an MI5 informer/agent. His motive was to distance the UDA from Stone, and to cast Stone as a crazed psychopath.

By now, the IRA and Sinn Fein saw some advantage to be gained from exploiting the press scrutiny of the events. They were in possession of the Ruger revolver and Browning pistol. Sinn Fein circulated photographs of the weapons, indicating, if without proof, that the Ruger was a police-issue weapon, and alleging that a woman seen in the cemetery had acted in collusion with Stone.

The RUC were also concerned about the Ruger, but made no public mention of their fear that it might have been a police weapon. Superintendent Derek Waites had the issue firmly fixed in his interrogation agenda on the morning of 17 March, but found Stone non-committal on the origins of the gun.

Instead, Stone persisted with details of his dress and demeanour as he left home for the cemetery. He said he was cool-headed, had not taken drugs or alcohol, and didn't smoke. His approach to interrogation proved frustrating; intermittently he detached his thoughts from his dialogue.

'Did I miss the boy in the van?' he asked Waites.

'What van?' retorted Waites.

'Beige van, big one, two in it. I cracked at one of them,' Stone replied. He then offered a vivid description and Waites made the following note:

I opened my clothes, got out two grenades, pulled the pins, I lobbed them into the people wearing berets and the flags. Everyone turned and looked at me. I pulled out the Browning. On lower ground there was women and children. I was on lower ground again. Emptied the mag into the mass of people on higher ground. They were the main republican mourners from all over the country. I was wanting them. I wanted to kill. Not ordinary women and children. If I wanted Catholics I could get them down the street. Turned round to walk again. Wasn't goin' to run. I took out the Ruger. A skinny fella went to jump out from a beige van, passenger side. I fired in his direction. There was a fattish man in the van. Crowds started closing in. Popped one more grenade at these boys. They were throwing bits of gravestones and wee urns at me. They were cowards. They were shouting 'Orange bastard'.

Stone's language was delivered staccato, as though reliving everything he described. Waites listened to Stone's stark account, detail omitted as the monologue increased in pace.

I got up and started firing the Ruger at these cunts coming at me. I was at the end of the fen. I had two empty guns. I sat down to reload the Browning, dropped clip of Browning and reloaded. I banged off two from where I was sitting. She jammed. Crowds shouted: 'he's out of ammo'. I threw a grenade. You want to have seen the water it threw up, and the screams of the boys.

When he completed his story, Waites asked why he gave police a fictitious name. He said he gave his stepfather's name and he was 'an old boy'. His motive concerned his suspicion of hospital porters. He did not trust hospital staff because they might be republicans.

Waites terminated the interrogation at midday to permit Stone to have lunch, and recommenced at 12.40 p.m. In the court record of Stone's trial, Waites's statement contained the following account of his interview with Stone:

He was questioned, was he sure he was the only one there and he insisted he was. He was asked by myself, 'Do you know a man called Robert Montgomery?' Stone replied: 'Ah fuck, spin-'em Rab.' He was asked what he meant. Stone explained he was always spinning yarns, and laughed. Stone kept joking and said, no way he was on his own, Montgomery wasn't there, and explained because Montgomery was ex-Army he thought he was in on it and that was not the case. He insisted that he (Stone) is a loner and said: 'I was on my puff.'

Stone provided Waites with information of the killing of Brady in Boucher Road adding: 'I done him with a pump [pump-action shotgun]. I left a number 4 cartridge in the car.' He didn't reveal the type of gun but convinced Waites of his role in the killing. He listed other killings and attempted murders and much of his dialogue was littered with expletives when he discussed his abortive attempt to murder Sinn Fein official, John Joe Davey, he told Waites:

I was carrying the Ruger, the one I had yesterday. I fired four at Davey in the car. Davey got out of the car through fields. Big fat cunt really moved.

He refused to name his accomplices in each operation, but was pleased to offer graphic descriptions of his individual actions.

The following morning Det. Superintendent Harry Colgan and Det. Chief Inspector Wilson replaced Waites and Russell. Stone told Colgan he was willing to make statements about all his crimes because he had no wish to be rearrested at a future date, or released from prison, and charged with something he could now reveal. He set familiar terms of reference for his interrogation, pointing out that he would not name accomplices, and would resist all attempts to make him do so. Then, he gave them a statement outlining his role in the killing of the milkman at Boucher Road.

The interrogation sessions continued for days and on one occasion Stone showed a slight element of regret when he confided in Waites he had not killed McPolin with greater efficiency. 'I felt bad I didn't do the job right and caused him to suffer,' he told Waites, an example of Stone being concerned more with his killing methods than the victim's fate. He took pride in his use of guns, and was embarrassed when he learned how McPolin crawled from his car along the roadway. He revealed to Waites his annoyance at reading press accounts of how McPolin died, and he justified the killing by trying to encourage Waites in the belief that his victim was a member of an IRA active-service unit.

On 21 March, Det. Constables Nixon and Cunningham, who had worked extensively during Stone's numerous interrogation sessions, visited his hospital room at 3.30 p.m., briefed by Waites, Colgan and Russell to pursue a line of questioning about the origins of the Ruger pistol. Waites knew that loyalist paramilitaries had acquired 9mm Brownings in arms deals, but not Rugers. It was important to isolate the Ruger and discover its history; the RUC hierarchy were concerned the gun might have been given to Stone by a rogue policeman. Their fears were exacerbated knowing that the Provisionals were now in possession of the weapon, and might trace its history. If a police-issue gun, the IRA would derive propaganda from such a revelation – which would further fuel suspicion of RUC involvement in the Milltown killings. Unknown to Waites and his team, the gun was indeed an RUC weapon and Stone knew its history. While Stone was in hospital he reflected on his possession of it, and became concerned on two counts: firstly, if he revealed how he came to be in possession of it he risked retribution from his terrorist accomplices, and secondly if the police discovered its history, by coincidence, their disclosure of that knowledge might lead his accomplices to believe him responsible for such a revelation. From the outset of his interrogation he repeatedly asked police, particularly Waites, whether the guns had been recovered?

Before Milltown, Stone had tried unsuccessfully to remove the serial number of the weapon by which it could be traced to its lawful owner – according to a loyalist source, the gun belonged to a serving policeman; he committed suicide prior to Stone's trial. Over a year later, the IRA used the gun to kill two policemen at security gates in High Street in Belfast city centre.

Cunningham and Nixon kept a detailed note of their questioning of Stone *re* the Ruger:

Q. The Ruger revolver you had with you on Wednesday, where did you get it?
A. I was given it and told it came from a burglary.
Q. What part of Northern Ireland did it come from?
A. I don't know.
Q. Do you remember the serial number of this weapon?
A. No.
Q. Did you see a serial number on this gun?
A. Yes.
Q. Was it clearly visible?
A. Yes.
Q. Did you remove the serial number from this gun?
A. No but someone tried to rub it off with a file but failed.
Q. Are you sure you never removed any number from the Ruger?
A. Positive. When I had it with me on Wednesday the serial number was still on.
Q. Can you remember any of the digits of this number?
A. No it was stamped at the bottom of the grip and on the side.

The questioning proved futile, as did police attempts to pin other murders on Stone. Waites was convinced that he had killed someone in July 1987 in East Belfast, and Colgan was detailed to question him about it.

The victim, a Catholic, Kevin 'Mungo' Mulligan, died of gunshot wounds, coincidentally on the day of the Milltown massacre. He had been shot in the stomach with a shotgun, and Waites believed that the killing had the hallmark of a Stone-style operation. Despite Mulligan's extensive injuries, he survived for over eight months. Stone refused to admit responsibility, saying he would never have operated 'close to home', being, he claimed, too well known. Waites and his colleagues had a long list of killings similar in character to those admitted by Stone, but they failed to encourage him towards a confession. Among the crimes which he denied was the double killing of Mrs Mullen and her son, and in denying those he stressed he did not kill women. His denial rang hollow to these policemen investigating the carnage at Milltown, in which many women were injured terribly by shrapnel, and were considered lucky not to die. Stone mesmerised his interrogators with his detailed recollection of events in which he was involved, and he constantly referred to security forces' photographs of his targets, photographs taken at IRA funerals.

On 22 March at 4.10 p.m. Stone was led to the police office at Townhall Street in Belfast, and confronted by Waites, who arrested him and preferred six charges of murder. The first three related to the Milltown deaths, and Stone listened intently to the charges but did not speak, until Waites completed a reading of the names of the three victims.

In answer to the three charges I want to say that I alone carried out the military operation as a retaliatory strike against Provisional Sinn Fein, IRA in response to the slaughter of innocents at La Mon, Darkley, Brighton and Enniskillen. I would state I am a dedicated freelance loyalist paramilitary. No surrender.

Waites, unimpressed by the well-rehearsed speech, continued with the other charges. In respect of the other charges, namely the murders of Brady, Hackett and McPolin, Stone replied to each: 'I read his file. He was a legitimate target.'

Stone says that, to his pleasure, while he was in a police cell at the police office, and during subsequent court hearings, policemen guarding him requested his autograph. He claims that he signed his name on copies of the police gazette with messages such as 'good wishes'. In loyalist areas, people had begun writing songs about him, and painting his name on gable walls. The UDA remained publicly detached from him, and the UVF refused to reveal its relations with him except to state privately that it would not disown him.

Arrested, in custody, and charged, Stone's contribution to violence was not over. His awful spree at Milltown was yet to unleash the revenge motive in the Catholic community – with tragic consequences.

13

Violence Breeds Barbarousness

The 'Milltown Massacre' increased tribal divisions, and generated a clamour for revenge. Heightened tension became the cumulative effect of the killing of the Gibraltar trio and the cemetery murders. Particularly in Catholic districts of West Belfast, Catholic anger was directed at the security forces and loyalists. Catholics who harboured guilt about the IRA atrocity in Enniskillen were now, to a degree, liberated from their guilt, and felt more comfortable in supporting IRA claims that the security forces had colluded with Stone in the Milltown killings. The atmosphere in West Belfast grew tense, with violent passions willing to be ignited.

In West Belfast, twenty-four hours after the Milltown tragedy, multitudes of young men stood on street corners, their glances directed at every passing car, suspicious that it might harbour another Michael Stone. In this part of Belfast, people were conditioned to detect the presence of strangers. Years of violence, which had included incursions by loyalist killer-squads, and shootings by undercover soldiers in unmarked cars, engendered suspicion of anyone entering the area who was not instantly identifiable as a non-combatant. The area resembled a fortress, with police and military watchtowers on every approach road and exit. Every security-force command post was screened by high fencing, and protected by elaborate security surveillance systems. The fencing was designed to prevent mortar shells or RPG7 rockets from entering the inner compound.

The military did not restrict its surveillance operations to ground posts but established heavily guarded observation towers on high-rise flats, which offered a panoramic view of the sprawling estates of West Belfast. On the roof of Divis Flats, soldiers hidden in a concrete bunker scanned the streets with cameras and high-powered binoculars every moment of every day. In the sky above, two helicopters with 'heli-teli' (long-range cameras) supplied constant pictures of the life below. These pictures were transmitted to monitors at Woodburn Army base, and relayed to other stations in the district. The concentration of security devices and personnel made inhabitants and visitors alike uneasy and wary.

The whole area was the theatre of war for undercover soldiers from the 14th Intelligence Company (sometimes known as the 14th Independent Company) and the Special Air Service. They operated in unmarked cars, on foot or concealed in derelict buildings, and the secret of their success was to blend into the atmosphere of the streets, and to look and behave as though they lived there. SAS teams of four men often spent weeks in the roof spaces of abandoned houses watching streets through holes in the brickwork or in the slating. Members of 14th Intelligence regularly travelled in cars, generally two-man teams with a back-up team operating at a distance which permitted swift support action. Within 14th Intelligence were several female operatives who accompanied their male colleagues. The female soldiers were not simply there to ensure that a male colleague appeared to be accompanied by a wife or girlfriend, but to act with the same clinical ferocity when required. Women in 14th Intelligence were equally adept at surveillance and eliminating terrorists, though they did not always display the marksmanship of their male counterparts. In 1989 a female operative pursued a UVF hitman from the scene of a sectarian murder in North Belfast. The killer was the pillion passenger on a motorbike, which was then rammed by a car driven by 14th Intelligence operatives. A female undercover soldier in the car was tasked to kill the UVF hitman, and she emerged from the car and quickly fired four bullets into the back of her target. She did not succeed in killing him, and quickly rushed forward to where he lay immobilised and injured, where she dispatched him with two bullets to the skull. An internal 14 Intelligence investigation found that she failed to immobilise the killer with her first two shots, and she was returned to base in England to undergo further firearms training. Her superiors had concluded that she left herself at risk by not removing accurately the threat to herself with the first fusilade of bullets. The UVF hitman staggered but was still on his feet after the first volley of two bullets hit him. She eventually returned to Belfast, and was based in the west of the city in 1991.

The operations of undercover soldiers worried the paramilitaries in both communities, and increased their suspicion of strangers. In republican districts, where security forces concentrated most of their efforts, the arrival of a car unknown to residents attracted the attention of IRA scouts, who stood on street corners observing all passing traffic; in West Belfast all cars belonging to residents were known to all IRA volunteers. IRA and undercover operatives played a deadly cat-and-mouse game, in contrast to the early years of the conflict when street confrontations and gunbattles characterised the violence.

In the 1980s, the conflict became a dirty war, in which under-cover tactics determined the failure or success of security policy. SAS and 14th Intelligence were not designed for street warfare, but for eliminating the enemy wherever possible, thus reducing the debate about whether there was a 'shoot-to-kill' policy by the security forces to a mere academic exercise. Sufficient evidence now shows that SAS and 14th Intelligence operatives were, and are, tasked to kill rather than arrest suspected terrorists. The recurring tactic of disabling terrorists with bullets to the torso and then shooting them through the head clearly validates the claim that extirpation was and remains a military objective: 'to termi-nate with extreme prejudice'.

In many controversial shootings by secret military groupings, whatever the merits of subsequent military claims that targets were armed, or were escaping unarmed from an operation, in the majority of cases the order was to eliminate the terrorists. They do not seek to arrest them, on the basis that a dead terrorist is preferable to one who might serve a prison sentence, and be back on the streets within 5–10 years. Many people believe this to be an admirable and necessary military tactic, but it raises difficult questions, not least in that it offers a form of counter-terror. This in turn presents problems for any democracy seeking to isolate the terrorist on account of his inhumanity. In several instances terrorists and common criminals have been swiftly immobilised, and thus pose no threat – yet have then been dispatched clinically, and by security forces charged with upholding the rule of law. Such incidents reinforce the view of assassination techniques as an acceptable method of warfare. In Northern Ireland, this exacer-bates suspicion among Catholics that justice is unattainable; it also provides the IRA with much-needed propaganda. The presence of a shoot-to-kill policy becomes irrelevant if there is a perceivable tacit agreement in official circles that such methods are not only permissible but necessary. Such activities undermine the RUC's attempts to present a fair and impartial, if not wholly moral, security policy. It remains crucial, and increasingly so, that those empowered with responsibility for security can ensure that the need to combat terrorism is undertaken with a respect for the general sanctity of human life, something terrorists do not possess. Undercover soldiers may be essential to protecting society in conditions such as those prevailing in Northern Ireland, and it is understandable that they are required to defend themselves and the public, but not at the expense of demonstrating a casual and barbaric disrespect for life.

In 1989 three common criminals were shot outside a book-maker's in West Belfast. Two of the men carried imitation weapons; each was struck by several bullets while they posed no threat; on the ground they were then shot through the head at close range. The third criminal, unarmed, and sitting in a getaway car, was shot dead from close range. A member of the security forces, from the 14th Intelligence who carried out the triple killing, spoke to me in 1991:

The military team was run by an experienced operative who was older than his colleagues. He shot the guy sitting in the car. He said when he delivered the first shots he watched the guy twitch as the bullets struck him. He described it graphically and the way the guy's body reacted to the impact of the bullets. He reckoned he was still alive and told his colleague, the youngest member of the team, to finish him off. It was his way of letting the younger operative experience the sensation of killing someone.

(The older member of the team was still working from a West Belfast base in the autumn of 1991.)

The killings illustrated this entire, deeply questionable tactic; and the shooting of the unarmed criminal amounted to murder. Yet, no member of 14th Intelligence was charged in respect of any or all of the three deaths, suggesting afresh that such tactics had become an acceptable part of military policy.

Too many journalists have ignored the nature of the undercover war, and have acquiesced with official accounts of shootings. The tabloid press contends that the killing of every terrorist is justifiable homicide and government reprimands those who disagree with that view. In British society, one of the most closed in Western Europe, it becomes every day more vital that writers scrutinise the activities of any military groupings operating outside of the law.

Many obstacles face police officers who attempt to examine such operations, or shootings carried out by undercover military units. RUC CID is not permitted access to the working of secret units, or those who control them such as MI5; Military Intelligence prefer no scrutiny of their operations.

Now, and alarmingly, the issue is much more serious than simply the activities of the SAS and 14th Intelligence. In Northern Ireland, there have been groupings run by MI5 and Military Intelligence who are not listed on Army files – so that their existence can be denied. In the past, some covert units have been given bogus names, which implied a role for which they were not designed; e.g. 'Field Survey Troop' was an MI5/Military Intelligence organisation which undertook duties in Northern Ireland in the 1970s, with a base of operations in South Armagh, although it did not confine its activities to that area.

One of its workers, Captain Robert Nairac, was captured, interrogated and killed by the IRA. In answer to a parliamentary question in 1978, the group's existence was revealed, but all files relating to it were destroyed. The government minister who made that revelation had the audacity – or the lack of information – to assert that the role of Four Field Survey Troop was reconnaissance and map-reading, and that it was affiliated to the Royal Engineers. His story epitomises the willingness of government to ensure that secret groupings would never be accountable for their actions, nor would government.

On 19 March, three days after the Milltown killings, amid IRA claims that Stone operated with the connivance of undercover units, the RUC maintained its policy of a low profile, as the IRA prepared to bury 30-year-old Kevin Brady. The only Milltown fatality with republican affiliations, his funeral provided the Provisionals with an opportunity to capitalise on public anger and sympathy. Local priests in Andersonstown received assurances that there would be no paramilitary trappings, aside from the habitual leather gloves and beret placed on the coffin after the requisite church service from St Agnes on the Andersonstown Road. Women and children were discouraged from attending the funeral procession and, in particular, the burial service at

Milltown. IRA and Sinn Fein spokesmen stressed the risk of another loyalist attack, but reassured people that they had prepared for it. The Provisionals organised elaborate security precautions and detailed a large number of their men to patrol streets leading to St Agnes' Church, the funeral route along Andersonstown Road, and the grounds of the cemetery. These IRA spotters wore walkie-talkies to connect them to a base in a house within Andersonstown. Mary Holland, an experienced journalist with the *Irish Times*, later reflected on the nature of the IRA security precautions:

Police were nowhere to be seen and the only evidence of a security presence was a British Army helicopter hovering over Milltown Cemetery. The Provisionals had made their own arrangements to protect mourners. All of us arriving at St Agnes' Church on the Andersonstown Road were searched, no cameras were allowed inside, and stewards with walkie-talkies patrolled the area.

The priest officiating at the requiem mass spoke to mourners of a desire for peace in a 'bewildered community'. At noon, the cortège left the church followed by leading members of Sinn Fein and thousands of mourners. On the roadway lined with people, it soon became apparent that fewer women and children were present; many young men appeared prominently in the cortège, and within the ranks of the pavement spectators. Ahead of the hearse a line of London-type cabs led the entire funeral procession, designed, it seemed, to provide a battering ram in the event of a frontal assault on the funeral procession. The cabs, locally known as 'black taxis', originated on the streets of Belfast at the beginning of the Troubles, providing an alternative means of transport to the beleaguered city's bus service. When they were first introduced, they were illegal and drivers paid a weekly subsidy to the IRA. Government frequently tried in vain to remove them from service; each time legal steps were taken to end their service, the IRA responded by burning buses. Eventually, in a stand-off, government concluded it preferable to permit the taxi operation and make it legal, thus ending retaliatory action against the bus service. The government decision did not prevent taxi subscriptions to the IRA, nor the creation of a black-taxi service in loyalist districts. Black taxis offered cheaper rates than buses, and suited the anti-government lobby, particularly in republican neighbourhoods where the knowledge that the bus service was owned by the State gave sufficient justification for supporting an alternative service.

The history of black taxis, and their obvious connection with paramilitaries, ensured that their drivers became terrorist targets. On the one hand, loyalist murder-squads constantly used the taxis to carry out atrocities; whereas in West Belfast, many of the drivers were republicans. The political character of 'black taxi' drivers in republican areas was best illustrated when the undercover soldiers shot the three criminals at Graham's betting shop. As the soldiers made their escape several taxis were used to block their route and almost succeeded in leaving the soldiers to the mercy of mob violence.

On 19 March, the 'black taxis' moved ahead of the Kevin Brady funeral procession. Within two hundred yards of the church, a silver Volkswagen Passat approached the cortège at speed. The driver of the Passat recognised that his path countrywards was blocked, and he attempted to drive into a sidestreet – but his route was blocked by 'black taxis'. The silver car mounted the pavement, and with its retreat citywards now blocked by a phalanx of black cabs it turned towards the hearse at speed. Within seconds it came to a halt, hemmed in by taxis and a surging mob.

Two men were in the car, one of them dressed in a pale green sweater. Television cameras captured the scene as the mob, many of them mourners, descended on the car. Mary Holland of the *Irish Times* heard a shot ring out and saw youths surging towards the car; a man armed with an iron bar climbed on to the roof of the vehicle. Wheel braces were used to smash the windows of the car, as the mob tried to drag the occupants from the vehicle.

The televised sequences of the incident resembled a lynching scene – violence and uncontrolled hatred on the faces of the attackers; terror on the features of the car's occupants. To a casual observer, who did not know Northern Ireland, or who was unaware that these events were news coverage, it might have looked like a scene from a low-budget American movie.

One of the men in the car, a pistol in his hand, levered his body upwards out of the driver's window. The fury of the mob was unrelenting; nothing was going to intimidate them. The two occupants of the car, both of whom were armed, probably sensed that their guns provided no protection or deterrent. They were soon repeatedly beaten with wheel braces, and pulled clear of the car interior. Members of the IRA then took the pair from the mob and dragged them into the grounds of Casement Park, a centre for Gaelic football and hurling.

The IRA had obviously prepared for such an eventuality, and in the park they savagely beat and interrogated the two men; the gates to the park were locked and the press denied access. IRA men stripped their victims to their socks and underpants and continued to kick and strike them, asking who they were, and why they were there. The victims replied they were soldiers from the Royal Corps of Signals and protested their innocence. After five minutes the almost lifeless soldiers were hurled over a wall into a lane at the side of Casement Park. A 'black taxi' reversed into the lane and several IRA men bundled the soldiers into the vehicle and drove across Andersonstown Road into an area of waste ground near St Agnes Community Centre. Mary Holland heard shots and made her way towards the community centre.

Shopkeepers started pulling down their steel shutters as I walked up the road and into the car-park. A small crowd which had gathered there began to melt away. One young man passed me and said: 'Short and sweet, good enough for him.' I saw a priest kneeling beside the body of a young man, stripped down to his underpants and shoes and socks with blood on his chest and head. Fr. Alex Reid was administering the last rites, making the sign of the cross on the young man's lips. His eyes were open and he was moving his head from side to side.

Fr. Reid said: 'He's still alive.'

The priest asked Mary Holland if she knew how to give mouth-to-mouth resuscitation, but decided she should phone for medical assistance. He gave the kiss of life to the dying soldiers but his efforts proved futile. Mary Holland later wrote that Fr. Reid's actions 'redeemed us all'.

It sent one image of Ireland across the world that spoke of human pity in the face of death rather than the savagery of the mob. A local bookmaker's shop let me in and people inside helped me to phone for an ambulance. Their kindness too throws back the lie that the people of West Belfast are savages. When I came out again there were two bodies; I suppose the other one had been there all along and I hadn't seen it. The ambulance and the Army and police had arrived. Both bodies were covered with tarpaulins and blood was seeping from them.

Both soldiers were shot moments after they were taken to the waste ground. Beaten repeatedly on the short journey from Casement Park to the place of execution, one of them still had sufficient determination to struggle with his captors, as they prepared to kill him. Hours after the murders, the victims' names were revealed: 23-year-old Corporal Robert Howes, and Corporal Derek Wood, aged 24.

Within twenty-four hours, the Commander of the Royal Corps of Signals praised the restraint of the two soldiers in not firing into the crowd of attackers. Lt. Col. Martin Roberts, Commander Communications, Northern Ireland told reporters that the soldiers mistakenly drove into the cortège, and in making their escape were cornered by 'black taxis'. To refute IRA claims that the corporals were engaged in undercover duties he offered an explanation for their movements:

Their car was in motion all the time. They only left Howard Street Mill [*Army compound*] shortly before 12.00 and the incident took place shortly after 12.00. They could not possibly have been stationary. They were obviously moving, I suspect probably got lost.

In the light of the suspicious movements of the transit van at Milltown, the IRA and Sinn Fein reacted quickly to events. They knew the value of propaganda, and the need for swift publication of their version of the story. Both soldiers they told the press, were members of an SAS 'dirty tricks' operation. Within twenty-four hours the IRA, worried by world revulsion at the televised barbarisms, altered its initial statement.

What happened was terrible, but it must be seen in the context of the conflict created by the British presence and of the battle of the funerals, especially the Milltown massacres. Those mourners who attacked the undercover car and its occupants acted in exactly the same way, and with the same motive, as those young men who pursued, and were praised for pursuing, one of the Milltown attackers. It was in that atmosphere that the car drove into the cortège.

The IRA statement, a clever exercise in damage limitation, represented a departure from its earlier position that the soldiers were an SAS team on a dirty-tricks mission. They hoped to reduce the scale of the revulsion towards the IRA by appealing to those who had praised the three men, Brady, McErlean and Murray, all killed in the pursuit of Stone. The IRA fully recognised the power of television, and the ghoulish nature of the murders of Howes and Wood. Not only was sympathy for Milltown erased, they considered, it was replaced by a savage act graphically portrayed on world television. Denunciations rang out from their own community, summarised by the apposite comment of Fr. Toner from St Agnes' Church, who said the parish was 'dripping in blood'.

The guilt which typically emanates from mob violence, and the horrific expression of anger, turned inwards upon the IRA in a manner unparalleled in recent history. Fr. Reid, who ministered to one of the soldiers, accurately reflected the ghastliness of mob rule, when he said that possibly the most humane act that day was that of a local woman placing her coat over the head of one of the dead soldiers. Fr. Reid heard her say: 'He's somebody's son. God have mercy on him.'

Two days later, amid the news pages of condemnation, no satisfactory explanation had emerged for the presence of the soldiers in such proximity to the funeral route. David McKittrick, writing in the *Independent*, observed the folly of the corporals' actions, and admitted confusion at their actions. Like many enquiring journalists, he had been told that the pair, on routine signals work, were returning to their base at Lisburn outside Belfast. According to an Army version of events, they foolishly chose the funeral route. McKitterick was not persuaded by the Army's story, as his article of 21 March testified:

Tensions have been running high in West Belfast for weeks, particularly since the deaths in Gibraltar of three IRA members, all of whom came from that area. But even at the best of times the idea of any unarmed military vehicle driving into a republican funeral, demonstration or parade in this most hostile of streets would be considered most outlandish and suicidal. The probable result would be the deaths of any soldiers or policemen who did so.

According to the Army version, the two corporals were making their way from a military base to Army HQ at Lisburn. It is a fact that soldiers do traverse West Belfast in civilian clothes in unmarked cars. Sometimes these are surveillance patrols undertaken to keep an eye on the district, to look for anything suspicious or to watch for individuals, chiefly IRA suspects.

McKittrick also revealed how he once travelled in an unmarked car with an Army officer and discovered that the vehicle had been fitted with a radio transmitter hidden behind the dashboard. He also pointed *Independent* readers to the choice of routes the corporals could have taken to Army HQ, any of which would have presented little or no risk to them. One of the points made by McKittrick may never be resolved – whether the corporals possessed a hidden radio transmitter. The issue remains imponderable; the IRA burned the car to erase fingerprint evidence, and did not scrutinise the car's interior.

Tom King, Secretary of State for Northern Ireland, told the House of Commons that he could not speak with certainty about the reasons for the soldiers presence in Andersonstown.

If the most likely explanation is that they decided to take the shortest route back to their base, without appreciating the presence of the funeral, this can only be conjecture, and it will probably never be known why they were there.

Ironically, IRA claims that the soldiers were part of an undercover operation received the support of loyalist terror groups, who had little affection for the SAS or 14th Intelligence. The shooting of the UVF volunteer by the female undercover soldier at Crumlin Road made the UVF strange bedfellows in the IRA propaganda war, and they supported the contention of the Provos that the corporals were members of the SAS.

While the reasons for the presence of the soldiers at the funeral preoccupied many observers, others began to ask an equally relevant question: 'Why were they not rescued?' James Molyneaux, leader of the Official Unionist Party, alleged that a political directive prevented the security authorities from attempting a rescue mission. He said that no one could have been certain such a mission would have failed. He pointed an accusing finger at 'Stormont', as a place symbolic in British government policy-making, and added he was informed that 'men on the ground were prevented from exercising their judgement by orders from Stormont'. It appeared a wild unsubstantiated allegation which presumed the presence of British officials watching the televised events from parliament buildings out at Stormont, and yet refusing permission to police and soldiers to act. However, Molyneaux's question was valid and demanded an answer which was never forthcoming.

The *Belfast Telegraph's* London correspondent, Desmond

McCartan, wrote a story on 22 March, which offered Molyneaux an answer:

The Government today declined to respond to allegations by an unnamed RUC officer that a heavily-armed police mobile support unit was on standby at Andersonstown Road RUC Station at the time the corporals were attacked and killed. The RUC officer, quoted by the London *Evening Standard* from an interview with Independent Radio News, complained bitterly that a 30-strong police support unit was ready for action only a mile away from the attack. He says the 'heavily-armed unit had been ready to go, but had not been ordered to do so'. The police officer claimed: 'We were chomping at the bit but there was indecision at Headquarters.'

McCartan hardened his story by quoting from extracts of the source material from the *Evening Standard*, and Independent Radio News. He repeated allegations made to Radio News by the unnamed officer:

I was part of a mobile support unit – that's 30 heavily-armed and protected men and we knew exactly what was going on because we were getting feedback from the heli-telly. . . . Of course at that time we didn't know who the men in the car were – but that didn't matter. As far as we were concerned it was a policeman's duty to save lives – anybody's life – if he possibly can. I can't be certain we could have saved these two men but there were thirty of us, and we could have been on the scene in two minutes. So if we'd been given the 'go' as soon as things started to flare up, at least those two lads would have had a chance.

The unnamed source alleged that it took time to clarify what was happening, but he and his colleagues knew that no security forces' personnel were in the area.

The *Evening Standard* and Independent Radio News were dealing with an impeccable source, yet he did not reveal the whole story – which raises serious questions about some of the faceless men in charge of security when the soldiers were seized. For reasons I will reveal I began examining this story partly because it stemmed, I believed, from the events at Milltown Cemetery. I soon discovered its relevance to be much greater than my initial perceptions of it. To begin with, it is essential to clarify some of the events of 22 March, firstly addressing the question of whether the soldiers could have been rescued.

On 16 March a small number of policemen from a mobile support unit faced a mob and dragged Michael Stone from the clutches of his would-be executioners. Without firing a shot in anger they demonstrated courage and professionalism in a situation which was to be replicated in many respects three days later.

When Corporals Howes and Wood were seized, a mobile support unit stood in place at Andersonstown Station, half a mile from the point at which the soldiers fought for their lives. From the moment they were abducted, to the time of their deaths, fifteen minutes elapsed, all of it transmitted live from the cameras on board the helicopter which hovered overhead. As the corporals were taken to Casement Park to be interrogated and beaten, the helicopter descended to a height which offered a clear graphic portrayal of the events, and the IRA men who were present. Those live television images, with an onboard commentary, were relayed directly to Woodburn Army base on the edge of Andersonstown, and from there they were beamed to Andersonstown RUC Station. On two occasions a request was made by officers at Andersonstown for permission to rescue the two victims of the mob and each time the request was denied. A source who was there confirmed this, but such a serious and disturbing story requires an additional witness. In the autumn of 1991, another source, a member of the security forces present in Andersonstown that day, told me the following:

Don't ask me why the soldiers were allowed to die because that is one I cannot answer. In fact if you were in a position to ask others who were there with me they would give you the same answer. The one thing they would agree is that the soldiers could have been rescued. The support unit could have gone in. It was close enough to tear through the area and the men were of the calibre capable of handling anything. If you could get the files you would find some of them were involved in the Stone rescue. The whole event was relayed to our position and a first request was made to the Woodburn Base to let us go. I can't be sure of the exact time but it was sufficient to allow us to achieve the objective of the rescue. The request was denied, and no reason was given. There was complete dismay and frustration, and in desperation a second request was made, again there was enough time to get the job done. It was also turned down with no reason given. We didn't know the two guys in the VW car were soldiers. In fact I think even Woodburn believed they were loyalists. It would be easy to conclude that people at Woodburn or maybe Army HQ who would also have had access to coverage of the event, decided that since they were loyalists it was better to let them die rather than risk men in a rescue bid. Maybe that's too easy, but it's a cynical business and I can only guess, I can't offer a true explanation. You might ask – was it better to let two loyalists die, because the effect would wipe out the IRA's propaganda success after Milltown? I really don't know – but someone does.

Let's put it this way, they could have been saved but somebody, somewhere, decided to let them die. I know you're thinking I'm betraying my own people in the force but I don't think so. There were those of us who wanted to go for it, and who knew enough about terrorism, to succeed. It's that which forces me to be cynical about the person or persons who decided otherwise.

One of my colleagues suggested a theory which again is maybe far-fetched but it shows the extent to which many of us were prepared to speculate because of what happened. He reckoned the powers-that-be knew that the two men in the car were soldiers, but decided not to act because of the Milltown aftermath. His theory was this: a successful rescue of Howes and Wood would have reinforced the IRA claim that security forces colluded in the Milltown massacre. No one would have believed Howes and Wood simply strayed into a funeral, if a police or military operation was launched to snatch them. The IRA would have argued that their presence was evidence in support of their claim that Stone was connected to the white transit van. As it turned out, the terrible deaths of the two corporals overshadowed any case the Provos might have made about their reasons for being in the vicinity of the funeral.

The decision to refuse the RUC requests from Andersonstown caused ill-feeling and resentment among officers who had watched both the rescue of Stone, and the failure to attempt to save the lives of Howes and Wood. My evidence suggests that a decision was taken which prevented a rescue of the corporals; in the public interest an explanation should be provided for the apparent inaction.

Even without these revelations, the rescue of Stone should have indicated justification for questioning such decision-making. Who was responsible for individual security decisions during the fateful events of 22 March? The range of security groupings constantly on duty in West Belfast offered a wider set of options than, say, a mere mobile support unit. Security forces could well have effected a successful rescue jointly, or at least the immediate apprehension of the IRA unit who beat and shot the two corporals.

Contrariwise, it was tentatively suggested to me – by a security source – that the official version of the Stone rescue contained one important inaccuracy: the mobile support team in question *acted on their own initiative and not on orders*.

Though the veracity of the allegation remains impossible to test, the events of Milltown provided enough lessons to security planners. Three days later they could have anticipated the abduction of Howes and Wood and their subsequent murders, as well as the tactics necessary to combat such an atrocity. Someone, somewhere, should, in the public interest, reveal the reason why no action was taken to save the two soldiers.

Perhaps the reason for inaction sprang from political expediency, and fear that matters would be exacerbated by intervention? The story of Howes and Wood and its vast and crucial implications, requires answers to their reason for being in an area which was so dangerous.

On the day of their deaths, Andersonstown area was declared OOB, the code for out of bounds to uniformed military and police personnel. The OOB code is one which can be issued at any time to uniformed patrols, whether mobile or on foot. It signals the beginning of an undercover operation, and all patrols must respond by returning to base. It ensures that an area is cleared for an SAS action, or for an operation by members of 14th Intelligence. A security force source explained its significance:

When the SAS or a similar covert grouping are about to operate, say to take out an IRA unit, they need the area cleared because they don't want to end up in a shoot-out with police or soldiers. It's important to remember that to ordinary security forces' personnel they will look no different than terrorists. They prefer RUC or ordinary Army are not in the vicinity of their target area. the use of OOB presents problems, because the RUC only ever has the word of undercover soldiers for what happened in a shooting incident, but that's the nature of the business. Those guys in the SAS are a weird lot – nice guys – but some of them look like thugs, teeth missing etc. They get bored hanging around. In one base they constantly played pool in the police mess – they didn't like being with ordinary soldiers. They seemed to respect policemen, particularly the Special Patrol Groups, who were in the thick of it. To understand that type of camaraderie you've got to know the similarities of temperament. For example, there was a mobile patrol unit based at Bessbrook at one stage, and they were what a lot of us knew as rejects. They were in South Armagh because of misdemeanours or attitude problems. They were responsible for some dirty business down there, and at one time wrecked dozens of cars. The SAS preferred them to the squaddies. It's the same in Belfast. SAS or 14th Int. operate out of a base at Grosvenor Road, close enough to the Falls, but not too close where the IRA can maintain constant surveillance on the site. It means they are only minutes away from an action in the republican districts of the west of the city.

On 22 March the funeral route was – officially – not OOB to undercover surveillance personnel, such as those in 14th Intelligence. In fact, it was an ideal day for man-to-man surveillance, owing to the numbers of republican activists likely to attend; not, however, a highly desirable time for an operation because of the high level of IRA security.

The importance of man-to-man surveillance can best be illustrated by the way in which the SAS detected the Gibraltar trio. Generally, when an important IRA activist disappears from view, all surveillance effort is directed at finding the activist on the basis that his or her whereabouts will reveal an imminent IRA operation, its planning, and the identities of other IRA personnel assigned to the operation. The intelligence theory is – that IRA operators only detach themselves from their daily routines when they receive orders to travel to the area of a planned murder or bombing. Man-to-man surveillance marking provides a constant update on the whereabouts of known activists, and is constantly revised until the moment when the target person vanishes. At that moment alarm bells ring within intelligence circles and all means are concentrated on locating the person. When he or she is located they are likely to be in the presence of others who have been brought together for a terrorist objective. The tracing of one person, sometimes two persons, is preferable to extending resources to the point where too many people are being tracked.

From reliable contacts, it transpired that Howes and Wood belonged to neither SAS nor 14th Intelligence. The official version said – here were two young, inexperienced members of Signals who had strayed unwittingly into a dangerous area. According to the Army's version of events, Corporal Wood, completing his fourth year of duty, was showing his colleague a republican stronghold. Unfortunately they lost their way. An Army officer told journalists that Howes was a relative newcomer, and Wood was probably trying to impress him by letting him watch an IRA funeral. The latter theory unofficially emanated from military sources but remained simply another explanation impossible to confirm: nobody mentioned man-to-man surveillance.

But – before the cortège left the church, the corporals were detected by IRA personnel, suspicious of them and their vehicle. A communication reached IRA officers that a strange car, containing suspicious-looking men, had been seen in the vicinity. A message was sent to IRA volunteers to challenge the occupants, and to use black taxis to block its path. Howes, dressed in a pale green sweater, did not familiarly resemble a West Belfast resident; the car registration was not known to IRA watchers. Some media people, parked in the area, had stickers on their cars signalling 'Press'; or if not, immediately anticipated suspicion, and produced press cards to identify themselves.

Howes and Wood panicked when challenged, and must have known that once spotted they were in serious trouble, with IRA personnel 'crawling' all over the whole district, nor could they be sure whether the men approaching them carried arms. When their car was about to be engulfed by the mob, Wood emerged from the driver's window, his body leaning across the door frame, and fired a shot in the air. His restraint in not killing his attackers had an admirable quality; deliberately or accidentally, he saved the lives of others rather than his own. Many people who later wrote about the event argued that Wood didn't shoot to kill simply because he was not SAS; an SAS officer would have taken several with him or held the mob at bay. But would his fear, his training, not have convinced him the killing of members of the crowd would not have prevented his death or, for that matter, helped anyone who was in his position? Many people who witnessed both events remain reluctant to admit that a distinction could be made about the two episodes; to many more the horror of 22 March eclipsed the violence in Milltown.

There remains the question of the motive of the corporals on that day and it is within that area of investigation that I found myself presented with new evidence about their military roles. When I began investigating their service records, I was given the official line – they were 'rookies' who worked for Signals, not regular combatants. In 1991 I finally uncovered answers to the presence of the corporals at the funeral and the real nature of their military role. They were clandestine operatives, in a highly secret, shadowy organisation run by Military Intelligence.

14

Future Research Units

In 1990 a Catholic student – 'X' – from Queen's University left the students' union building in South Belfast intending to make his way home to a rural area of County Down. As he walked down the steps of the building he failed to notice a car pointing citywards, and four occupants watching him. When he reached the pavement, two men emerged from the vehicle and approached him. They appeared to have police badges but his initial fear at their sudden appearance distracted him from scrutinising the precise nature of the badges, which seemed of the type used by the New York Police Department. The men allowed him little time to interpret the nature of their approach, and bundled him into the car with an assurance that he was 'wanted for questioning'. Initially he accepted that they were *bona fide* policemen, and that resistance was futile, if not dangerous. He did not question their right to detain him, and felt it 'pointless'. Then, he quickly became suspicious and frightened, but was unable to analyse the matter owing to the swiftness with which the men bundled him into the rear seat.

As the car drew away from the pavement, a gun was pressed into his back, his head was pushed downwards and a hood placed on him. He was held in a prone position out of sight of passing motorists and the only sounds he heard were the car engine and passing traffic.

The journey from the University was not lengthy and 'X' admits that it was difficult for him to assess the distance travelled. Frightened to speak, his captors' actions, and their silence, convinced him of the little point in asking questions.

The car came to a halt, he was dragged unceremoniously from it, lifted bodily by two men and thrown into the rear of a vehicle. He was convinced, that the vehicle to which he was transferred was a landrover; cold metal floor, sound of a diesel engine. The doors of the vehicle closed behind him with a resounding metallic reverberation. He was pinned to the floor by someone's feet and a journey of similar duration took place in silence. When the vehicle stopped he was removed and made to walk a short distance with strong hands pinioning his arms. He was led up a flight of stairs and a metal door closed behind him.

Next, he was led across a wooden floor, pushed into a chair and the hood withdrawn from his head. His surroundings resembled a room in a typical Belfast terrace, except for the fact that the door into the room was reinforced by a metal frame. He saw no evidence of a window; a single light bulb, without a lampshade, hung from the middle of the ceiling. Three men in the room had their faces covered by balaclavas. In front of him stood a television and video recorder, and alongside, a strange type of battery, larger than a normal car battery.

One of his captors tied his hands, then feet, loosened his trouser belt and pulled his trousers and underpants to his knees. As he watched in terror another man attached wires from the battery to his genitals.

A VHS cassette was placed in the video machine and the television set was switched on. One of the men operated a video remote-control device while another knelt beside the battery. 'X' was told to concentrate his eyes on the television; the third captor stood over him.

Television images appeared of 'X' walking with friends in the vicinity of the University district. The images were mixed footage taken at different times of day and showing a range of people. Each time a new face appeared, the hooded man standing over 'X' ordered one of his companions to freeze the frame depicting 'X' with another companion. 'X' was asked to name the person and his political affiliations. 'X' was not aware of the political affiliations of some of his friends or associates and when he failed to answer a question to the satisfaction of his captors, the one interrogating him nodded to a masked colleague who was seated by the battery to deliver electric shocks to 'X''s genitals.

The three hooded men in the room appeared to be building a dossier on all those filmed with 'X'. They were concerned to know which person was in the IRA, his rank and any crimes he had committed.

'X''s ordeal lasted, he believes, several hours before the hood was placed over his head. He was warned that he should never reveal what happened; if he did, he and his family would be assassinated. He was told that he would be taken to a vehicle and released, but when he was free he was to walk away and not look back. They would be watching him and any attempt to look at his captors, or their vehicle, would result in his death.

He heard the warnings through a semi-conscious haze and as he was lifted from the chair he collapsed, and reckons that throughout his ordeal he lost consciousness several times, on account of the excruciating pain of the electric shocks. He was lifted from the floor and heard the metal door being opened. Unable to walk, he was then lifted off the ground, but his feet connected with stairs and the sensation convinced him he was being removed from the building. They tossed him into the rear of what he believed was a landrover, and took him on another journey. He recalls the vehicle stopping, and his being lifted bodily and placed on hard ground. The hood was removed from his head and he was left in a prone position. When he was sufficiently confident to stand he found himself in an alleyway in Belfast city centre. He eventually made his way home too frightened to contact police. The threat from his interrogators resounded in his head.

The interrogator was the only one of his captors to talk during the ordeal, and 'X' detected a Belfast accent which suggested to him that he could well have been in the hands of loyalists. He was, however, puzzled by the sensation of being in what he believed was a landrover, which encouraged him to surmise that he could well have been abducted by undercover soldiers, or rogue members of the RUC or UDR. It felt unlikely that they could be IRA, because the questioning was designed to discover whether his friends and associates were Provisionals. 'X' was not a republican. He was an ordinary respectable student, with no criminal background or political affiliations. To his knowledge his friends and associates possessed no paramilitary connections.

He may not have been aware that Queen's University was known to harbour people with IRA affiliations; by the end of the 1980s a majority of the students were Catholics. A Unionist politician who lectured in law at the University was shot dead by the IRA, and there was a growing republican militancy among a considerable section of the student population. Until the 1960s few Catholics entered Queen's University; but by then the 1947 Education Act had made higher education possible for Catholics.

In the autumn of 1968 Catholic radicals, republicans, communists and Trotskyists formed the People's Democracy in the University. On 1 January 1969 they defied the Civil Rights movement and the Unionist government by organising a march, in contravention of an agreement between Catholics and Unionists that marches should cease until the tension on the streets, and in both communities, eased sufficiently to permit dialogue. The march, known as 'the Long March from Belfast to Derry', was designed to inflame passions. Its leaders chose a route which included staunch loyalist districts in the sure knowledge that Protestants within the police, and the auxiliary 'B' Special constables, would collude with loyalist extremists and attack the marchers. People's Democracy wished to push the state to its limit, prove that the police and its reserve were partisan and as a consequence that Northern Ireland was irreformable. The marchers were ambushed at the countryside halt of Burntollet by loyalists and 'B' Specials with the connivance of policemen. As a result of the Burntollet ambush, tension heightened, and the power and control of the Catholic Civil Rights movement began to fade.

Burntollet drove the two communities farther apart, banished the concept of peaceful protest and was a critical factor in leading to the complete breakdown of the social order in August 1969. Now, twenty years later, the University contained people with more radical ideas than those who led People's Democracy. The 1947 Education Act had begun at last to release a growing population of Catholic students from working-class areas, where politics were essentially republican, particularly the romantic nationalism of the IRA. Security authorities knew throughout the 1980s that a small core of republican sympathisers and activists attended the University. Many surveillance operations were mounted, and attempts were made by Military Intelligence and Special Branch to recruit students to spy on the University population. One security source told of a constant scrutiny of Queen's students from the 1969 period to the present day.

Universities are a natural place for radical politics, and in Northern Ireland more so than elsewhere. Special Branch and other intelligence services keep a close watch on Queen's as well as the University of Ulster centres in Jordanstown and Coleraine. The IRA, unlike the loyalists, attracts educated types, like many terrorist organisations throughout the world. The loyalists don't seem to possess the educated, intelligent thinkers found in Provo ranks. Mairead Farrell, shot in Gibraltar, was an educated girl and that is the type of person we look for in places of higher education. It's not simply the universities but the technical colleges. Some of the IRA's engineering expertise and propaganda has been devised and shaped by people with education. Miriam Daly, who was shot by loyalists, was INLA and the theoretician for the INLA's political wing, the IRSP. She was a lecturer in political science at Queen's. Ronnie Bunting, who led the INLA and ordered Airey Neave's death, was a former student of Queen's, and was in the Peoples Democracy. That's a few, but there were many others. No intelligence community can afford to ignore university campuses in Northern Ireland.

There is an obvious danger in assuming that all students are in some respects affiliated to traditional politics, or to paramilitary objectives. Not so: the majority of students in all institutions of higher education do not support the combatants of terrorism, nor do they provide vocal support for violence. However, it is clear that Queen's University, with a considerable student population from troubled parts of Belfast, is more vulnerable to the charge that it has been a centre for the activities of a small number of republican activists.

'X''s ordeal was an example of the paranoia which grips intelligence analysts. Neither a republican sympathiser nor activist, he was unaware of any aspect of his friends' lives which would fit into a republican framework. He told his mother about his experience and she recommended that he talk to the RUC. Initially, he resisted her advice, and remained at home, frightened that every time the doorbell rang it would signal the return of his captors. Within a short time he relented, approached the police and recounted his experiences. The police took a statement but did not encourage him to believe that they placed any reliance on his story. Within the RUC, the statement was scrutinised and analysis was divided between those who believed he was a Walter Mitty figure to those who felt he might have been held by members of the UVF or UDA. Experienced officers dismissed a suggestion that any Army covert grouping could be guilty of the crime. However, one seemingly irrelevant part of his story attracted the attention of advisers to the RUC chief constable, Hugh Annesley.

'X' appeared unwittingly to describe the battery used in his interrogation, and he offered details which both puzzled police investigators, and gave a dimension to his story which intrigued one of the sceptics in the investigating team. He described a battery not in common usage, and certainly not known to a student. Of a sort manufactured for certain types of military vehicles, it could not have been in the possession of paramilitaries. Chief Constable Annesley, formerly a counter-insurgency expert within the Special List Operations at Scotland Yard, was equally intrigued, and he ordered a secret investigation to discover whether a rogue grouping might exist within his force, or whether 'X' could have been the victim of secret counter-insurgency operations by the military. Within a short time, rogue police or UDR involvement was ruled out – which left investigating officers wondering about possible military involvement.

Scrutiny of the military, particularly Military Intelligence, presented the RUC with insurmountable problems. Firstly, Military Intelligence resented any intrusion by RUC or their CID, and did not permit examination of its classified units. CID officers approached Special Branch, who liaised with both MI5 and Military Intelligence, but they proved equally unhelpful. They had no wish to be drawn into something which might rebound on them. Ironically there was little respect for Military Intelligence within the Special Branch, owing to a long-running dispute between the two services. Special Branch had complained to MI5 for years that Military Intelligence was recruiting Special Branch agents without consultation. Consequently, some agents possessed several handlers, with the result that a number of operations got compromised by inefficiency and confused loyalties. Special Branch also held the opinion that Military Intelligence operated units which acted without proper control, and in a fashion which could lead to another Stalker-type investigation. Some of the units used terrorists, particularly in loyalist terror groups, to carry out acts of violence in the role of *agents provocateurs*. Military Intelligence agents also failed to pass on information about proposed acts of violence to the RUC, so that murders could be prevented. One Special Branch contact told me of his concerns about Military Intelligence operations.

The Stalker Affair was a symptom of the problem that arises when secret groupings are not properly controlled. Stalker was getting close to a much better story than the one he published. He knew Military Intelligence was using very dubious methods, and was prepared to sacrifice anyone to keep its agents in place, and its operations intact, and it didn't matter if it was policemen. Stalker looked at the deaths of three policemen in a landmine explosion, and I can tell you that their deaths were allowed to happen because Military Intelligence was concerned that if the whereabouts of explosives were revealed, their agent within the IRA would be compromised. Military Intelligence planners were prepared to allow three policemen to drive into an IRA booby-trap – a fucking landmine – knowing it was in place, and that the policemen were travelling to their deaths. We've watched secret groups come and go and, believe me, there are some wild boys in them. You can't hide the shit for ever. We got to the stage we didn't want our fingerprints on the shit. MI5 are more likely to condone some of the wayward military schemes, provided there are a few terrorist bodies produced, but even they have become cautious. We saw it all before – the use of terrorist agents. It happened in the early 1970s, and the military then made a mess of it, but they never learn. They think they can do whatever they like, and then fly their men out when something goes wrong. Everybody else in the intelligence community is left to sort out the pieces. They set up these secret groups and because they are not officially listed they can do almost what they like and it can be blamed on the IRA etc. We soon find out from our own agents what is happening on the ground. The problem is we have to live here and this war is a long one. Nobody knows when an agent will decide he can get a better deal from the authorities and blow the whistle on the whole intelligence game. After Stalker we had Stevens, and you can blame that one on Military Intelligence. Their flirtation with loyalist paramilitaries created the problem. They were giving loyalists information on republicans knowing what they would do with it. Stevens investigated the leaking of intelligence material to loyalists, and in the process picked up loyalists who were Military Intelligence agents, as well as guys working for us and MI5. They start to blab and look for a deal but Stevens says no, so they turn on their handlers who are not able to protect them. The shit begins to hit the fan, and we all suffer in our game. Our own agents become edgy and feel vulnerable that if they are in a fix they will be left unprotected by us. That starts a rot.

The Special Branch reluctance to assist the team investigating 'X''s ordeal left the detectives with no choice but to make informal contacts with regular Army personnel, and with military officers who maintained good relations with the RUC. Enquiries were made in the utmost confidence at several military bases in Belfast but realised no new dimension to the case.

An official approach to the Army was out of the question; it possessed its own internal security, the Special Investigation Branch, and military establishments were out of bounds to RUC or CID personnel, unless permission was granted by senior military staff. The police officers were also concerned that an official approach might alert the culprits, if they were indeed soldiers, and they could be flown from the Province if they had been operating under orders. One of the officers was aware that in previous investigations soldiers simply disappeared, and their existence was then denied by the military command. Whenever RUC officers were granted permission to enter Army bases, they were only allowed to interview soldiers in the presence of Special Investigation Branch personnel.

The case of 'X' presented the RUC with a dilemma; they had no concrete evidence, no descriptions of military personnel and, as such, a request to enter military compounds for a search or interrogation exercise would be denied. The only course open was to establish informal contacts with leading Army commanders in Belfast, with a view to testing their reaction to the student's story.

Senior Army officers, asked privately about the possibility of military involvement in the 'X' abduction, reacted predictably by dismissing suggestions of covert military involvement; and in some instances they expressed an unwillingness to discuss the secret world of military intelligence, its links with MI5 or the types of groups both organisations controlled. One officer made it clear that he preferred 'to know nothing' of the activities of groupings operating from his compound.

The two covert groupings most likely to figure in any allegation related to undercover work were 14th Intelligence and the SAS. One of the features, and obvious advantages, of secret groupings is that their members can disappear from sight to avoid investigation. An RUC officer put it this way:

When a shooting happened and there were allegations of military involvement we had the unenviable task of seeking information from the Army. Now if the culprits were part of a covert organisation not registered on Army records there was no way we could trace them. Without witness identification there is no one we can look for. Covert personnel can be flown out of the Province immediately and their previous presence denied. It is much the same with the SAS. Before a CID officer can get near any person involved in undercover military work, there is an elaborate procedure. By the time an investigator is given access, the alleged culprits have their stories in place. There is a general reluctance within the system to permit scrutiny of the activities of all covert personnel. It appears to be an area of operations controlled from above by people who have the ultimate exercise of veto over police powers.

In 1990 a male/female team from 14th Intelligence were guilty of a breach of the unit's security. They were busy having a sexual dalliance in the Europa Hotel in downtown Belfast when their car containing documents and guns was stolen from the hotel car-park. The matter was within the remit of police investigation but the undercover operatives were flown from Northern Ireland before RUC officers could interview them.

The investigation into 'X''s abduction and torture met with silence, if not downright harassment. Military Intelligence, Special Branch and MI5 were all finally approached, and refused co-operation.

They were harbouring a secret; a highly classified operation, which they did not wish exposed by the RUC. The secret – a new organisation, known in intelligence circles as the FRUs, Future Research Units. They operated throughout Northern Ireland, and particularly from two centres in Belfast, one of them in the grounds of the Army compound at Ladis Drive in the Castlereagh district of East Belfast. Members of the units frequently used landrovers to take them from, and return them to, the East Belfast base. Unlike other regular units, they employed special signals by means of battery-operated torches when entering the base. The signal provided them with unhindered access, and regular soldiers on sentry duty knew not to stop, search or question the occupants of any landrovers who gave the required signal. The purpose of this was to maintain the secrecy and identity of FRU personnel from the regular Army. It may also have been designed to allow the transport of victims such as 'X' into a specifically constructed room.

FRU personnel regularly drove unchecked through the compound to a special building, where they were based out of sight of regular troops. Military Intelligence did not place trust in regular soldiers who were likely to talk to each other, to policemen with whom they shared patrols, or to girlfriends in the community. Some members of the Ladis Drive unit were based within the community, and like Howes and Wood lived seemingly normal lives. Their role was one of surveillance and liaison with informers within the Ulster Defence Association in Stone's stomping ground of East Belfast. It seems more than likely that they could have been privy to knowledge of Stone's presence, and could have heard of his plans to attack the IRA leadership in Milltown Cemetery. I put to one source the thesis that Military Intelligence must have known about Stone's approach to the UDA leadership, and his plan to enter Milltown:

Military Intelligence undoubtedly knew about Stone, and probably so did MI5 because they both had him on file. MI5 may not have been told about the planned massacre at the cemetery, but I would be surprised if Military Intelligence were not aware of it. They were both running guys in important positions with the UDA/UVF but Military Intelligence, in particular, had one agent who was very close to the planning of violence within the UFF. I know of one example where Military Intelligence was informed by one of its operatives that a prominent lawyer was selected for assassination, but they let it happen, and the RUC was not informed, or given the chance to prevent it. I couldn't see them acting to prevent Stone doing what a lot of us would like to see, and that is the deaths of the Provo leadership. If you ask me were they running Stone, I would have to say I doubt it, but anything is possible. If you ask me were they or MI5 running McMichael or Bingham, I would say it was more likely because they would have been obvious targets for recruitment. They would have viewed Bingham or McMichael as people who could sanction operations, and if they controlled senior figures, they effectively controlled the actions of those under them, such as Stone. Some of us thought long and hard about Stone, and certainly wondered if he was run by one of the Military Intelligence units. He was an ideal recruit because he was clever and committed, and therefore was potentially reliable; the kind of guy who would accept his fate if caught. You'll never know if he was, but for the sake of conjecture I would say it was more likely the person controlling him was the agent. Howes and Wood ran agents, relayed orders to them and received communications from them. When it comes to organisations like the FRUs, their role would include unusual operations beyond the scope of orthodox groupings such as Special Branch or E4. The case of 'X' is an example of the unorthodox nature of their work and that is probably only the tip of the iceberg. There are probably many people who have suffered a similar experience, and are too scared to talk about it, or have been recruited in the process. It's a dirty business but it's also a dirty war.

A secret police memorandum was presented to the Chief Constable linking Future Research Unit operatives to 'X''s ordeal, but the existence of the units is officially denied by the intelligence community. The covert grouping calls to mind the counter-insurgency work of the Military Reconnaissance Force in the early

1970s. They recruited agents, and trained some of them at Palace Barracks, employed counter-insurgency techniques such as the sectarian killing of Catholics to inflame tension and draw the IRA into a sectarian war, with the aim of detaching them from their ideological conflict, and portraying them as common criminals.

'X''s ordeal suggests a worrying dimension to the conflict and a return to military tactics long discredited – which raises the question of Howes and Wood and their military roles. Wood was a member of a Future Research Unit and, at the time of his death was in the presence of the newest recruit, Robert Howes. After their deaths their description as 'members of the Royal Corps of Signals' was standard procedure when any covert soldier was killed in action. Captain Robert Nairac worked for Four Field Survey Troop, but his parent regiment, the Grenadier Guards, claimed him as a fellow officer when he was murdered. Soldiers who work under-cover maintain their regimental allegiance as a cover for their undercover roles, and both Wood and Howes were originally Royal Corps of Signals personnel. At the time of their deaths they lived in a house in Bloomfield Avenue in East Belfast, territory of Michael Stone and of many UDA members. Bloomfield Avenue is situated in a Protestant heartland less than half a mile from UDA HQ. A loyalist paramilitary source confirmed for me the presence of the two corporals in East Belfast. It is not unusual for military personnel to visit girlfriends in that part of the city where no enmity exists towards soldiers. Howes and Wood lived in an upstairs apartment and led a quiet life with one or two exceptions.

We knew two young Englishmen lived in the house, just as we know most people who come into the area – that's our business. They made no attempt to integrate into our community so they posed no threat. I was told by a neighbour that once or twice, loud noise, such as shouting or screaming, was coming from the apartment, but that could have been an ordinary row. After their deaths I saw their faces in the newspapers and recognised them. If they were undercover people, they were good.

My source failed to mention that in the aftermath of the two soldiers' deaths, the UFF supported the IRA contention that they had been covert military personnel. Their military roles did not fully explain their appearance at the funerals, although it added weight to the allegation they had gone there for a purpose, such as ground surveillance, linked by hidden radio to the Army heli-copter. This leaves room for the oft-repeated theory that Wood took Howes there to impress him with his experience of operations in Belfast. But Wood knew Belfast, and his undercover training would have equipped him with sufficient knowledge to dispel any desire to visit West Belfast as a day-tripper, or mistakenly to take a route which led him into a republican funeral cortège. To everyone in Northern Ireland, and the outside world, the events of that week demonstrated the dangers constant in that part of the city.

Perhaps we may never know fully why they were there, and perhaps the human factor, namely bravado on the part of Wood, became the deciding factor in their ill-fated journey. Captain Robert Nairac worked undercover in South Armagh, and on the night he was abducted he was drinking and singing in a pub in a republican area, believing his training and knowledge of the conflict accorded him invincibility. Nairac's presence, without appropriate back-up, dispelled the myth that all undercover soldiers behave with an impeccable sense of danger, and with the specialised knowledge to extricate themselves from the most dangerous situations.

15

The Aftermath

A Belfast courtroom became the final stage for Michael Stone, and it gave him an opportunity to display the coolness of the professional killer. The prosecution, with the aid of television footage, provided Stone with a 'high-tech' record of the events in Milltown. He went into court with the deliberate purpose of forcing the prosecution to tell his story, even though he was not prepared to offer evidence in his defence. This was the archetypal Stone, the narcissist, the egocentric, who wished everyone to know the extent of his crimes, and to oblige them to sit with him while his most infamous exploit was played and replayed for the benefit of the press, onlookers and the judge sitting, as in all such Northern Ireland trials, without a jury.

Many other men in Stone's position would have pleaded guilty, and have ended the indignity of having to relive all the detail of their crimes. Stone has never seen himself as a criminal, as a man who regretted his actions. Proud of what he had done, he wanted the world to know the totality of his crimes, and determined to erase the tabloid portrayal of him as a madman, a 'Rambo' figure. He sought to convince the sceptics that the Milltown massacre was not the product of an impulsive, deranged mind, and he knew that the weight of the prosecution case would show him as a long-term, dedicated killer. 'Mesmerised', as he said, by the courtroom, and by the film footage of the Milltown massacre, he had another reason for craving the public forum of a courtroom, as he explained in a letter to me:

It was strange for me because even though I had done it, it was as if I was able to relive it. It seemed fantastic even to me. It certainly didn't look like me. In court I looked respectable. I could see everyone in the courtroom was fascinated by it all.

'It certainly didn't look like me' was one of the most telling statements when assessing his reasons for enduring the lengthy judicial outline of his career. He was always concerned to assure me that the person I met in prison, or the man in Milltown, was not the real Michael Stone. In court he was well dressed and did not resemble the cemetery killer. Throughout many of my conversations with him, he self-consciously referred to his shabby appearance in the cemetery, and pointed out that he did not always dress in that fashion. He was, after all, as he told me repeatedly 'a ladies' man who wore expensive suits'. Curiously he revelled in the adulation of the professional hitman, but abhorred the archetypal tabloid image of the unshaven, wild-eyed terrorist. He betrayed no emotion in court, his overall performance a testimony to a man consumed with self-importance, a man who wished to make his bloody imprint on history. For him court would always be a charade and, undoubtedly, for his lawyers, a futile exercise: he was not prepared to enter the witness box and face cross-examination which might concentrate on his personal life or his motivation. He later claimed that he chose to act in that fashion to express his distaste for non-jury trials.

Behind the scenes Desmond Boal QC, a celebrated lawyer, once a Unionist politician for the loyalist heartland of Shankill, tried to devise a strategy for defending his client. Boal had defended many terrorists in the conflict, members of the IRA as well as loyalist paramilitaries; renowned for his fine mind and persuasive handling of legal argument, he was a curious, some would argue eccentric, figure, who rarely gave media interviews. In the 1960s he was a fiery politician during the turbulent years before Northern Ireland moved towards chaos, and one of several Unionist politicians who opposed the reformist policies of the Northern Ireland prime minister, Terence O'Neill (1963–69). On one occasion in 1966, he formed part of a Unionist deputation which arrived at the house of Brian Faulkner, a cabinet minister, seeking his support for a plan to topple O'Neill and reinstate Faulkner as prime minister. Faulkner, a hardliner in O'Neill's government, opposed O'Neill's liberalising approach to Catholics and was often described as an arch-bigot. Boal was and remains a friend of the firebrand orator, Ian Paisley. In the 1970s I watched some of Boal's performances in court and marvelled at his expertise in addressing juries.

In this case, whatever the difficulties of his client, Boal fulfilled his role with propriety and skill, ordering a private psychiatric evaluation of Stone – perhaps to discover if Stone was mentally competent to stand trial, or was of a disturbed state of mind, which required a plea of diminished responsibility.

Stone agreed to two evaluations by independent psychiatrists, one of them a woman. He says he resented the psychiatric sessions; he knew he was sane, and his participation implied that he required psychiatric help. Any lawyer dealing with Stone would have been obliged to seek a medical analysis; his actions in the cemetery, considered in isolation, seemed to many to symbolise the actions of a deranged mind.

Stone withheld crucial evidence in the psychiatric sessions: his childhood, his feelings of rejection. During a conversation with the woman psychiatrist he became abusive and resentful when she enquired if he was a 'wife-beater'. Such a question touched a raw nerve in his self-image. He professed love of women, and an admiration for their role as mothers remained central to his self-image; and then he refused to permit the psychiatrists to examine his early life, forbade them to speak to any member of his family circle. They were reduced to analysing him in a narrow environment, without access to many of the factors which shaped Stone's life. Both psychiatrists concluded that he was sane, with the consequence that when Boal was asked by the trial judge whether Stone was of sound mind, he replied: 'I have no reason to believe he is not.'

Stone was found guilty of six murders, five attempted murders, conspiring to murder, causing explosions and possessing firearms. In sentencing him to life imprisonment, the judge described him as a danger to society. In a letter to me on 13 November 1990, Stone reflected on the judge's comments:

My trial judge was Mr Higgins. As I've said before I had a fair trial. In his summing up, amongst a few derogatory, smart-arsed remarks, he stated I had taken the law into my own hands, and that I was a threat to society. I have never been a threat to society, i.e. the law-abiding nationalist population, but I most certainly was a threat to those PIRA terrorists who wage an unjustifiable war against Ulster's innocent mixed populace.

In the same letter he addressed himself to the prospect of spending the remainder of his life behind bars:

Some may think that I now find myself in the unenviable position of surviving a life sentence with a thirty-year stipulation – 'Tomorrow is promised to no one' – I have faced death several times in my life and I can honestly state that any form of life is preferable to death. There ends the sermon by the Revd M.A. Stone.

In some of his letters, he offered a rhetoric riddled with observations intended to depict him as a caring individual.

As in all wars the opposing factions have their volunteer-soldiers, and they in turn have families and dependents. These are regrettably the hidden victims of this war. Given that the most hardened terrorist or dedicated freedom fighter inevitably has someone who cares for him, may it be a mother, wife, children, etc. As I jot this dribble down, I now have been an Ulster Volunteer for some twenty years and in those years the cost to me and my family has been incalculable – two broken marriages, several long-term relationships and all those moments of innocence and devilment I've missed as my children grow into maturity. Yes, even those families of my actions, whilst their political and religious affiliations are alien to mine. I can still think of them much like my family. They are but a few of this war's hidden victims.

If Stone has regrets, they are to be found in the confused rhetoric which depicts him as a casualty, and his victims as a necessary consequence of war. He never expressed remorse for killing anyone, apart from one indication of distress at not causing instantaneous death to McPolin. Relying on a vague emotionalism, he recognised his own family's sorrows in the pathos of the families of his victims, and he continued to perceive the killing of his victims as justifiable. His failed marriages and extra-marital relationships he attributed to the conflict and not to any inadequacy or infidelity on his part. Forever the narcissist, he saw himself as a Macbeth, a tragic hero.

In another letter he reminded me of the moment when he encountered a former gang member, turned Provisional, within Long Kesh internment camp.

There was one thing I'd forgotten to mention, and that was the look he and I exchanged during our short stay in that integrated environment. It was one of compassion, sadness if you will, not apologetic – but one that said: 'Well pal, this is where it is at. We have left our gang behind and joined our tribes. The fists and feet of our youth have been replaced by the bombs and bullets of our future'. Long-winded or what?

Many of Stone's letters were laced with a penultimate aside as if indicating his embarrassment with his colourful representation of his past. His letters give him a means of revising his history, and their phrasing rebels against the truth of his actions, and his statements to police after Milltown. The letters conflicted with the bitterness which symbolised his killings, and with his regret that he only murdered three people in Milltown.

He told me he enjoyed the spectacle of a public trial, but rejected my contention that he needed the trial and the history of his terrorist life-style to dispel the tabloid portrayal of him as a psychopath. His preoccupation with self-image, and his detest-ation of the newspaper evaluations of him, grew sufficiently relevant for him to refer to them in a letter to me in September 1990.

I have been called a sectarian killer along with a few choice inaccuracies. I have never knowingly taken action against an innocent person. The names attributed to me, such as 'crazed' or 'mad gunman', run off me like water off a duck's back. The 'sectarian killer' I find insulting. I can assure you I didn't travel the length and breadth of Ulster to 'sanction' innocent constitutionalist nationalists.

Throughout our conversations, it was clear that he hoped the trial had refuted the claims that he was mad, but he feared that he could not erase the allegation of having been motivated by sectarian hatred. The 'sectarian' label caused him much disquiet; it impinged on his life and touched on his suspicion that he came from an Irish Catholic background. Press reports that he was born Catholic also distressed him, as did suggestions that his desire to hide his religion motivated him to kill Catholics, and so convince fellow loyalists of his total adherence to the Protestant cause. More importantly, he did not wish to be branded a sectarian killer because it conflicted dramatically with his self-image, his self-esteem and his desire to be regarded as a 'soldier' fighting 'a just and honourable war' in the traditions of his forebears. 'Sectarian-ism' was a dirty word, it epitomised mindless violence, thuggery and despicable motive. Stone preferred to be hailed as a hero who liquidated a ruthless enemy – but an enemy he was obliged to respect, if he were to accord himself the role and persona of a soldier at war. The latter point was clearly illustrated when Ed Curran, editor of *Sunday Life*, interviewed Stone in 1989, and asked him how he felt when he shot the IRA volunteer, Kevin Brady during the Milltown operation:

As I drew out my Ruger and aimed at him he looked at me in disbelief. He kept coming forward not believing what he'd seen. He'd gotten too close to me. He and I knew he'd gone too far. He fell dead where he stood. I didn't want to shoot him. He had something it's hard to describe. You have to see it to understand. I salute this republican. He was a man, a real man.

He admired the IRA, and one can surmise that had he been born in Andersonstown, he would have become a hardened Provisional. He evidently craved the adulation accorded to IRA heroes, and in Milltown Cemetery on 16 March 1988, found himself captivated by the paraphernalia of hero-worship – exactly what he desired for himself, except that it belonged to the enemy.

In the same conversation with Ed Curran he offered curious insights into the confused thinking of the police officers who held him in custody after Milltown:

'Who is he. Is he one of ours – are you SAS? Are you Branch?'
An RUC officer leant over me. He asked me in a whisper, 'Are you RUC, Army or UDR?'
'That's some job you did up there,' he said.

Sunday Life, 12 November 1989

While he was awaiting trial, Stone enjoyed the admiring looks and comments from prison warders and police who guarded him; he was requested to autograph several copies of the RUC magazine. Shortly before his trial, he was overjoyed to learn of the killing of Sinn Fein councillor, John Joe Davey. He told me that Davey's death was particularly pleasing, because the killers were trained by him, and operated with him during McMichael's reign as UUF supremo.

I might have failed in my attempt to kill him but I knew he would be hit sooner or later. I was pleased the people I was associated with got the job done.

Stone said news of Davey's death outshone the gloom of prison, and it proved that he trained his people to 'finish the job'.

He quickly resigned himself to the rigours of prison life content in the knowledge that he was a hero to many in the outside world, and feared by his fellow loyalists in the Maze Prison. Exercising constantly, he developed a physique which conveyed muscular power and toughness – his way of warning others, including republican inmates, that he was not to be intimidated.

Prison may be a secure establishment for housing terrorists but it did not prevent Stone and other inmates from sending messages to their associates in the ghettoes. He has played a prominent role in the loyalist paramilitary structures in the Maze and has participated in a series of prison interrogations, in which loyalist leaders interviewed their fellow inmates to uncover information about the murders of UFF leader, John McMichael, UVF leader of the Shankill Butchers, Lenny Murphy, and several other figures associated with both organisations in West Belfast. Stone, according to a loyalist source, was prominent in questioning several inmates, and the information communicated from prison helped to identify West Belfast UDA leader, James Craig, as the person responsible for providing republicans with the necessary information and back-up to kill rival loyalist terror chiefs. Craig, a murderer, racketeer and an informant for the IRA and INLA, ruthlessly maintained brutal control over his subordinates, and clinically eliminated anyone who interfered with his racketeering exploits. He bought immunity from IRA assassination by colluding with them in the deaths of leading loyalists including McMichael, and formed a racketeering alliance with members of the INLA, carving up parts of the city with their approval as part of a profit-sharing arrangement. A police informer, too, he gained a limited degree of immunity from prosecution. On several occasions, he phoned Tennent Street police station in West Belfast to inform officers of the location of a murder victim, and in some instances he had been the killer. While Stone languished in prison, the UFF, with the approval of Stone and other inmates, passed a death sentence on Craig; and he was lured to an East Belfast pub frequented by loyalists, and one of Stone's previous haunts.

Craig travelled across the city with a promise of people waiting to sell him an assortment of gold objects, the proceeds of a robbery. Several young men waited near the pub, dressed in overalls, a trait Michael Stone developed in his terrorist career. While Craig sat in the pub drinking, they entered and killed him with bursts of automatic fire. Fleeing to a nearby house, they removed their overalls, track shoes, gloves and balaclavas and burned them.

In 1991, Stone was divorced from Leigh-Anne. In a letter to me, he attributed the divorce to his illegal political activities and added: 'It's tragic but that is life. Now there's a touch of unwarranted bravado.'

He told me that he had encouraged Leigh-Anne to seek divorce; in fact, she initiated proceedings because she had met another man and had hoped to form a permanent relationship.

Leigh-Anne left the family home, changed her surname and moved into another part of East Belfast to establish a new life and avoid press scrutiny. In February 1991 a parcel addressed to Leigh-Anne Stone arrived at her former home, and the occupier immediately delivered it to Leigh-Anne at her new address. She was not expecting a package and reckoned it had not been sent by her friends, all of whom were aware of her new surname. She summoned the police who removed the package – a booby-trap bomb concealed in a VHS cassette.

Stone reacted to the news of the bomb by summoning prison officers and demanding to talk to the prison Governor. His request was granted and he told the Governor he believed the IRA was attempting to murder his wife in revenge for Milltown.

The Governor noted his comments, but declined to comment on the specific allegation of IRA involvement. Stone angrily declared his wish to meet the IRA spokesman in the prison to discuss the matter. The Governor replied that it was not possible to arrange and would constitute a clear breach of prison regulations; the matter was one for the civil authorities not prison staff.

I told him if he didn't organise a meeting with the top Provo, whose identity we both knew, I would deal with it. He asked me if I was threatening violence and I told him I would lean over a cubicle during a visiting session and snap a republican's neck; that would make the prison authorities take notice. I knew I could do that. I had the strength and it would have been easy.

According to a senior prison official the threat was sufficient to persuade the Governor to accede to Stone's request. There was a meeting between the Governor and the IRA spokesman in the prison and a message was relayed to Stone to the effect: 'We don't target the families of prisoners. Look to your own people.'

The IRA was not involved in targeting Leigh-Anne, and Stone believed them. He concluded that associates of the late James Craig were behind the murder attempt as a warning to 'keep his mouth shut'.

I knew some of Craig's associates had worried that they would also be assassinated, if it became known that they had colluded with their former boss in the murder of McMichael. They knew of Stone's close relations with McMichael, and the fact that Stone had met McMichael several days before his death. At that time McMichael was compiling a dossier on Craig and some of his henchmen. Some of those henchmen were indeed worried that McMichael might have confided in Stone about Craig, and might have named others suspected of assisting Craig in providing the IRA with information on loyalist terrorist leaders. Craig's death left behind a lot of anxious men, all wondering if they would be next on the list.

When IRA involvement was ruled out I reflected on the possible motive of Craig's former colleagues, and decided to contact some of my sources within loyalist ranks. One source said that if loyalists were intent on murdering his wife they would not have sent a package to the wrong address.

From the moment of his incarceration Stone insisted that Leigh-Anne visit the prison with their two children. She, unhappy about the arrangement, became increasingly disturbed by the prospect of her children visiting a notorious killer. Her concerns were not voiced until she began a new life by changing her name and forming a relationship with another man. In January 1991 she told Stone that she intended to end the children's prison visits, and had sought legal and social services advice, and they assured her she was within her legal rights to deny him access to the children. She believed the experience of prison visiting to be detrimental to their upbringing, conflicted with her attempts to make a new life for them, and resulted in them being subjected to constant scrutiny – as well as the stigma of being 'the kids of the Milltown killer'. Stone, furious and verbally abusive, said he was their father and, as such, had the right to demand access to them. She pointed out that he was in no position to make such a demand, and that it was the children's welfare which was at issue.

Leigh-Anne probably never understood the intensity of Stone's feeling provoked by such rejection. She was, in effect, repeating the actions of his natural parents, by forcing him to reject his own children. Able to cope with the divorce, though not pleased, she had found love with another man, the hurt caused by the divorce was minor compared with the overwhelming loathing he directed at her when she proposed an end to the children's visits. His professed love for all his children was expressed to me in a letter in September 1990.

As for my family life, I've married twice and divorced likewise. I have nine children, five from the two marriages, four to four girlfriends. I love all my children. They are my life and my future. My children when married were planned. Those outside were also planned but their mothers neglected to tell me of their plans. I have my own thoughts on why these accidents occurred but I'm glad they did.

Even at the moment he delivered his homily to his children, he qualified the circumstances surrounding those born out of wedlock. His comments signified a deep-seated guilt about fathering children beyond marriage: it also implied a form of rejection. He assuaged his guilt by subliminally suggesting the four children born out of wedlock were brought into the world by the deception of his girlfriends but he, nevertheless, accepted them and recognised them as his. Stone never offered me an explanation of the phrases 'these accidents occurred', or 'the mothers neglected to tell me of their plans'. I was left to conclude that he was trying to say that his girlfriends deliberately became pregnant without consulting him, but he still acted honourably and remained 'a father to the kids'. He undoubtedly maintained contact with all his children – it was important for him to prove that parents did not need to disown their offspring.

On Sunday 10 March 1991, the *Sunday News* carried a front-page story headlined: 'Stone Cries Mercy'. A *Sunday News* reporter, Una Brankin, visited Stone in prison and her story carried a plea from him to 'the terrorists to leave Leigh-Anne and the kids alone'.

She quoted him admitting those responsible were 'almost certainly fanatical loyalists', angered by rumours that his ex-wife had abandoned him.

He begged them: 'If this is the case, desist. You're doing me a great disservice. Your actions have caused me great harm. As a result of this incident I have given up all access and visiting rights I had to my youngest children. I did this to save them from further attack.'

Stone neglected to tell the reporter that access to his children was a critical personal issue before the murder attempt. His newspaper plea was his method of placing on record that the ending of his children's visits was made by him to protect them, and at great distress to him. He did not tell the reporter that access was about to be denied, irrespective of his own wishes.

Stone's legacy today in his community is evident – in songs, and in gable-wall slogans, extolling his murderous career. The young men who shoot innocent Catholics regard him as a hero, and he has acquired the status he long craved. Like so many young men he came out of a society where tribalism extols the cult of the gunman, and human life has grown cheap. His efforts to portray himself as a soldier in the British tradition failed, and in time, he may become a sad figure in the knowledge that no one believes the persona he continues to fashion – nor was he mad, but bad.

Many factors in his life conditioned his inadequacy and shaped him as the ideal recruit for terrorism. None of those elements can be considered a mitigating dimension to his actions; he killed people and he enjoyed it. He was not an aggressive psychopath in terms of the medical definitions, but sane with a psychopathic personality; he could be kind to his children but, ultimately, cruel to the children of others. The comment made by the woman who bent over the tortured body of one of the dead corporals contained a sentiment which Stone could not express: 'He's somebody's son, God have mercy on him.'

God never figured in my conversations with Stone, with the exception of a passing answer to a question about the loyalist slogan 'God and Ulster'. Stone casually remarked that he believed in God, but declined to elaborate on his conviction. He possesses a disarming personality, wit and a powerful presence. In prison he has refined his view of life, constantly reminding me of his attractiveness to women, not at all, he said, the man I observed in prison, he loved his children and killed only those who were in the IRA.

I was constantly forced to remind myself that I could have been one of his victims, and that the persona I witnessed in prison was fashioned for my benefit, and that of his admirers in the outside world. His eyes betray a coldness and his body a tautness which suggest explosive qualities. My prison visits illustrated the unreal quality of Stone's demeanour; reality was suspended, terror and bloodshed were not evident. It was too easy to forget that the man beside me was a cool, clinical killer without normal feelings of remorse, devoid of respect for human life outside his tribe.

In prison he became adept at dealing with his incarceration; if the gates were opened he would probably deal in death again. Unfortunately not unique, his story illustrated the futility of Northern Ireland's violence, its flawed rhetoric and the glamour of the cult of the gunman. The newspapers described him as a 'Rambo figure', but unfortunately Stone was real and Rambo a mere celluloid creation.

His legacy was evident on the streets of Northern Ireland in 1991, when loyalist violence reached a peak reminiscent of the 1970s and early 1980s. The killings of Catholics were characterised by a professionalism of the type exhibited by Stone, and by those he trained. Many of the victims were republicans, or people with republican affiliations and their names would have been included on many security forces' dossiers of the type used by Stone and his former associates. Parallel to the selective targeting ran the indiscriminate killing of Catholics. These random murders testified to the gut sectarian savagery endemic in loyalist ideology, a reflection of Stone's own career, and that aspect of it which he professes to abhor. On 22 December 1991 as another bloody year of IRA and loyalist violence claimed innocent victims, I received a letter from Stone in which he expressed a 'sense of foreboding' about this book. He also informed me of his involvement in a prison project, initiated by fellow loyalist inmates, aimed at producing a book of verse and short stories.

Nothing heavy – just reflections of our lives – no politics unfortunately because it's funded by the prison welfare department.

The letter also included a poem, preceded by a self-conscious preamble:

Has he seen the light? Yes I see the sodding light as it flashes by my cell window! Seriously, use the poem if you can. Have a quack analyse it as it may prove interesting reading. POEM [He did not give it a title and it was written in capitals in keeping with the nature of all his correspondence with me.]

GENTLE SLOPES OF CASTLEREAGH CARESSING MOTHER EARTH.
HEDGEROWS ABUNDANT WITH NATURE'S BOUNTY PLAYED HOST TO
MELODIOUS SONGBIRDS.
CLEAR SWEET AIR PERMEATED MY INNER SOUL.

SHIMMERING CRYSTAL RIVERS TRICKLE TO OBLIVION
LUSH GREEN EXPANSES NOW ENDANGERED, AS ANCIENT OAKS
SILENT WITNESS KEPT
OH PROTECTIVE SENTINELS HOLD STEADFAST.

TENTACLES OF CIVILISATION SPREAD THEIR CANCEROUS SHADOW
VIOLATED LAND, SLASHED ASUNDER AS GREED AND IGNORANCE
TAKE PRECEDENCE
ENCROACHING REGIMENTED DWELLINGS DEVOUR ONCE BEAUTIFUL
GLADE.
GONE NOW THE ENCHANTMENT OF MORNING CHORUS.

HORIZON SCARRED BY TALONS OF CONCRETE AND STEEL
SCREECHING CONTRAPTIONS SPEW FORTH MOST VILE EXCRETIONS
DULL-GREY PIGEONS ROOST ON GRIMY DILAPIDATED CONSTRUCTIONS
OF OUR PAST
TRANSPARENT GUARDIANS BLOATED WITH SELF-RIGHTEOUSNESS
BELEAGUERED PEOPLES JADED BY INSURRECTION AND BETRAYAL
COLD DAMP ENVELOPING SMOG CONSUMES ALL EXISTENCE.

SHATTERED CITY OF SORROW, YOUR BEWITCHING HOLD HAS
   AFFLICTED US ALL. . . .

[The poem was accompanied by a PS.]
I've been rather controversial (I think) – a dark cloud – on purpose. Well,
   maybe it will get your readers going 'inside' the mind of the mindless.
   Maybe I'm not beyond their experience!!?

The PS illustrated the self-deprecating way he addressed himself to
personal matters, but the overall letter displayed the conflicting
aspects of his character: humour, charm, self-conscious embarrassment, fear and insecurity. The poem depicted starkly his
darkness, anger and despair. He ended the letter with an IRA
slogan written in Gaelic – 'Tiocfaidh Ar La' – which translated
means 'Our day will come'. Under the slogan, he included a
paradox symbol – a half-moon with two dots above it which
resembles a smiling face.
   While writing the book I was captivated by Stone's dual
personality. On some occasions I found myself sympathetic to the
person Michael Stone would like to have been, and could still
become, and appalled by the Michael Stone who wallows in his
notoriety. His humour had an appealing quality, and there was a
sadness within the insecurity which littered his self-expression. I
was constantly obliged to remind myself that he, like many killers I
had interviewed, was a human being with genuine feelings,
aspirations and the ability to form warm relationships. He was the
product of a society in which killing for Jesus was not incompatible

with the orthodox expression of the political aspirations in both communities. A living victim, he bore testimony to the cult of violence which shaped Ireland. I never lost sight of the fact that he was able to express his flawed humanity, while denying the expression of humanity to his victims. One of the lines in his poem adequately describes those like him, who deem themselves the moral arbiters of life and death: 'Transparent guardians bloated with self-righteousness'.

Postscript:
Terrorist Agents

In January 1991, the British public was afforded a rare insight into
the workings of Military Intelligence, when one of the Army's
terrorist agents appeared in a Belfast courtroom charged with
twenty offences, including five of conspiracy to murder. Much to
the dismay of the media, who were hoping for a full trial with
controversial revelations, the agent pleaded 'guilty'. The judge, Sir
Basil Kelly, a former Attorney-General in the days of Unionist rule,
passed a ten-year sentence. The agent, 44-year-old Brian Nelson,
doubled as a top ranking loyalist terrorist in the UDA/UFF. His plea
of 'guilty', and the fact that the Director of Public Prosecutions
decided to overlook two additional charges of murder, ensured
that there could be no detailed public scrutiny of the double life led
by Nelson and his military handlers.

In an unprecedented step, a colonel in Military Intelligence
appeared in court as a character witness for Nelson, perhaps
hoping to encourage leniency in sentencing the Army agent. The
colonel portrayed Nelson as a 'courageous man' whose 'mistakes
were understandable'. He stressed that the 'mistakes', notably
conspiracy to murder Catholics, were 'very understandable', but
none the less Nelson was always loyal to the British Army, and had
never given allegiance to the UDA. He claimed that Nelson saved
the lives of many people, perhaps 200, including that of the
Provisional Sinn Fein leader, Gerry Adams. He told the judge that
no guidelines existed for the running of agents who, in the context
of Northern Ireland, were bound to become involved in criminal-
ity. Moral responsibility, he added, lay with the system which had
not yet found ways of coming to terms with the problems faced by
an agent.

A Belfast journalist was later heard to remark 'When is a terrorist not a terrorist? When he is working for Military Intelligence.' Certainly the case was bizarre. If Nelson were so loyal and brave, why his involvement in terrorism? Surely, unquestioning loyalty to his handlers would have ensured that he told them everything about his life as a terrorist?

The use of terrorists in the employ of the intelligence services began in the early 1970s with the creation of the MRF (Military Reconnaissance/Reaction Force). It recruited members of the various terrorist groupings, mostly the Provisional IRA, trained them, and used them as *agents provocateurs*, and informers. Such agents, of that period, were encouraged to participate in IRA violence, as a means of maintaining their credibility within the organisation. They were also used by their handlers in sectarian killings in Catholic areas, at a time when the military objective was to detach the IRA from its armed struggle with the British Army, and force it into a shooting war with the loyalists, thereby leaving it vulnerable to the charge of being an organisation built for tribal murder. When the IRA uncovered such agents, it executed them, and buried them in unmarked graves. Agents recruited from within the loyalist paramilitaries – the UDA, UVF, UFF – were similarly employed in what had become their natural tendency, namely counter-terror against the Catholics.

The *modus operandi* of terrorist agents of the early 1970s never changed, nor was there any serious scrutiny of the part they played in terrorism, as opposed to defeating violence. Essentially, a successful terrorist agent is capable of remaining undetected within terrorist ranks; to achieve that objective an agent must necessarily engage in actual terrorism in order to maintain the trust of other terrorists. A former British Intelligence operative offered me this explanation of the role of a terrorist agent:

When we recruit a terrorist as an agent it is important that he is highly placed within a terrorist network. We accept that to maintain his role and credibility with his associates, he necessarily must play the role of the terrorist, with all that implies. There is no point in moralising about this. If he is going to be of any value to us he must display to terrorist leaders that he is loyal to them, and willing to do whatever is required of him. It is essential to his survival, and his success, that he has their trust. If they ask him to kill people, or if he has to order the deaths of people so be it. This is war, and sacrifices have to be made, and the normal rules of law suspended. You cannot ask the normal authorities to adjudicate on the role of a terrorist agent because you are asking people to decide whether it is right within the normal framework of the law to justify murder in pursuit of defeating terrorism. The real problems arise for the handlers of a terrorist agent when he tells them that he is required to order somebody's death, or to take part in a bombing or shooting. You have to weigh up the possibility that if you act to prevent your agent taking part in a killing, or act to prevent a bombing, you risk compromising him and he is unmasked. When an agent tells you that his associates are about to kill someone, but warns that several terrorists are privy to information about the intended kill, you have to reckon that if you act to prevent it, that the terrorists will order an enquiry into how the security forces uncovered the murder plot – and then suspicion will fall on those in possession of the information. Which includes your agent. Now if that agent is useful as a regular source, one may well feel that the murder or bomb outrage should be allowed to take place. It is a nasty, dirty business, and gains are often only achieved with sacrifices.

Brian Nelson was such an agent, and assuming that the colonel was correct in his testimony, Nelson informed his handlers of all his activities including the terrorist offences to which he pleaded 'guilty'. Nelson was an agent in the tradition of operatives of the early 1970s, like those in the MRF, which was publicly discredited after a shooting in which several of its members, dressed like terrorists, and equipped with IRA-type weapons, fired into homes in a Catholic estate in West Belfast. Another example of the use of such agents was the Littlejohn affair, an intelligence sting run by MI6. Kenneth and Keith Littlejohn, two English-born criminals, were recruited, sent to Ireland as spies, and then encouraged to become involved in terrorist activity.

Throughout the 1970s and '80s, numerous secret groupings were created by the intelligence services, particularly Military Intelligence, and then disbanded once their role became known to the public, or when their activities came under scrutiny from the media, or the RUC. The latest creations by Military Intelligence, especially MI5, included the Future Research Units, to which Howes and Wood belonged. The *modus operandi* of the various covert groupings seem not to have changed; as the Nelson case appears to confirm, and it bears a striking resemblance to that of Albert Walker Baker, the UDA assassin. Released from Franklands Prison in England in February 1992, Baker, a former soldier, also worked in the engine-room of UDA terrorism. Baker's claims that he was a terrorist and agent were easily discredited in the 1970s, but become more credible with the revelations in the Nelson case.

Nelson was a soldier who returned to Belfast, joined the UDA and was recruited by Military Intelligence in the mid-1970s. It is not known whether he had been recruited as an agent before he joined the UDA, whereas Baker always contended that he himself had been recruited before he left the Army.

Nelson, first with the Black Watch, later joined the Ulster Defence Regiment. Recruited as an agent by RUC Special Branch, he was run by a variety of handlers during the 1970s. During that period he came to the attention of Military Intelligence, who also recruited him. There was nothing novel about this procedure: Military Intelligence often recruited Special Branch agents, sometimes without the knowledge of Special Branch – thereby creating considerable internal rivalry between the security agencies. In Nelson's case Special Branch happily shared him with the military. During the early 1980s Nelson took time off from terrorism, and life as an agent, and went to Germany, where he undertook manual work. His wife and two children later joined him there, and he began what appeared to be a new life; secretly, he maintained contact with UDA leaders, and with handlers from within Special Branch and Military Intelligence. He had been a considerable loss to the intelligence community, and eventually MI5 persuaded Military Intelligence to arrange a meeting with Nelson at a London hotel at the beginning of 1987. Nelson duly travelled to London and met a Military Intelligence officer and an MI5 operative. They told him he was needed in Northern Ireland because of a lack of high-grade intelligence on the activities of the UDA, and promised him a regular income, plus finance for a house-purchase deposit in Belfast.

Nelson returned to Belfast in April 1987 and became a co-ordinator of UDA intelligence, which involved the gathering of intelligence on Catholics and republican suspects for use in assassination. In this role, he acquired extensive security forces' documentation on members of the Catholic community, particularly those suspected of involvement with Provisional Sinn Fein, or the Provisional IRA.

At this point, a provocative question arises: was his success as a terrorist actually aided by those who were running him as an agent? Nelson was trusted and admired within the UDA leadership for building extensive dossiers, and for his card-index system used by UDA murder-squads in their campaign of sectarian killings; Nelson stored much of his information on a computer in his home. All the while, he kept his handlers informed of all planned killings by the UDA, and by other loyalist terror groups such as the UVF, who often operated with the connivance of the UDA. None of the information which he passed on to Military Intelligence found its way to the RUC, who later felt cheated that they had not been permitted to prevent many killings – which Nelson knew all about at the planning stage. While he was in place, the UDA was responsible for at least twenty murders.

In 1988 Nelson became a member of the newest Military Intelligence grouping, the Future Research Units, and in that role he may well have come into contact with Howes and Wood, then living in East Belfast close to UDA HQ. He may even have used them as a conduit for information which he wished to pass to his handlers. As a coordinator of UDA/UFF intelligence, he was also in a position to know about Michael Stone and the planned massacre at Milltown Cemetery: a close confidante of John McMichael, Nelson had been involved in McMichael's reorganisation of the UFF. At the express wishes of his handlers in the FRUs, he discussed with McMichael a plot to bomb shops and offices in Dublin. Military Intelligence reckoned that if loyalists bombed Dublin, the Irish government would later seek the extradition of the offenders, and in doing so would leave themselves vulnerable to pressure from the British to reciprocate by relaxing Irish extradition laws. The plan to bomb Dublin, codenamed 'Operation Snowball', never happened.

In September 1989, press reports of collusion between the security forces and loyalist terrorists renewed calls from Catholic politicians and the Dublin government for an inquiry. The eventual impetus for such an inquiry was the revelation that loyalist terrorists were in possession of security forces' files on republican suspects. The person chosen to head a subsequent enquiry was John Stevens, Deputy Chief Constable of Cambridge-shire, who went about the job of investigating the allegations of collusion with vigour and resourcefulness, clearly sparing nobody's blushes, notwithstanding many efforts to block his inquiry. Stevens lost no time in ordering the arrests of leading loyalists, particularly those within the UDA leadership. It was his swoop that netted Brian Nelson, who, within several months, provided Stevens with a clear picture not only of terrorist activity, but also of his role as a terrorist agent, and of the existence of the highly secret Future Research Units. Before he was seized, Nelson handed over much of his documentation to the FRUs; he had realised that Stevens might seek him out.

The documentation consisted of leaked police and military files on suspected and known republicans. It was months before the Army, under pressure from Stevens, revealed the contents of the Nelson hoard. The room in which Stevens and his team of investigators stored their files – a heavily guarded police building with specially installed electronic surveillance safeguards – was damaged by fire in January 1990, and the computerised records destroyed. The RUC, at a loss to explain the cause of the fire, suggested that one of Stevens's investigators accidentally dropped a cigarette butt in a waste bin. Forensic scientists failed to establish the real cause of the fire, discovered when the Stevens team returned to the offices three hours after they had vacated and locked them. Although Stevens later conceded that the fire had probably been accidental, several members of the RUC who worked closely with the Stevens team became convinced of arson; they still insist that only people within the security services could have breached the security of the building. Suspiciously, no one was alerted to the fire, and the sophisticated technology which should have warned of the blaze was not activated; when it was detected, a member of the Stevens team rushed to a telephone in the building to summon the fire service, but discovered the telephone line out of order. The fire occurred the night before Brian Nelson was scheduled for arrest.

Index